Culture
.com

Culture
.com

Building Corporate Culture in the Connected Workplace

PEG C. NEUHAUSER

RAY BENDER, PhD

KIRK L. STROMBERG

JOHN WILEY & SONS CANADA, LTD

Toronto • New York • Chichester • Weinheim • Brisbane • Singapore

John Wiley & Sons Canada Ltd
22 Worcester Road
Etobicoke, Ontario
M9W 1L1

Canadian Cataloguing in Publication Data

Neuhauser, Peg, 1950–
  Culture.com : building corporate culture in the connected workplace

ISBN 0-471-64539-7

1. Corporate culture. 2. Organizational change. I. Bender, Ray. II. Stromberg, Kirk L. III. Title.

HD58.7.N48 2000   658.4'063   C00-931657-4

Production Credits

Cover & Text Design: Interrobang Graphic Design Inc.
Printer: Tri-Graphic Printing

Printed in Canada
10 9 8 7 6 5 4 3 2 1

3 2280 00870 9743

Contents

Preface

A ROAD MAP FOR MOVING TO A .COM CULTURE

Corporations, nonprofit organizations, and government agencies are racing to transform themselves into e-business enterprises.[1] For traditional organizations this represents a massive shift in business strategy and infrastructure. The purpose of this book is to provide a road map for building a corporate culture that can help companies succeed in carrying out their business strategies in a connected business world. Leaders and managers in the corporate, government, and not-for-profit sectors can use the ideas in *Culture.com* to find practical tools to ensure their organization's culture fits the demands of the connected workplace.

Because the transition into e-business is still so new, there is very little research to draw on about how to build a .com corporate culture. This was our biggest challenge in writing *Culture.com*. We gathered our data from scratch by interviewing the people living through the changes and inventing what to do as they go. We also reviewed articles in journals, newspapers, and books on e-business, looking for stories about its effects on how work is now being conducted in

---

[1] In this book the term e-business as used refers to the broad application of the new technologies, including e-commerce, business-to-business, and e-government processes. E-commerce is used when we are referring specifically to business-to-consumer processes.

organizations. We found that culture.com is a moving target. No one knows for sure what will happen or how to make it all work. In many ways, we are all living in the middle of a grand experiment. When we mentioned to one colleague that we had to do our own research through interviews, he laughed and said the word "research" was an old one that may not even apply in this case. And he is right. In this book we observe and report on a fast-changing moving target. We also coach and offer some tips for proceeding down this road.

Our sources for the ideas in this book were you: the people who are living through it. We interviewed people from a wide variety of corporations, making sure to include start-up .com companies,[2] as well as older, traditional organizations. We collected ideas on what worries them, what they are trying to do to change their enterprises, and what frankly has them stumped at the present time. We collected their advice, added our combined expertise on corporate culture, and wrote this book as a practical road map of ideas and advice on how to build a .com culture. It is the best current thinking but certainly not the end of the story. Actually, it is just the beginning of the journey.

To track the ongoing culture evolution inside companies in the coming years, we have set up a web site and will continue to do research on what is happening out there. We will probably continue to avoid the traditional academic forms of research to track the trends, because the process of conducting and analyzing that type of research is too slow and would likely leave us with obsolete information rather than useful updates about current workplace developments. We will keep you posted with updates, articles, and interviews on our Web site at **www.culturedotcom.com.**

 Companies around the globe will spend $600 billion a year by 2003 on e-business, according to marketing researcher International Data Corp.[3]

---

[2] Companies that are called .com companies are usually start-up enterprises founded since the mid 1990s. Usually their lines of business are primarily focused on using Internet technologies to sell products or services directly to consumers. This is known as business-to-consumer processes. When we refer to a .com company, we are describing this type of business (for example, Amazon.com).

[3] Ira Sanger, "Inside IBM: Internet Business Machines," *BusinessWeek* (December 13, 1999), 26.

NINE CHALLENGES FOR TURNING
YOUR CORPORATE CULTURE INTO A .COM ASSET

The first chapter of the book summarizes the corporate culture issues facing traditional companies who are moving into a clicks-and-mortar world. Chapters 2-10 address each of the nine culture challenges every company must confront when moving into the e-business world. Each chapter contains stories about what other people are doing to tackle these challenges and practical tips on how to take action in your company to build a corporate culture for the connected workplace. The nine challenges covered in this book are summarized below. Decide which of these worry you the most. What keeps you awake at night? As you read this book, you will likely spend the majority of your energy on the issues that worry you the most.

1. MAKING THE JUMP TO WARP SPEED

Net time is often referred to as operating at a ten to one ratio. Everything is moving ten times faster than the prenet world and getting faster all the time. Debugging on the fly has become standard procedure in many companies. A finished product is one that is too late to market in the e-business world. Companies must get to market as quickly as possible and let their customers help them develop and debug products. "Launch and learn" is the phrase often used to describe this strategy of getting started rapidly and continuing the refinement of products in real time. Companies are struggling with how to meet the demand for .com speed and at the same time maintain quality. This shift to rapid product launch means that companies have to take greater risks if they are going to operate on net time. Everything and everyone inside companies must move at much faster speeds, and for most traditional organizations this means changing the culture.

2. BUILDING A CORPORATE CULTURE IN A VIRTUAL ORGANIZATION

As companies move into the e-business world, the idea of employees gathered in large corporate office buildings will become less common. Employees will be scattered all over the world in small team clusters or home offices or they will be perpetually on the road. The virtual organization where there is little cohesion, trust, or shared experience among employees can be a lonely place to work. One person describes it as, "bowling alone." What are the key elements of culture that will function as the glue to hold the organization together? How do you create a strong corporate culture in a virtual organization?

3. LIVING WITH PARALLEL CULTURES DURING THE TRANSITION TO E-BUSINESS

There is a transition phase during which most companies must keep the old business going while bringing the new e-business enterprise up to speed. For some organizations this phase may last for a long time. Living with two such different cultures side by side is a challenge few companies have had to face before. If you decide to create a separate Internet group for the early development phase, how do you reintegrate these groups with contrasting cultures when it is time to merge their operations back into one business strategy and structure?

4. A NEW BREED OF TEAMS IN A .COM CULTURE

As the structure of organizations changes dramatically, the old subcultures break apart and people form new functional groups. Many of these new groups are short-lived as teams assemble and reassemble to meet changing customer needs. Employees at all levels must adapt to constantly changing team memberships. A .com culture will have to enculturate people rapidly into new teams and quickly create loyalties among team members. Historically, team building has been a slow process, but it cannot continue to work that way in the future. What will happen to the traditional problems caused by rigid organizations structures that create functional silos, triggering conflict between the "tribes" that organizations have dealt with in the past? Will the problem disappear or will it resurface in new forms?

5. COMMUNICATION BELONGS TO EVERYONE IN A .COM CULTURE

A wired company is an "open-book" organization. This changes the entire landscape of communications and distribution of power because employees at all levels are far better informed about the operations, strategy, and finances of the company. They have access to tools that allow them to communicate with each other instantly, and they are more willing to second-guess leadership decisions and company direction than ever before. Companies must find ways to maximize the benefits and minimize the potential problems of communicating in an open book corporation.

6. KNOWLEDGE MANAGEMENT IS MANAGING PEOPLE'S BRAIN POWER

Managing people's brain power and the company's collective memory require new skills. Traditional managers must become facilitators who guide, but do not control, the knowledge management processes in their companies. Everyone needs easy access to knowledge and must tap into that collective base to improve their work. Organizations must uncover and leverage employees' knowledge more quickly than ever before, and they must develop tools for managing knowledge in both routine and unstructured work. Learning from mistakes so everyone can benefit from the new knowledge is an important cultural trait to develop if a company is to be successful at managing people's brain power.

7. THE NEW CORPORATE IQ AND GETTING SMART

Mistake learning, just-in-time learning, stealth learning, and rapid learning become the backbone of the new corporate IQ. Organizations that do not build an intense focus on learning into their culture face repeated mistakes stemming from lack of systemic thinking and wrong or incomplete models for implementation. Those organizations are missing the opportunity to tap into their collective IQ. The corporate IQ that fuels the organization is the sum of the intellectual, creative, and emotional capacities of all employees and their ability to learn rapidly from each other. Every member of the organization is responsible for learning, and the organization must provide tools, time, and resources to enhance learning.

8. LINKAGES AND RELATIONSHIPS OUTSIDE THE ORGANIZATION: A CULTURAL CHALLENGE

Creating alliances is a way of life in the e-business world, because there are too many good ideas out there for any one company to buy them all up. Buy-or-make options are being replaced by decisions to team up with other companies and produce joint products. There are many different types of alliances that companies can establish—which ones to choose depend on the company's business strategy and its culture. Some of the alliances require high degrees of trust and cooperation between organizations. However, if high trust and cooperation are not the norm inside the company, it is very unlikely that these traits will be present in the alliance.

9. LEADING THE JOURNEY TO THE WIRED ENTERPRISE

Leaders are the most influential cultural carriers in the organization. The leader's core beliefs and actions set the tone for the entire company, which is why cultural fit between the formal leaders and the organization is essential for building a strong corporate culture. In a .com culture, informal leadership takes on greater significance than in traditional business settings. The demands for speed and innovation at all levels of the organization make the traditional command and control management approach by a few formal leaders too cumbersome. Eight key leadership activities for shaping the culture are addressed.

PRACTICAL TIPS THROUGHOUT THE BOOK

The book describes hundreds of examples and stories that people told us about what is happening in their companies and how they are handling the transition to the .com world. In addition to the stories, each chapter has practical tips and how to advice to help decide what steps to take next in your company. Many of these tips are boxed to make them easy for you to find.

At the end of each chapter, we include questions to ask about your company. This book is a practical guide that helps you answer the question "so what?" The questions will help you get started in asking the right questions about your company's current culture. We want you to walk away from this book with some concrete ideas of what to do next about the issues that are worrying you.

The case examples and interviews from the following list of companies are included in this book. The sources for these stories and quotes were interviews, journal and newspaper articles, and books on e-business.

3M Corporation
Ace Hardware Corporation
Acxiom Corporation
Amoco
Amazon.com
American Airlines
AOL/Time Warner
Apollo Team
Apple
Arinso International
AT&T
Barnes & Noble Booksellers
Bingham Dana LLP
Borders Bookstores
Boston Consulting Group
Brandwise.com
British Petroleum
Brunswick Corporation
Buckman Laboratories
Burlington Northern Santa Fe
   Railway
Canadian Rock Entertainment

Canadian Tire Acceptance Limited
CD Plus
Chapters Inc.
Charles Schwab and Co.
Chase Manhattan Bank
Chase Manhattan's Chase.com
Cisco Systems
CMGI
Computer Sciences Corporation
   (CSC)
Critical Path, Inc.
Cyberplex, Inc.
Daimler/Chrysler
Deep Woods Technology Inc.
Dell Computers
Delphi Group
DMR Consulting Group, Inc.
EDS
Eli Lilly
Ernst & Young LLP
Fairfax, Virginia Public Schools
FedEx

Fleet Boston Bank
FLYCAST
Ford Motor Company
Fordham University
Gartner Group
Gateway, Inc.
General Electric
General Motors
General Services Administration
    (GSA)
GTE
Hallmark Cards
Henry Ford Health System
Hewlett-Packard
Hire.com
Home Depot
Honeywell
Hospital Corporation of America
    (HCA)
HPL
IBM
Ideo Product Development
Industrial Light & Magic
Intel
Intelisys Electronic Commerce
    LLC
iVillage
Johnson & Johnson
Kaiser Permanente
KPMG Consulting
Lexmark International
Los Angeles Times
Lotus Development
Lucent Technologies
MCI WorldCom
McKinsey & Company
MDS International
Merck
Microsoft
MIT Center for Org. Learning
Monsanto
Morningstar, Inc.
Nations Bank

Nike Corporation
Nortel Networks
Northop Grumman
National Aeronautics and Space
    Administration (NASA)
NASA's Apollo Team
OnTargetInternet.com
PG&E
Phillips Lighting
Proctor & Gamble
Ratheon
Reflect.com
Rock Entertainment
ROLM
RSKCo of CNA Insurance Co.
Schneider Automation
Scient Corporation
Sears
Seimens Building Technologies
SiteSpecific
Sony
Southwest Airlines
Stein, Roe & Formham
Southwestern Bell
Sprint
Talk Visual Corporation
Team EcoInternet
UNext
Unisys
United States Air Force
United States Army
United States Marines
U.S. NASA and Apollo Team
University of Augsburg, Germany
University of Phoenix
Xerox
W.W. Granger, Inc.
Wal-Mart
Whirlpool
Wingspan
World Com
Xerox
Xerox's PARX

Acknowledgements

Writing Culture.com was an experience that matched the world we were describing. It was a high speed, "invent-it-as-you-go" creation. The e-business models are so new and changing so rapidly that our most reliable and useful sources of information were the dozens of interviews with the people living through the changes and figuring out how to make this new world work in their organizations. Their ideas and stories became the backbone of this book. We would like to thank all the people who took the time to be interviewed and allowed us to quote them extensively throughout this book. Without their examples, advice, and sense of humor about learning to live in the .com world, this book would not have been possible. We hope you enjoy reading their stories as much as we enjoyed gathering them.

The process of writing a book always involves many people beyond the authors. We would like to thank our editor, Karen Milner, and all the people at John Wiley and Sons Canada, Ltd for their belief in the book and their skill in helping us write it. Steve Engler, Martha Zivley, and Lee Dillard spent countless hours helping us edit and refine the writing. Denise Bugg converted dozens of taped interviews into transcripts at a speed that kept us on track with the tight deadlines we had set for ourselves. Hal Kooistra kept our computers running and communicating across three writing locations using a motley mix of hardware and software that had not been designed for a high speed team project.

A number of people gave us advice and insights as the manuscript developed. We deeply appreciate their contributions and extend our thanks. Ira Chaleff reviewed our initial idea for the book and encouraged us to find a publisher. Glen Goold and Dr. Albert Hollenbeck reviewed the manuscript and helped shape the ideas contained in this book. No one spent more time and energy helping us than Linda Goold. She worked with the conceptual development, editing, and review at every step along the way. She was our most enthusiastic supporter and most valuable advisor throughout the entire process.

Friends and family are always drawn into the writing of a book. It is a life-consuming process, and no one can do it without a great deal of personal support. Ray would like to thank his daughters, Ginny Tucker and Lee Dillard, as well as Pat Bender for years of encouragement and support that made his contribution to this book possible. He is appreciative of Elton Zimmerman who sparked a lifelong interest in Sociology and Bob Steinerd who understands the difference between leadership and management. Kirk thanks Neal A. Maxwell, Frank Mensel, John Mulholland, Colonel Dana Peck, and Dr. J.D. Williams. All were great mentors who saw a spark of potential in him and helped fan it into a life-long love for learning, exploring new ideas, and finding new tools. Peg thanks her friends Ruth Pincus and Mary Walker for their enthusiasm and support for this book project. And as always special appreciation goes to her mother Nancy Neuhauser and the memory of her father Paul. Over the years, whenever Peg needed encouragement from her greatest fans, all she had to do was call home.

Peg would also like thank Ray and Kirk for agreeing to join the project to write this book. They must have wondered about the wisdom of that decision at times. Peg has written two other books and knew the toll it takes. Anyone who knows Peg has heard her declare each time that she will never write another one. Writing as a team with Ray and Kirk has changed her attitude. She would write with these two again anytime. Don't worry, that's not a suggestion, just a thanks.

Peg Neuhauser
Ray Bender
Kirk Stromberg

CHAPTER ONE

Your Corporate Culture in a Clicks-and-Mortar World

CORPORATE GRAFFITI MOVES TO THE WEB

"The bathroom walls are cleaner and the water cooler isn't as crowded anymore. They've all gone to Yahoo," related Bob Kulbick, CEO of one of CNA Insurance Company's newly merged subsidiaries, RSKCo. If he wants a quick check of the mood among the 2,500 employees on any given day, all he has to do is sign on and read. The reactions to the latest RSKCo news are there for the world to see.

"This is what you have to keep in mind about a Web site on Yahoo," said Kulbick. "Everyone can see it, including our competitors, current customers, potential recruits or new customers. The information is not necessarily accurate and the views of the employees that sign on to leave messages may not be representative of the whole company, but it is still there for all to read. It's difficult to know what to do about it. I loved the time they announced on Yahoo that I had been fired from previous jobs. It isn't true. I've never been fired, but what can you do? On something like that, you just laugh it off and keep moving."

So what do you do? In some executive suites, you will hear the first angry reaction, "Who are those people? We need to track them down and fire them." When that tactic is quickly abandoned as unrealistic, often the next comment is, "Then, we just have to ignore the whole thing." And yet, those with the most experience of living in the .com business world will warn that you cannot ignore the net. Business communications have changed forever, and everyone has to figure out what to do about it.

In a .com workplace communication belongs to everyone. Adjusting to the "open book" corporation is one of the many new challenges facing companies as they move into the e-business arena. Chat rooms on the net have become the place where employees gather to compare notes on the latest company news, vent their anger, or entertain themselves with gallows humor. A vast array of financial and strategic information is easily available to anyone who wants to access and discuss it on-line. Any illusion that senior management or the communications department controls the corporate messages anymore has been destroyed. A .com culture must develop new ways of dealing with internal communications and the redistribution of power inside the company. Hoarding information used to be a source of power. In this new era, the rules of the game have changed. Now information hoarding is more likely to set you up to be the next target of discussion on net chat.

THE RULES OF THE GAME ARE CHANGING

We are living in a .com world. The old rules are changing, but it is not yet clear what the new rules are. It has been said that going from an analog to a digital world is like moving from living on land to living under water.[1] Everything is in flux. The speed and complexity of the changes are difficult for many of us to absorb. Futurists, historians, and social scientists tell us the transition to a networked economy is the biggest shift in the way the world functions since the Industrial Revolution. The people working today are the bridge generation, spanning the gap between the old and new ways of doing business.

---

[1] Chuck Martin, *The Digital Estate: Strategies for Competing, Surviving, and Thriving in a Internetworked World* (New York: McGraw-Hill, 1997), 15.

I have been in this business for 33 years and I'm a cynic by birth and training. I have gone through the death of mainframes, the PC revolution, client/server hoopla, as a researcher, participant, and manager. And I have never seen anything that has had (and will continue to have) the profound effect of the Internet. There is a true paradigm shift taking place where the basic business model is fundamentally changing. The catalyst for that change is the Internet.

I don't think the Internet itself did it. Everything had to be in place for it to happen. The amount of digital data that was available was very large, the computer literacy was relatively high, the applications were set up, and people were already attempting to communicate via telecom. Then the Internet came in and created an easy way of doing it all. It suddenly blew the lid off what was holding everyone back. The Internet by itself is overblown, but as the catalyst it changes everything. It is a profound change that will affect literally the way people live. We have only faintly begun to see the effects.

—*Tom Shipley, Group Vice President, Gartner Group*

The business and professional world is working feverishly to learn how to change its business strategies to capitalize on this .com world. A great deal of attention is directed at the external business issues of designing, marketing, selling, and delivering goods and services in the networked environment. In contrast, the internal infrastructure changes in individual companies have received very little attention so far. When a company does address these infrastructure issues, it tends to focus on hardware and software and getting its technology up to speed. Think of a company's infrastructure as being composed of hardware, software, and peopleware. The corporate culture is the peopleware in action.

The next issue that must be tackled is how to create a corporate culture that matches the new .com business strategy. Corporate culture is a major component of the infrastructure engine that either drives the organization in the direction it has set for itself or creates obstacles that block its route. Culture is often defined as "the way we do things around here." If the way a company does things does not match its business strategy, the culture wins every time. No matter what a company says it intends to do, the way people actually behave, think, and believe determines what really happens.

THE first e-business challenge that companies must face is to develop a new business strategy, and the second is to build a corporate culture that fits that strategy. If they do not change the culture to match the new strategy, the inertia of the old culture will derail the strategy. Make sure you have a two-part plan for moving to the clicks-and-mortar world:

- develop your e-business strategy
- change your culture so it supports the strategy.

WHAT IS CORPORATE CULTURE?

There are many different definitions of corporate culture. Some of the best ones are quite simple.

- It's the way we do things around here—the HP or the IBM way.
- It's the personality of the organization.
- Culture is what people do when no one is watching.
- Walk the talk. Say what matters and then do it consistently.

All of these definitions are accurate and work well as a base for reading this book. Pick the definition that makes the most sense to you or fits best with the way people in your company would say it. The language you habitually use to describe things within your organization is one element of your culture. This is your dialect. It is easier for you to understand each other if you use the dialect that makes the most sense to you.

KNOW as much as you can about your current corporate culture before you try to change it.

For this book, we used the following description of corporate culture.

1. Shared Underlying Assumptions and Core Values of the Group: The Deepest Layer of Culture.
2. Behaviors and Habits: "The Way We Do Things Around Here."
3. Symbols and Language: The Most Visible and Simplest Level of Culture.

Figure 1.1: Three Layers of Culture

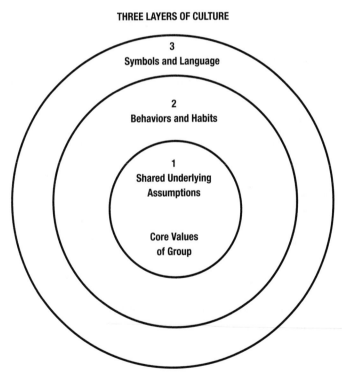

THREE LAYERS OF CULTURE

3
Symbols and Language

2
Behaviors and Habits

1
Shared Underlying
Assumptions

Core Values
of Group

Layer 1
Most stable and unchanging

Layers 2-3
Changes frequently as environment and business strategy changes

SHARED UNDERLYING ASSUMPTIONS AND CORE VALUES OF THE GROUP: THE DEEPEST LAYER OF CULTURE

The underlying assumptions and core values are the deepest part of the culture (Figure 1.1). They are the hub of the wheel for everything else about the culture.

Examples of Underlying Assumptions

- Is primary importance given to the group or the individual? Do you believe that society should be organized around the group/community or should it be organized around the individual?

- What is time? Is it a linear resource once spent can never be regained? Or is it "circular" where it is acceptable to do several things at the same time and sticking to schedules or meeting deadlines is less important.[2]

Often these assumptions are so deeply ingrained that the people in the organization find them difficult to put them into words. It is simply the way things *are*, and questioning these beliefs would cause offense. For example, it would not be wise to walk into a hospital and ask employees if they thought it mattered whether the staff purposely harmed patients. The question sounds absurd. And any health care staff member from the physician to the housekeeper would be insulted if you even asked the question.

Examples of Core Values

Cultural core values are easier to describe because they are the more conscious level of beliefs and are often discussed and written down in organizations. Some examples are:

- Customers come first.
- Individual initiative is the source of success.
- Keep your promises. Your word is your honor.

---

[2] Edgar Schein, *The Corporate Survival Guide: Sense and Nonsense about Culture Change*, (San Francisco, Jossey-Bass, 1999), 52-55.

Underlying assumptions and core values are inextricably intertwined in any culture. They are the most deeply held beliefs of the group, the beliefs that drive the actions of its members. When Jim Collins and Jerry Porras, authors of *Built to Last*, give their often-repeated advice to "preserve the core," they are mainly talking about the underlying assumptions and values of a company.

 ... a fundamental element of... a visionary company is a core ideology—core values and sense of purpose beyond just making money—that guides and inspires people throughout the organization and remains relatively fixed for long periods of time.[3]

Here are a few famous examples of underlying assumptions and core values held by well-known companies. These organizations are famous for their corporate cultures because they consistently act on what they say they believe.

3M

- "Thou shalt not kill a new product idea."
- Tolerance for honest mistakes.
- Respect for individual initiative and personal growth.[4]

Amazon.com

- "Our vision is the world's most customer-centric company. The place where people come to find and discover anything they might want to buy on-line."
- Six core values: customer obsession, ownership, bias for action, frugality, high hiring bar, and innovation.[5]

[3] James C. Collins and Jerry I. Porras, *Built to Last: Successful Habits of Visionary Companies* (New York: HarperCollins, 1994), 48.
4 Ibid, 68.
5 Joshua Quittner, "On the Future," *Time* (December 27, 1999), 50.

Procter & Gamble

- Product excellence.
- Continuous improvement.
- If you cannot make pure goods of full weight, go do something else that is honest, even if it is breaking stone.[6]

IMPORTANT questions to consider about the core layer of your corporate culture.

- What happens to the core as your company transitions to a .com workplace?
- Have the fundamentals of your business changed so much that you must change the underlying assumptions and core values of your culture?
- Will a little tweaking and updating of this core layer of culture be enough to bring the company into the net world?
- Is this core element of culture what remains the same while everything around it goes through dramatic change?

BEHAVIORS AND HABITS: "THE WAY WE DO THINGS AROUND HERE"

The behaviors and habits of people working for the company make up the middle layer of culture. This is the layer described when people say, that's just "the way we do things around here." In the field of social sciences this layer of culture is called norms. These behaviors and habits include everything from the formal policies and procedures to the informal habits and tactics employees use to function effectively within the company.

---

[6] James C. Collins and Jerry I. Porras, *Built to Last: Successful Habits of Visionary Companies* (New York: HarperCollins, 1994), 70.

Examples of the Cultural Behaviors and Habits

Formal policies and procedures:

- Answer the phones in three rings,
- Don't transfer a customer to someone else if you can solve their problem yourself.
- Everyone needs to come in off the road to be in the office on Friday for face-to-face team meetings.
- Don't bypass your supervisor for permission.

Informal habits and customs:

- Chat with people and be friendly on the elevator.
- Sit only with people from your department or grade level in the cafeteria.
- Speaking up to disagree with boss in a meeting is allowed (or not).

> Most people I talk with about recruiting them into these companies have not had experience in the .com world. I had a discussion recently with a candidate who asked me for an org chart. I told him, "I can't send you an org chart. Our organization is very fluid." He is coming from a setting where he is used to a hierarchy instead of the flatness that is typical of a .com organization.
> —*Patti Tobenkin, Contract Recruiter for .com companies*

These behaviors and habits operate as the ground rules or guidelines. By carefully watching how veteran employees act, a newcomer figures out quickly which actions are encouraged and which ones are not. When you take a job with a new company, much of the first weeks are spent trying to catch on to this layer of culture. You do not want to make too many mistakes when you are new because it can trigger the age-old tribal reaction—they will declare you "dead" and freeze you out, never letting you become a full-fledged member of the group. Everyone can think of people in their organizations who were declared dead years ago and still do not seem to realize it. In a company with a .com culture, you would probably be declared dead and frozen out for some of the following behaviors: insisting on working only 40 hours a week; not participating in the games and "play" that are a key element of the daily life; or not carrying your weight on a product team for both quantity and quality of work.

Some of the cultural behaviors and habits that are most noticeable are the eccentric actions that the organization tolerates or even encourages. The reason the organization allows these is because they tend to produce results that move the company toward success in meeting its goals. For example, in some brokerage firms, high producing salespeople know they can get away with asking five different people to solve a problem without telling any of the five they are all working on the same task. This increases the odds the salesperson will get a quick answer. It annoys everyone else because it wastes their time, but the salesperson does not get into trouble for this tactic as long as he or she has a reputation for keeping customers happy and producing revenue.

Another example of a condoned behavior that an outsider to the business might not expect occurs in consulting and speaking firms where reliability is a core value. The company makes it clear to the consultants that the client is counting on them to show up, so they are to go to great lengths to do so. For example, in many firms, consultants know that it is acceptable and even expected to take on extra expenses that will be absorbed by the firm if necessary. They do not have to call for permission, because they know the priority is to get to the event on time. In one case a consultant paid a $400 taxi fare to get to the client site. In another, the speaker chartered a private plane after being delayed by weather. "Do what it takes and we don't bill the client" is the ground rule in these companies.

Art Fry, inventor of the Post-It Notes, is one of 3M's most famous examples of the company's tolerance for allowing its developers to use tactics that stir things up in their efforts to bring a product to life. The marketing group conducted a survey during the product development of the Post-It Notes. The results were terrible, indicating that people did not want pads of somewhat sticky paper.

But Fry was not going to take that lying down, so he distributed samples to people throughout the 3M complex and did his own market research on usage. The reaction of people when their supply ran out was remarkable. Fry observed, "From my own personal experience of people clawing and scratching to get these things, and the use rate compared to Scotch Tape, I extrapolated that there was a large market."[7] Needless to say his independent market research did not put the marketing department in a good light. In some companies, behavior like that would get you into trouble, but at 3M these stories become corporate legend. It is acceptable behavior in this culture.

SYMBOLS AND LANGUAGE: THE MOST VISIBLE AND SIMPLEST LEVEL OF CULTURE

The symbols and language of the people who work for a company make up the third key element of its culture as illustrated in Figure 1.1. Symbols and artifacts of the company are all the tangible items you can see, touch, and hear (e.g., corporate colors, logos, hats, t-shirts, songs, Wal-Mart's famous yell, dress codes or lack of them, and office layouts). Think of these culture elements as the simplest and most visible layer of culture.

 LOOK around your company at the buildings, grounds, and the people. What stands out as the identifiable "look" of your company?

Does wearing a suit and tie tell people immediately that you are an outsider because everyone who works for the company wears jeans? Is your cafeteria a friendly gathering spot where people sit together in large groups at lunch, talking and laughing? Does your building have glass partitions and doorless offices? What are your company's trademark symbols and visual cues that give you clues about your culture traits?

---

[7] Gifford Pinchot III, *Intrapreneuring: Why You Don't Have to Leave the Corporation to Become an Entrepreneur* (Toronto, Harper and Row, 1985), 140.

Amazon.com is a classic illustration of a company using a concrete symbol to reinforce the message about one of its core values—frugality. In the early days, Amazon.com was located in a modest two-bedroom home that Jeff Bezos and his wife rented in a Seattle suburb. They converted the garage into a workspace and brought in three Sun workstations. Extension cords snaked from every available outlet in the house to the garage, and a black hole gaped through the ceiling—this was where a pot-bellied stove had been ripped out to make more room. To save money Bezos went to Home Depot and bought three wooden doors. Using angle brackets and two-by-fours he hammered together three desks, at a cost of $60 each. That frugality continues at Amazon.com to this day. Employees, many of them millionaires from stock options, still work two to an office at Bezos-designed door-desks. Helen Owen, Design Director, made a bet with *Time* writer Joshua Quittner that she would still have a door-desk in five years, even if Amazon.com flourishes.[8]

Language includes the industry lingo, insiders' phrases, and favorite words of company employees. Some of these words are generic to the industry, but many are unique to the individual enterprise. In fact, each organization has its own distinct dialect that an outsider will notice immediately. For example, the management team of a large medical center may make repeated references to the "BBA" during a meeting. An outsider might pick up the tension and frustration connected to the phrase: however, he would have to ask to learn that BBA is the abbreviation for the Balanced Budget Act, which affects reimbursement in the health care industry and this organization's bottom line. In a more informal example at MDS, a health and life sciences company based in Canada, the senior management group refers to "the piano lessons" during a meeting and laughs. This is a well-known insider's phrase that represents one of MDS's core values supporting MDS employee efforts to balance work and personal life. To do this, they have rescheduled senior leadership meetings so the CFO does not miss his jazz piano lessons.

---

[8] Joshua Quittner, "On the Future," *Time* (December 27, 1999), 50.

WHAT DO YOU CHANGE AND WHAT DO YOU KEEP?

 If an organization is to meet the challenges of a changing world, it must be prepared to change everything about itself except its basic beliefs as it moves through corporate life. The only sacred cow in an organization should be its basic philosophy of doing business.[9]

Unless you are a new company starting from scratch, one of the most important questions you must answer as you enter the e-business world is what to change in the culture and what to keep the same. Historically, the hub of the wheel (underlying assumptions and core values, as illustrated in Figure 1.2 tends to be the most stable element of a culture. These core beliefs rarely change. As the market demands, technology, or products change, everything except the core layer changes. You change your behaviors, habits, symbols, and language but not the core.

Figure 1.2: E-business Strategy and Culture

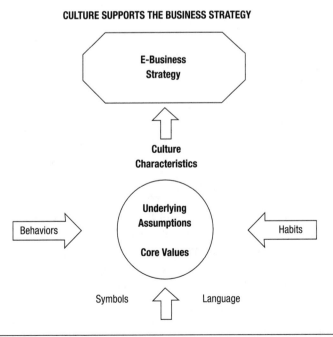

---

[9] Thomas J. Watson, Jr., *A Business and Its Beliefs* (New York: McGraw-Hill, 1963), 5-6, 72-73.

Collins and Porras repeat over and over that you must preserve the core while stimulating progress.[10] Stability of the culture comes from the core. Flexibility comes from everything else. It is possible that some companies will have to change their core beliefs to survive in a .com world. If the underlying assumptions of the corporate culture are hostile to speed, risk taking, or collaboration, a company may face the daunting task of changing the core of its culture. This is the most difficult cultural change to make. In the past, changing the core was rarely necessary, but it is not certain whether this will hold true in the future as companies move into e-business. Changing the core of the culture is discussed in detail in Chapter 6.

Because it is so difficult, there is no reason to change the core layer of your culture (shared underlying assumptions and core values) unless you are convinced that you must do so to be successful in the e-business environment.

The following four statements give you a quick road map for how to think through what to change and what to keep (Figure 1.2).

1. Know what makes up the core beliefs of your company. To determine what these underlying assumptions and core values are, look for the themes in the frequently repeated stories about the company. If people like to tell a story over and over, it contains some "truth" about life in the organization—good or bad. For example, the theme or message of a particular story may be that telling the truth to senior management makes you a hero (or is suicidal). Or if stories about customers take the form of cynical humor or belittling, respect for the customer is not a core value, no matter what the formal mission statement says.

2. Know your current business strategy. Make sure it is consistent with the core. For example, Procter & Gamble would not set a new business strategy for producing low-quality products. If your business strategy calls for high levels of rapid innovation, but your core beliefs are that people must be controlled and monitored to ensure they follow all the rules, your old core does not match your new business strategy. You must change that core belief to survive in the e-business world.

---

[10] James C. Collins and Jerry I. Porras, *Built to Last: Successful Habits of Visionary Companies* (New York: HarperCollins, 1994), 81.

3. Change *anything* in the two outer layers of culture if that will help you achieve your business strategy without destroying the core. For example, if your company currently requires five sign-offs before a team or lower level employee can implement a decision, cut that back to one or two sign-offs. To learn where your cultural barriers are, all you have to do is ask. Tell employees at all levels what the new business strategy is and then ask them, "What are the barriers in this organization that will keep you from being able to deliver these results?" What policies, procedures, or habits do we currently use that will be stumbling blocks to making this strategy a success. Listen particularly carefully to your best producers. People with a track record for getting things done will not waste their time complaining about issues that are not important. They will tell you exactly what will cause them delays and problems in trying to pull off the next success for the company. Listen carefully to what they have to say.

4. Whenever your business strategy changes, you need to change symbols, language, behaviors, habits, and policies. But you are not likely to change the core. Collins and Porras use IBM as an example of a company that lost its way for a few years by forgetting to change everything but the core. "No where in IBM's 'three basic beliefs' do we see anything about white shirts, blue suits, specific policies, specific procedures, organizational hierarchies, mainframe computers—or computers at all, for that matter. Mainframe computers are not a core value... It stuck too long to strategic and operating practices and cultural manifestations of the core values."[11]

CULTURAL CHANGE IS DISRUPTING AND UPSETTING TO EMPLOYEES

A few words of warning about changing your culture are in order at this point. Changing the core elements of the culture, underlying assumptions and core values, is quite difficult and is very disruptive to the people living through the transition. Usually the transition requires massive changes of personnel, especially in the leadership

---

[11] Ibid, 81. Three core values are: give full consideration to the individual employee; spend a lot of time making customers happy; and go the last mile to do things right.

ranks. In most cases, the only effective way to make this fundamental change to the core, especially if you need to change quickly, is to bring in new leadership with new values and core beliefs. This new leadership then makes sweeping changes throughout the organization, and many people lose their jobs. If you find you cannot enter the e-business world successfully without changing basic beliefs governing the organization, then fasten your seat belt, you are in for a bumpy ride. The good news is that in most cases it is not necessary to tinker with the core, in fact, it often would be damaging to the company to do so. What you need to change is your business strategy and the simpler elements of the culture that back up the strategy with action.

 We should have no illusions about the possibility of major cultural transformation, without massive human costs. For old cultural assumptions to be destroyed, the organization has to convert or get rid of the culture carriers.[12]

The second warning is that even though the other two elements of culture are easier to change, it is still a struggle. People get attached to "the way we do things around here." Everyone has encountered the ever-popular expression, "but we've always done it that way." People do not like it when you change the structure, the building, the teaming procedures, the technology, the levels of accountability, the rewards, or the rules about what gets you into trouble or makes you a hero. No group of people in any part of the world has ever been known to live through cultural change happily or quietly. Most people will gripe, complain, and resist their way through the entire process. We are truly creatures of habit.

 BE prepared for the disruption and disturbance that cultural change triggers. It is not possible for you to be so skillful and persuasive that everything goes smoothly. It is a messy, frustrating process. People will be upset by the changes. Count on it.

---

[12] Edgar H. Schein, *The Corporate Culture Survival Guide: Sense and Nonsense about Culture Change* (San Francisco: Jossey-Bass Inc, 1999), 168.

A third warning is for companies that have worked hard to ensure that employees understand the culture of the organization, especially the core values. When you change policies, procedures, and habits of the organization, people often accuse the company of abandoning its core values, because it is easy for people to confuse the core values with the behaviors associated with them. It is possible to take one key value, such as 3M's focus on innovation, and find hundreds of behaviors and procedures that illustrate that value in action. If employees are used to the ways the company has always done things, they will not like it if you take one procedure away and replace it with a different one, even if it is geared toward the same goal. If 3M decided to discontinue its practice of allowing employees 15 per cent of their time for experimentation and replace it with a different practice to encourage innovation such as new team structures or technologies, people would resent it and would probably question the company's commitment to the core value.

An example of this occurred at Canadian Tire Acceptance Limited (CTAL), the credit card processing subsidiary for Canadian Tire Corporation a leading retail hardware and automotive supply chain in Canada. One of CTAL's core values is respect for the individual employee, and it has an impressive history when it comes to formal and informal behaviors demonstrating this value in action. In the past few years CTAL experienced great success in its business strategy and has grown rapidly, adding personnel at an extremely rapid rate. Because of this, the company had to change many of its inclusive habits such as inviting large numbers of people to many meetings, having frequent off-site culture days and other events for all employees, and other processes geared toward treating the company like one small group. It could not be done anymore. The company was too big and moving too fast. It had to find new ways to respect the individual that were consistent with its current business strategy and pace.

Some people focused on these "take aways" and a common refrain was that the company was "going against its values." Because CTAL really was trying to find new ways to continue living its core values and was involving people in department and division level events and decision-making, the complaining eventually died down. People formed new habits and moved on. CTAL leaders knew they needed to stay the course and wait for people to adjust. When you are changing a culture, you have to be prepared to weather the storm. If you truly are committed to maintaining the core values, people will eventually see that commitment in your actions and adjust to the changes.

> CTAL's values actually allow us to move faster because we operate in an environment of trust. These are the values upon which we continue to build our business and culture, day by day, one person at a time. Even though CTAL did get too big for us to gather everyone in one place very often, employees are more involved in the business more than ever before through such vehicles as focus groups and project teams. Employees are represented and involved in every initiative CTAL takes. Their commitment and energy enables CTAL to grow and move faster.
> —*Janice Wismer, VP of Human Resources,Canadian Tire Retail*

The bottom line is that change inconveniences people, frightens them, and usually leaves them in a bad mood. The employees did not ask to go through this experience, and it is very hard on them. If you are hoping to make these kinds of changes and keep everyone happy during the transition, you are being unrealistic. You need to face reality and prepare for the flak. If you are confident that you are focusing on keeping the core and accomplishing the business strategy, then everything else in the culture is negotiable, even if it is a rough journey along the way.

BREAKING OLD HABITS AND FORMING NEW ONES

Changing a culture entails breaking old habits and forming new ones. It is a bit like quitting smoking or taking up jogging. It takes a great deal of repetition before the new habits become second nature to the individual. When changing group behavior, even more repetition is required, because you have to convince a large number of people you are serious and the change is really going to happen. A common way to avoid change in an organization is to simply wait it out. Do nothing and wait. Eventually the instigators of the change may give up or lose interest, but if the changes that died were essential to the company's ability to enter the e-business arena, stonewalling cultural change will have devastating effects on the organization's ability to survive in its marketplace.

Every time you get an individual or team to take an action that represents the new culture, you have made one step in the right direction. For example, in the e-business environment, decisions have to be made much faster than they were in the past. Every time you get a team or individual to expedite a decision in two days instead of two weeks, you have a small culture win. Now multiply that by hundreds of similar actions throughout the company and you have a culture that is changing. The larger the number of these actions, the faster your culture changes. If you are a leader of the change, one of your main tasks is to inspire, encourage, and reward these individual actions representing the new desired behaviors for the new culture. Chapter 10 describes the role of the leader in detail, but there is one key behavior of a leader that is essential in changing a culture—paying attention to the right details. Employees at all levels watch carefully to see what (and who) leaders pay attention to and what they ignore. For example, if increasing product development speed is a key requirement of the new culture, the leader needs to pay a great deal of attention to the teams that are delivering results at the new, faster pace.

The devil is in the details and so is the successful change to a new culture. It takes large numbers of details to create real change. Think of it this way. You get one point for each action and to win the game of changing the culture you need lots of points. A common mistake made by cultural change leaders is to think one or two big glitzy events will enlighten and inspire people to move in the new direction. They assume that will do the trick or at least those events will take you far down the path in the change effort. This is rarely the case. The big lavish, expensive retreat or company meeting may be great, but you only get one point for it. You will probably get more mileage from 20 or 30 small, everyday actions that focus on the new direction. That is not to say that big leadership or company-wide events are useless. They can be very effective, but just be realistic. They are only one step in your cultural change strategy. You need a steady stream of actions occurring throughout the company to form new habits that stick. Every action counts: when a team delivers results more quickly than in the past, two employees use the new knowledge management process to exchange information about a client or product, a team does an "after action review" to learn from their successes and mistakes, or an individual employee speaks out in a team meeting and is listened to without retribution. Each action is moving your organization one more step closer to building a .com culture.

TIP

REMEMBER that you only get one point for each new behavior that represents the new culture no matter how grand or impressive. It takes many detailed actions all over the company to trigger a real change in the culture.

APPLYING THIS INFORMATION IN YOUR ORGANIZATION

Below are some questions to help you determine what kind of culture you currently have. If you are going to try to change a corporate culture, it is important that you know this. You may want to discuss these questions with others to see how different people in the company respond.

1. What are the words and phrases you would use to describe the core values in your company?

2. Think of your favorite stories about your organization at its best. These include hero stories, success stories, and responses to crisis.

- What do those stories say about you as an organization?
- Do the messages match your core values statements?
- Do actions in the stories match the official descriptions of core values that you described in Question 1?

3. Think of stories about when you fell short as a company or made mistakes.

- How did the company handle these problems?
- Did people work hard to improve the situation or did they try to bury it and ignore the shortcomings?

   (Note: Cultures, like individuals, are not perfect. The key to understanding your culture—or the personality of an individual—is to watch how the imperfections are handled.)

4. When it comes to making the transition into an e-business culture, which of the nine challenges listed in the Preface worry you the most? What keeps you awake at night? Spend the majority of your energy on the issues that worry you the most.

CHAPTER TWO

Making the Jump
to Warp Speed

LIVING IN NET TIME

> We want to change GM from being an automotive com-
> pany that moves on an automotive time frame, to an
> automotive company that moves on an Internet time
> frame. To do that, we have to have our employees think
> about things completely differently than the way they
> think about them today.
> —*Mark T. Hogan, Group VP of E-GM at General Motors
> Corporation*[1]

"Net time" is a term that has entered the business vocabulary,
describing the speed with which e-business is moving. It is generally
assumed that net time is a ten to one ratio, meaning that business is
transacted ten times faster than as it was traditionally (even a few years
ago). This means that changes that once took ten years to develop are

---

[1]Brian S. Akre, "GM Plans to Expand Use of Internet to Cut Costs, Increase Speed for Customers," *Associated Press Newswires* (August 8, 1999), 23.

now taking place in one year. The actual increase in speed, of course, varies dramatically depending on the situation, but in all cases things are moving much faster than the traditional mind-set.

Cisco Systems is known for consummating acquisition agreements in days or weeks rather than the old model of companies taking months or years to reach merger agreements. Chase Manhattan launched its new company ChaseShop in partnership with ShopNow.com and took only 18 weeks to get all its lines of business to sign off on the new infrastructure and have the Web site designed, tested, and rolled out. Mike Mazza, VP of Chase's Internet project office said, "Traditionally, in a large corporation, in 18 weeks, you can't even have two meetings. The bank gets it."[2] Lexmark International slashed production cycles for computer printers by 90 percent. A printer that used to take four hours to assemble now takes 24 minutes. Another new word that has entered business jargon for the speed and aggressiveness of the new business environment is coined from one of the .com world's most famous companies: *getting amazoned*. Move fast, or your traditional business model will be overrun by a .com start-up company. For Barnes & Noble, Borders, and Chapters bookstores, the world changed forever when Amazon.com took the bookselling world by storm.

There is a three-clicks rule for Internet usage. This is a guideline that Web site designers keep in mind. Most people have only enough patience for three clicks, and if they do not find what they want by then, the fourth click takes them elsewhere. In many ways this is a good metaphor for business in general. It is a three-clicks world. People are looking for value immediately, if your company does not offer it now, someone else will. If companies must develop business strategies based on net time for a three-clicks world, they need a three-clicks business culture to support their plans. Making the jump to warp speed is what many people identified as their biggest e-business challenge.

[2] "Chase Manhattan Forges E-Business Alliance," *Information Week* (October 18, 1999), 104.

Think fast... Speed must include everything—the Web server, firewall, backbone and back-end services. If a Web page takes longer than eight seconds to download, the consumer is likely to go elsewhere.[3]

ACXIOM'S 100-DAYS STORY

Most companies know by now that they need to speed up significantly, but figuring how to make it happen is not so easy. Acxiom Corporation is an example of a company that pulled off a major success in increasing its speed on one of its very important projects. The effort was such a success that the methodology the project teams used has spread like wildfire through the entire company and is now being used to deliver faster results on all types of projects. Acxiom Corporation is an information services company that specializes in enabling technologies for customer relationship management and has been in business since 1969. The company needed to develop new software and databases for a revolutionary new data linking process essential to Acxiom's success in the future. In 1999 the company found a way to get the work done in about one-fourth of the time of original projections, design more software than originally targeted at the beginning of the project, and produce stunning results in terms of quality and cost reduction. When the teams finished their work, they had removed 98 percent of the steps from some processes, producing faster technology at a much lower cost.

This term, 100-Days Project, has really caught on throughout the enterprise, not just in product development but in all areas of the business. People are approaching their work in 100-day increments of time. One of the people said she believed she has gotten more work done since we started using this approach than she did the rest of this calendar year due to nothing but energy level and enthusiasm. It tends to galvanize people to a common cause, and people like that.

[3] David Hildebrandt, "10 Tips for e-transformation," *Beyond Computing* (October 1998), 50.

> Another thing that is critical here is leadership. You can't just go off and issue a mandate and then abdicate. Charles Morgan [company leader] got involved. He worked 60 to 80 hours a week during the project, taking a role where people would send him work saying, "Charles, you need to make some corrections on some coding you did." In most companies, doing that is unheard of, but in this case, he was a part of the team. The leaders have to roll up their sleeves and work alongside you with the message, "We are in this together."
> —*Pete Hoelscher and Cindy Childers, Acxiom Corporation*

This is not a start-up .com company. It is a mainline, established company that is figuring out how to change its pace. Here is the story in the words of Charles Morgan, a 30-year veteran of Acxiom, who is the company leader (CEO in other companies—Acxiom has no titles). One amazing part of this story is that Morgan was a team member and actually did 10,000 lines of coding himself on the new business-to-business software they created during the 100-Days Project. It is a revealing indicator of the culture at Acxiom that a 30-year veteran CEO still even knows how to code, let alone would join the team and do the work. When telling the story, Morgan did not seem to see anything unusual about that role. When asked about it, he simply said, "I realized from my experience I had about as good a chance of figuring it out as anybody else."

Charles Morgan tells the Acxiom 100-Days Story

We had been developing this data linking technology that is the heart of the issue from Acxiom's standpoint. We have been working for years on building the software and databases. The problem we had was like many other companies: the projects get bigger and more complicated, and delivery schedules stretch out. Things slowed to a crawl. This technology is absolutely break-through for us. It would totally transform everything about our company, but for that to happen we have to get it created and deployed. At the rate we were going, it would be another year before we could start talking about broad-scale deployment.

In my frustration I said, "Let's commit to getting a deploy-ment in 90 days." The team wanted a little more time and sug-gested September 1 as the target date. Someone calculated that as 100 days. So we all agreed that at the end of those 100 days we were going to have this technology ready to deploy. It imme-diately became known as the 100-Days Project. What we were asking people to do was clearly a year's worth of hard work. And we were going to do it in 100 days.

We had about eight teams working on the project with about 50 people who were really critical to the project. They were committed. No person on any team was going to let their team down and no team was going to let the project down. As we got into the work, we realized that the requirements that we had defined on day one had significantly underestimated the project. So, not only did we have this incredibly short timeline for the original goal of creating extensions to the consumer product, but we also needed to develop a prototype of the business-to-busi-ness product which we hadn't even invented yet. That was the part I got involved with, helping to complete the invention of the business product. I did about 10,000 lines of prototype software development. I buried myself in it. It was really complicated stuff. We didn't know how to do it.

It was an enormous hill to climb. Do all the data workup and finish our negotiations with one of our key partners, Dun & Bradstreet, and keep the rest of the company running as well. During the final week some of the teams brought in cots and worked around the clock. The software was ready, but we had to process mountains of data. There were last-minute software bugs. People were making an incredible effort, working all night and all weekend. They had people staffing this project 24 hours a day, 7 days a week. Programmers were working in the middle of the night trying to get things fixed. Everyone really had a "take the hill" mentality. Nobody wanted to be the one who failed the whole project. We made all of our objectives. It was a tremendous success.

The general business culture has to be supportive of doing such things. One of the real dangers is trying to do something like this and not having a supporting culture. In a command and control culture, people have to get permission to do things, and people who make decisions outside their authority are often punished. In this situation, you end up with a learned behavior that people are not going to take risks or do things that might get them in trouble.

If you are going to do a 100-Days Project, you've got to have a lot of risk taking and people just deciding themselves what they need to get the work done. They may decide they need to go buy another workstation, upgrade a server, or bring in more team members to help out. They are literally making decisions on the fly. They have to know that some project administrator isn't going to come in and get upset that they are busting the budget.

People have to feel safe and trust that they are going to be judged on results. You can't tell people in a traditional company with a command and control culture that now all of a sudden they are empowered. I know, because I tried it in the past, and it didn't work. They don't trust you, and they don't trust why the rules have suddenly changed. As far as they are concerned, the last guy who tried that got fired and they aren't going to go there. At least they are not going to be the first one to try it.

To change the culture of a traditional company, you have to define a vision of where you want to go for the whole company. For example, we needed to reduce the layers of managers and move into a more efficient structure. That is one element of the vision. Create a vision that is understood and that people buy into. At first, people will be skeptical. If it is a company of any size, you can't change the culture in less than two to three years.

LESSONS LEARNED FROM THE ACXIOM 100-DAYS PROJECT

How to organize a high speed project:

- Pick an important, high-profile project, meet with the key team leaders, and negotiate a finish date that is one fourth or one half the usual time it has taken to finish similar projects. Charles Morgan wanted 90 days—they were willing to agree to 100 days.
- Give the project a name that everyone likes. The group came up with the name the 100-Days Project. The wording was a fit for that culture. Everyone understood it, and it triggered enthusiasm and respect.
- The CEO or other key leaders need to join the effort and become a part of the team in some way. Not all senior leaders have the skills to program 10,000 lines of code, but each can take on some key role that demonstrates to the team that you are working as hard as they are.
- As the leader who is a part of the team, make sure people feel free to tell you when you make mistakes. Ask for their feedback frequently and accept their critiques with humor and appreciation.
- Create publicity within the company about the high-speed project. Talk about it frequently, praise the team members, and tell lots of stories about the heroics of the teams working on the project.
- Be prepared for the project to expand after you get started or to run into set backs and problems that you did not foresee. Do not change your deadline. As you are getting started, talk about the fact that these things will happen, so the team is prepared to tackle the problems or new challenges as they arise. That is what a "take the hill" mentality is.

- Recruit team members who are enthusiastic about the project and the challenge of the tough deadline. These types of team efforts call for the best, the brightest, and the most determined employees you have available. Do not coerce people into participating.

How to create a safe culture where there is a high level of trust:

- Charles Morgan accurately pointed out that these team efforts do not work unless you have a high trust culture where people are confident they will be judged on results. In the past, individuals and teams were often measured more on how well they followed the rules, stayed within budget, or created impressive update documents and presentations. In a high trust, empowered setting the individuals need to consistently experience maximum flexibility and protection from their leaders in *how* they get to the goal and high rewards for successful results.

- Give people on the teams decision-making authority without having to ask permission before they can act on each decision.

- They will need access to budget and other resources so that they can implement their decisions. Cut out the red tape that prevent them from getting to the resources quickly.

- Protect people when they take a risk and make a decision. If someone goes out and hires some extra contract workers for part of the project, make sure they do not get in trouble for doing so.

- Make a big deal out of the first few independent decisions people make. Point out enthusiastically that those are the actions you support. Even if they did not make a decision that you would have made, coach them privately about what to do differently next time, but praise them for the initiative. In the long run it is more important that they feel free to take action than whether each action is exactly the one you would have taken.

- Reduce the layers in your organization and on your teams. Fewer layers lead to more power sharing and more outspoken team members.

- Create a clear vision of where the company is going, specific goals that must be accomplished to get to that vision, and how this specific project supports those goals and vision. Repeat these messages over and over. Use stories, examples, numbers, market research, and any other information you have to explain your message.

- Cancel projects that do not directly support the goals and the vision. Do not drain the company's resources, talent, and enthusiasm on peripheral projects. It blurs the message and slows your momentum.

LAUNCH AND LEARN IS STANDARD PROCEDURE

Chuck Martin coined the term "launch and learn" to describe the way companies are getting new products to market on Internet time.[4] Rather than design, build, test, and perfect products before launching them into the marketplace, companies are often launching products that are not fully developed. If you wait until you have a fully designed and tested product to put out to market, you are likely to be too late. Someone else is already ahead of you. Second to market is not good enough anymore. Think about how different the book buying arena might look if Barnes & Noble had been first into the Internet bookselling business. A start-up like Amazon.com probably would not have gotten a foothold as the second entry into that market behind an industry giant.

> We have found that once we got the initiative launched, we would have been far better off to launch the initiative based on the initial concept that was developed and gotten feedback from our customer partners, and in some cases, consumers. We found that we wasted a lot of time initially trying to overanalyze what something should look like versus putting it out. It's very important to get something of sufficient quality and make sure people know that this is the first release. The consumers know there are going to be updates. But be sure when you put it out there that you can support it. You know the release may not be perfect, but at least be able to respond to the things you do put out.
>
> —*Bob Sell, CIO, Brunswick Corporation*

---

[4] Chuck Martin, *The Digital Estate: Strategies for Competing and Thriving in a Networked World* (New York: McGraw-Hill, 1997), 13.

Procter & Gamble, the $38 billion consumer-goods giant, has been doing things its own way for more than a century and a half, but recently it has begun to aggressively transform itself into a company that can move rapidly into new markets. For example, the company developed a new product called Swiffer, a dust sweeper with disposable cloths electrostatically charged to attract dust, dirt, and other household allergens. This product took 18 months from test market to global availability. In the past, getting this same product to market worldwide might have taken five years. Mel Hughes, Financial Analyst at Stein, Roe & Farnham, an investment firm that follows P&G, said that in the past P&G's strategy was "ready, aim, aim, aim, aim, fire. Now it's ready, aim, fire, adjust. P&G is much more willing to move quickly, take risks, and make needed adjustments later."[5]

Chuck Martin pointed out that one dilemma faced by traditional companies in this kind of market environment is that consumers have different expectations for these companies than they do for the start-up.coms.[6] People expect half-baked products with bugs from the start-up Internet companies but would never tolerate that kind of performance from a General Electric or P&G. So how can traditional companies make the jump to warp speed and maintain the quality standards they bring from the old world of business? How do they create the internal culture that supports this complex mix of demands?

DO PRODUCTS ON THE FLY MEAN THE DEMISE OF QUALITY?

Jim Collins and Jerry Porras contrast two different mind-sets that they call "Tyranny of the OR" and the "Genius of the AND."[7] They found that great companies are not defeated by paradoxes and do not accept the notion that they must choose between two seemingly contradictory goals such as speed and quality. The companies Collins and Porras researched were determined to succeed at both goals.

---

[5] Marianne Kolbasuk McGee, "Lessons From A Cultural Revolution," *Information Week* (October 25, 1999), 56.

[6] Chuck Martin, *The Digital Estate: Strategies for Competing and Thriving in a Internetworked World* (New York: McGraw-Hill, 1997), 14.

[7] James C. Collins and Jerry I. Porras, *Built to Last: Successful Habits of Visionary Companies* (New York: HarperCollins, 1994), 43.

The pharmaceutical company, Merck, is guided by a set of altruistic principles *and* the drive for financial success. George Merck, founder of the company, described their ideals in this way, "We are workers in an industry who are genuinely inspired by the ideals of advancement of medical science and of service to humanity."[8] An example of these ideals in action at Merck was the company's decision to develop and give away Mectizan, a drug to cure "river blindness," a disease that infected over a million people in Third World countries. The company knew that the product would not have a large return on investment, and as it turned out it had none. They had hoped a government agency would purchase and distribute the drug, but that did not happen. At its own expense, Merck produced and distributed the drug to the millions of people at risk from the disease. Why did they do it? Leaders from the company explain that it would have been too demoralizing to the scientists who worked for the company. They view themselves as "in the business of preserving and improving human life." They go on to point out that there are often pragmatic payoffs for such altruistic gestures. Merck which brought antibiotics to Japan after World War II to eliminate tuberculosis, did not make any money from that particular venture, but today is the largest American pharmaceutical company in Japan. There is a belief in the company that good deeds and financial success are connected.[9]

In the long run, to be successful in the e-business environment, companies cannot choose between speed and quality. The companies that last will be the ones that figure out how to do both. The market in the .com world is already maturing in ways that may indicate less tolerance for 80 percent quality. Most e-commerce companies now have competition, so the consumer has choices if they are satisfied with the quality of vendor.

---

[8] George W. Merck, "An Essential Partnership: The Chemical Industry and Medicine," speech presented to the Division of Medicinal Chemistry, American Chemical Society, April 22, 1935.

[9] James C. Collins and Jerry I. Porras, *Built to Last: Successful Habits of Visionary Companies* (New York: HarperCollins, 1994), 47.

UNLESS a product or business model is very new and truly unique in the marketplace, the customers are not likely to tolerate 80 percent quality anymore, even in the .com world.

Dean Wolf, a Partner at Ernst and Young LLP, described the changes that are occurring.

"I don't believe that 'release and refine' or 'launch and learn' is true anymore unless you are carving out a genuinely unique business model where there is significant demand and little competition. If you and I were having this conversation a year ago I would not have said that. But now, a year later, you cannot put out something that does not work very well. There are so many choices out there for every product or service. If one on-line shopping site does not work well, you move on to another one. The bar has been raised quickly. As e-commerce moves to business-to-business areas, it must support the most demanding customers. In the B2B world, the value of transactions is very high; therefore, there is corresponding need for a high quality of service.

The need for e-commerce service providers to address market niches quickly has not gone away. What has really happened is life is more painful. Having 70 or 80 percent of the desired quality is not good enough anymore. If people or businesses have a bad experience, they don't click back."

HOW TO PRODUCE BOTH SPEED AND QUALITY

One distinction that companies may need to make concerning speed/quality demands is whether they will hold all products and functions to the same definitions of quality. For most companies the answer is probably "no."

Cindy Childers describes the way Acxiom approaches quality demands differently depending on which aspect of the company's output is under consideration.

"With software applications there is usually a general expectation that the first version will be about 80 percent right with enhancements in the pipeline. Version 2.0 is on the way. People are used to that. But in our company, data are a different issue. We can't be 80 percent right on the data. That's just not acceptable. Only having 80 percent data quality means that mail gets sent to 20 percent of the wrong addresses and wrong people. It gets to be a fine line, but the distinction is on the functionality side (software) where we are looking for 80 percent as acceptable, and on the data side or in areas that deal with dollars, the standard is much higher."

Every company must answer the question for itself about which functions or products they can release as 80 percent finished and which require zero defects to meet customer expectations. As Childers pointed out, it is a fine line in many cases. But if traditional companies continue to insist on long timelines for development before releasing new products or services, they are very likely to find themselves amazoned and at risk of losing their foothold in their markets.

 DEVELOP guidelines that employees can use to help them make judgment calls about when 80 percent is acceptable and when 100 percent quality is required.

If a traditional company operates with a learn-and-launch rather than a launch-and-learn method, the move to the new mind-set and procedures is a major shift in the culture. Developing a set of questions that are guidelines for making launch-and-learn judgment calls helps to provide a road map for a company entering unfamiliar territory. Here are some examples of questions that may serve as a guide for sorting out specific quality requirements.

1. What do the customers expect of us? Flawless quality or a new product that they will help refine.
2. Which products or processes will they tolerate 80 percent accuracy with upgrades to follow soon?

3. Which products or processes do the customers expect to function with zero defects and 100 percent quality?

4. Do we have the support mechanisms in place for the 80 percent accurate products and processes so we can respond quickly to bugs and feedback from the customers?

HOW TO USE A FAST/SLOW STRATEGY TO IMPROVE QUALITY

The second consideration for accomplishing the dual demand of speed and quality work focuses on the speed half of the equation. Achieving speed to market may not mean that all steps of the design and development process take place at top speed. A number of people described an alternating pattern of fast/slow. Stressing the importance of judging when to go fast and when to slow down. They pointed out that if you picked the right steps in the process to slow down to ensure that you get them right, the rest of the process could go much faster. You end up with a shorter delivery time overall than you would have if you tried to push the entire process along at top speed. So the wisdom or skill in high-speed development and delivery may center on knowing when to slow down.

 TIP   KNOW when to slow down during a project, so that you can accomplish both speed and quality during the remainder of the project.

When to slow down:

1. If the team has not worked together before, slow down for the project definition and role assignments, then you can scatter and move at high speed from that point on.

2. If the project calls for new ideas or inventing something that has not existed before, slow down and engage is some open-ended dialogue with colleagues before launching into the development work.

3. A third reason for slowing down is to measure how well the pilot or initial release is going. A new product or service may require a detailed set of measurements for quality that track customer satisfaction. Slow down for the quality measurements and then speed up again when responding to the problems as you find them.

 WHEN not to slow down. If you are slowing down to tip-toe around political conflicts or bureaucratic habits—beware. These delays will not gain you anything in quality and you are likely to end up with a project that is not only slow but also of low quality.

When *not* to slow down:

1. If you are a leader who has commissioned the project, one of your most important responsibilities to the team is to run interference for it. Protect them from the politics that may slow them down or derail the project.

2. If you are a team leader (or member), be realistic about whether or not the project has a powerful and interested leader who will help you navigate the political and bureaucratic land mines. If you do not have a committed sponsor, go looking for one. If you still cannot find one, abandon the project or prepare to fail. This is especially true in traditional organizations that are very political and have massive numbers of bureaucratic rules. Most .com companies are too young and small to have developed these corporate liabilities yet.

3. Keep a low profile. If you are on a team that may attract jealousy or trigger political controversial, do not go around the company unnecessarily publicizing your activities. This is not to suggest that you hide your work or are hostile to outsiders interested in your work. Just do not brag or flaunt your work and stir up trouble you could have avoided by keeping a lower profile. (This point is discussed in more detail in Chapter 5.)

QUICKER PROTOTYPING TO IMPROVE QUALITY AND SPEED

Prototyping or piloting more rapidly is another way of addressing the speed/quality demands of the e-business environment. Professor of Computer Sciences and author, Fred Brooks,[10] described the challenge this way. "The hardest single part of building a software system is deciding what to build. No other part of the conceptual work is so difficult as establishing the detailed technical requirements. No other part of the work so cripples the resulting system if done wrong." He went on to suggest how to deal with this challenge. "It is really impossible for clients to specify completely, precisely, and correctly the exact requirements of a modern software product. Creating a dialogue between people and prototypes is more important than creating a dialogue between people alone."[11] In other words, people need to play with prototypes at early stages in the development process, long before the prototypes are highly developed, sophisticated models.

Often the line leadership and the information technology (IT) designers detest each other because of past experiences that have gone sour. The pattern that led to this impasse looks like this. The IT software development people spend weeks performing extensive requirements analysis so they can determine precisely what the line management client needs. The clients are extensively interviewed and the interviews are translated into system requirements. These are circulated for approval, modifications are made, work flow charts are drawn up, and the client signs off on the requirements analysis. The software developers then build a working prototype, often taking as long as 90 days to design it. Then the trouble starts.

The "most important" meeting of the process is scheduled to demo the prototype to the client. The software developers are proud of their work because it not only captures all the client requirements, but also anticipates some possible improvements. The developers sit back and wait for the client's recognition of their skill and efforts.

---

[10] Fred Brooks, *The Mythical Man-Month: Essays on Software Engineering* (Reading, MA: Addison-Wesley, 1975).

[11] Michael Schrage, "Power Play," *Business* 2.0 (November 1999), 53.

Instead of the expected reaction, the corporate client says, "Well, you've given us almost what we discussed. But now that we have seen it, we realize it's not what we really want. We really need you to do is something different." In other words, the client rejects the prototype. By the end of the meeting, everyone is enraged and indignant. Charges fly back and forth that management doesn't know what they want or that the IT people are inflexible geeks who don't understand the business. This is not a good situation for producing the final product with high levels of speed and quality.[12]

This is a common pattern in many companies, so maybe it is time to change the approach. Fred Brooks made this suggestion: compress the requirements analysis dramatically. As quickly as possible identify only the top 20 to 30 requirements for the new system and stop. Then the developers rapidly develop what Brooks calls a "quick-and-dirty prototype" within a week or two. Meet with the clients, let them play around with the prototype, and have a discussion aimed at codeveloping with the client. When the clients can interact with an early version prototype, they can articulate what they want much more accurately than they can describe in detailed discussions of system requirements. There is another advantage. If the clients help develop the later stage prototype, they are much less likely to reject it, because it is, after all, partially their idea. The client is turned into a partner in the process. Making this simple change in prototyping or piloting vastly improves the speed and quality of the final results.

 TIP IDENTIFY a current pilot that might benefit from a "quick-and-dirty" prototype that the client can play with and codevelop the next iterations.

A California-based frozen food company used a version of this type of prototyping when they launched a new automated sales system. IT's original plan was to do a full-blown system that incorporated inventory control and other financial applications. The company decided to

---

[12] Ibid.

scale back the first iteration of the system and launched a system that only included two simple applications—order entry and a travel expense filing. Both were easy to use and were well received by the sales force. After they adjusted to the new system, IT and sales worked together to add other applications. The project was implement faster, with less resistance from the sales force, and better quality from both groups' perspective.

CREATING A CULTURE THAT SUPPORTS RISK TAKING

Having long periods of time devoted to development before you launch a new product or system is no longer acceptable in the e-business environment. Taking months or years to enter new markets will ensure extinction. Purposely choosing to be second into a new market has been one of the most respected and successful business strategies in past decades, but it no longer works in most industries. GE has had spectacular success under Jack Welch using a second into the market business strategy but has changed its approach. In 1999, Welch told all divisions at GE to develop first-into-new-markets strategies. His now famous "destroyyourbusiness.com" edict, delivered in January 1999 at a meeting of top GE executives, is commonly viewed as a milestone in the effort to rally corporate America to embrace the Net.[13] Welch told the division executives to find out where the threats to their business will come from and either enter that business themselves, or take action to protect against the threat. When Welch used the term "destroyyourbusiness.com," he was signaling a faster, much more aggressive, higher risk entry into new markets, particularly the e-business arena. From this point on, GE will not only be one of the two or three best in each of its markets, it will get there first. If this means the company must cannibalize current profitable products, it will do it. Better to destroy your own cash cows and replace them with the next generation of products than to have the competition come along and do it to you.

---

[13] Mark Veverka, "Get Ready for Dow.com," *Barron's* (December 20, 1999), 32.

It is no longer possible to take the safer, slower route. In fact, there is no safe route anymore. In today's environment, paranoia is not a sign of mental illness. Looking over your shoulder to see who is gaining on your company or is about to leapfrog past you is a sign you are in touch with reality. To thrive in the e-business arena, companies must be willing and able to take risks. And yet, risk aversion is one of the most common characteristics of traditional companies in traditional industries. The cultures of these companies are geared toward reducing risk in every way they can. In Charles Morgan's description of the 100-Days Project at Acxiom, he pointed out that a supportive culture is essential as a foundation for fast action. Employees must be allowed to make decisions and take risks without layers of approvals and fear of punishment.

In a risk-encouraging culture people are rewarded, not punished, for taking risks, even if those risks are not successful. If you institute broader decision-making and rewards for risk taking, and you want these to become a part of your culture, you must take this approach consistently with employees throughout the company. Having a trusted few who are given wider decision-making authority and rewarded for risk taking, creates an elite enclave, not a new culture. It is unlikely that a few privileged people will be able to drag an entire company into a successful delivery of Internet speed business strategies.

TIP

TO have a fast-paced culture companies must make risk taking one of its dominant traits.

1. Encourage risk taking by providing monetary and recognition rewards for risk taking.

2. Reward the risk takers whether they succeed or fail.

3. Reward the successes more highly, but everyone who took risks trying to reach the goal should be recognized and rewarded whether their risk paid off or not.

4. Loosen the controls over decision-making so that more people can make more decisions on their own.

> **TIP**
>
> 5. Protect teams from the corporate bureaucracy so they are safe to break the rules.
> 6. Make resources and budgets available to the team, and give them the freedom to use them without having to constantly ask permission before they can take action.
> 7. Recruit proven risk takers to come to work for your company and give them leadership responsibility for teams.

Remember Morgan's warning. People are leery of quick changes and test the waters carefully to see if the changes are real. They watch to see if the walk matches the talk. You can speed up this process by recruiting people to test the new strategy, encouraging some of your natural risk-takers to take new risks with assurances that they will be rewarded for their efforts whether they are successful or not. Then when these early testers make their moves, be sure the rewards are public and enthusiastic. Recruit the early testers from all ranks and functions and recruit as many as you can, as fast as you can and keep the rewards in the limelight. You will still have a lag time while the other employees see if the new culture is real, but you may be able to shorten the time it takes to change a culture.

MAKING DECISIONS AT WARP SPEED

Decision-making goes hand in glove with risk taking. When employees accelerate risk taking, they are making decisions, so if you want to change your culture to increase speed and risk taking, you need to take a look at the decision-making processes in your organization. If you have a slow, risk-averse organization, you almost certainly will find restrictive decision-making processes geared toward controlling and limiting people, not freeing them to move fast.

TO speed up decision making in your organization, count the number of meetings it takes to make a decision and how many sign offs each requires. Those two traits alone usually tell the tale about the slowness of your current decision-making processes.

To get to warp speed, you will need to:

- Simplify your committee structures—reduce the number of committees and the number of people on each committee, and shorten the amounts of time allotted for each meeting. Cut them all in half.

- Slash the number of approvals or sign offs needed to take action. If people have to jump through more than one or two approval hoops, it will slow decision-making and implementation down dramatically.

- Ask yourself why you need *any* sign offs. Give the team the resources, tell them the goal, and get out of their way. Let them accomplish the goal their way as long as they stay within the time frames and the allocated resources.

Peter F. Drucker gives advice to companies that want to be change leaders in their industries. By following his advice, a company can speed up its decision making, increase risk taking, and do these things in a way that increases the likelihood of focusing on the right priorities. Drucker said, "The *first policy*—and the foundation for all the others—is to *abandon yesterday*."[14] His reason for putting this first is to free resources from "maintaining yesterday," which always consumes time and resources. Innovation requires your best people to focus on new directions, and you cannot afford to commit them to maintaining yesterday. Drucker encourages an organization to adopt a policy of organized abandonment.

---

[14] Peter F. Drucker, *Management Challenges for the 21st Century* (New York: HarperBusiness, 1999), 74.

HOW to decide what to abandon. Drucker encourages companies to set up systematic reviews of what and how to abandon dying, resource-using elements of the business. His three criteria for deciding what to abandon are:

1. If it is fully written off.
2. If it still has a few good years left.
3. Most importantly, if maintenance of the old product, service or process causes a new and growing market to be stunted or neglected.[15]

Drucker also recommends that a company have two budgets to help it make better decisions that encourage innovation and risk taking. This allows the company to dedicate resources to an e-business initiative or other innovations. Two budgets will encourage decision-making that emphasizes speed and risk taking:

*   One is an operating budget that tracks expenditures for maintaining the present business, which are the products, services, and processes the company has not abandoned at this point. This budget is always scrutinized with the following question, "What is the minimum we need to spend to keep operations going." When times are bad, you cut this budget, but during good times you do not increase it.

*   The second budget is for the future and remains stable through good and bad times. The question that should be asked on a regular basis about this budget is, "What is the maximum this activity can absorb to produce optimal results?"[16] This budget should be used to exploit success.

Following Drucker's advice on organized abandonment and dual budgets can increase the likelihood that a company is focused on future opportunities and has resources available to make decisions and move at warp speed.

---

[15] Ibid, 75.
[16] Ibid.

CHANGING YOUR APPROACH TO DECISION MAKING

To keep up with the effects of energy deregulation as well as e-business, utility company PG&E has completely changed its decision-making process according to VP and CIO John Keast.[17] "We used to figure out what was needed to evaluate a new opportunity or initiative and then ask how long it would take to make a decision—say 12 weeks. Now we time-box it. The decision has to be made in four weeks, and we'll do as much as we can in that time frame." For example, PG&E completed a business plan in four weeks for the potential company-wide deployment of Web procurement of nonmanufacturing materials.

Keast sees this high-speed operating mode as the norm going forward. "Everyone has had to do a rapid project every now and then, but this is the standard way it's going to happen from now on. Time-boxing is a new way of approaching decision making for many companies. It is a change in the culture of how we do things around here.[18] The same concept of time-boxing can be applied to meeting structures, setting a limit on the number of meetings to make decisions, and the maximum length of meetings. Cut your meeting times in half and accomplish the same or more goals. People tend to fill any amount of time allotted for a task. When you shorten the time frame and keep the same goal, they often produce the results with no loss of quality.

TIP

USE time-boxing to complete projects more rapidly.

- Pick a high-profile project with significant potential payoff for the company and time-box it.

- Set a goal for completion that is three or four times as fast as the "normal" speed for a similar project.

- When getting started on a new project, first ask yourselves, "When do we need to have this project completed?" The second question is: "How do we have to organize and implement the project to meet the

---

[17] Clinton Wilder, "E-Transformation," *Information Week* (September 13, 1999), 56.
[18] Ibid.

> **TIP**
>
> goal within that time frame and at expected quality standards?
>
> • Quit asking the old question, "How much time do we need to complete this project? That leads to longer timelines.

David Roussain, VP of E-Commerce and Customer Service at FedEx, discussed his approach to decision-making.

"The truth is that you don't have to have agreements. You have to have a basis for a decision. You don't have to have absolute consensus. If seven of the nine people feel that it is the right way to move forward and two don't, then you acknowledge their contribution, understand their position, but ask them to refocus their efforts on the goal of the other seven. To make this work effectively, you have be skilled at collecting the intellectual property... constantly probing people for what the issues are that they see in their specific work areas and what the problems are. That is a big issue right now for teams and meetings in general where teams are trying to move ahead. There isn't rapid collection of intellectual property from members of the group."

The key to fast, high quality decision making is the ability to collect information concerning what team members think about issues and synthesize it. The goal is to make sure everyone on the team understands the range of perspectives, what issues already have been decided, and what issues are still open. Roussian explained that they use Power Point and the storyboard technique to visually communicate this kind of information among team members, especially on virtual teams where members are physically disbursed. The teams also use management briefings to move themselves toward decisions. The teams at FedEx make presentations at regular intervals during a project. According to Roussian, the importance of this step is not necessarily the presentation itself. What is most important about the presentations is that they "drive the team toward a consensus or decision point because the team has to shed a lot of excess baggage to come up with a position by the presentation date." The presentations are milestones marking key decision points in the team's progress.

Notice that there is an underlying assumption in Roussain's thinking about the presentations that represents an important element of the FedEx culture. The teams in that company must know that they are expected to tell the truth during the presentations to management. In some companies, presentations to management are well-known rituals for making bad news sound like good news and camouflaging any truths that might not be well received. In this case, a presentation to management is not an effective way to "drive a team toward consensus." Instead it is a time-wasting ritual that blurs and confuses the issues for the team.

HOW to make fast decisions based on high quality team input.

- Set your decision-making goal as reaching a basis for a decision, not reaching an agreement.

- Identify "continual research" as one of the key functions of the team. Everyone on the team needs to be responsible for collecting what David Roussain calls "intellectual property." This includes information about current issues, new trends, problems with specific aspects of the project, and changes in the company that might affect the project.

- Create meeting agendas (face-to-face or virtual) with an emphasis on dialogue and exchange of information among the participants.

- Schedule regular team update presentations with your sponsor or the leader who has commissioned the project. Use these milestones as a way to focus the team members on key decisions to do the presentation.

Major General Michael Kostelnik, Commander of the Air Armament Center at Eglin Air Force Base in Florida, discussed how they have used their management information system to speed up their review process. It has freed up hours of meeting time each month that can now be used with the people. "In the old style of military management, a general officer would make decisions based on written staff documents and meetings. The primary management tools were individual metrics oriented toward very specific management objectives. In the days of physical world management, progress on these performance indicators would be reviewed monthly by the general and 20 or more subordinate colonels. Once a month, every single performance indicator was reviewed by the general and his staff. This whole process was very inefficient."

General Kostelnik described two changes they made that saved time and improved the quality of their results. "First, we stopped managing things that were going our way. We color-coded our performance indicators and standardized the display formats of the management briefings. Green was used for metrics meeting expectations. Yellow for a process not meeting expectations, but experiencing only minor problems, and red was reserved for the metrics which were not going well and considered more serious in nature. With our 'virtual' approach, everyone now is looking at the same management data, and I no longer have to look at the green performance indicators. The yellow indicators don't have to be reviewed, but I usually do. The red metrics are where we now spend all of our management time." In addition to standardizing and focusing primarily on "red" items for review, Kostelnik points out that all the data is on the management information system and available to virtually everyone.

Now he can check the performance indicators anytime from his desk and can eliminate those time-consuming briefing meetings each month. "The great thing is that everyone can manage at their most productive time. Since this is a virtual system, you can use it when you are at your peak. I now have a lot more time for more important work and so do the colonels in my organization. So rather than have 20 colonels sitting around a desk trying to explain graphs to me, they now have time to get out where the work is really being done and spend more time with their people. I am able to go out more too. Today, we did two below-the-zone promotions, and I had time to do that because I no longer sit in all those meetings. In fact, every one of those meetings uses to take at least two hours. Multiply those hours by the number of people sitting at the table, and that's how much time was saved each month."

LOOSENING UP ON CONTROL CAN BE A DIFFICULT HABIT TO CHANGE

Loosening the controls and allowing more freedom to make decisions without bureaucratic oversight is one of the most difficult changes for the leaders of many traditional companies to make. This requires the skill and attitude to set clear but broad boundaries for the teams and individuals to function within and let them go within these boundaries to make decisions and chart their own course. Leaders must monitor progress along the way. This monitoring needs to focus on ensuring that the teams are staying on strategic focus and within the boundaries but should not spill over into interfering with the details of how the team is carrying out its mission.

Anyone coming from a command and control cultural tradition will probably have a tough time making that transition. But it is the linchpin in moving to a faster, more risk-oriented operating mode. There is no way to soften the message on this change. It may not be comfortable if it is not the way you are used to leading, but there is no choice. You must change if you want to succeed in the world of e-businesses.

COPING WITH THE RESISTANCE TO RAPID CHANGE

Leaders are not the only people in organizations who may be stressed by all the changes. People in general do not like change—they find it frightening; so people will often react by resisting the changes. Eventually, we may all get used to the increased speed and constant change and resistance may drop off, but for now it is still an issue. According to Daryl Conner, there are two different types of resistance—ability resistance and willingness resistance.[19] Ability resistance occurs when people do not have the necessary skills or know-how to perform in the new situation. The solution in this case is training. Willingness resistance occurs when people lack the motivation to apply their skills in the new situation. If you are dealing with willingness resistance, training will not help. You must find a strategy that changes motivation.

THE DIFFERENCE BETWEEN ABILITY AND WILLINGNESS RESISTANCE

- The most obvious source for this information is what people tell you. They may tell you that they do not have the skills or ability to perform in the new situation, or that they are unwilling to do so. If you have an outspoken corporate culture, as many .com companies do, their statements may be accurate.

- In some companies with more cautious or punitive cultures, people will be afraid to speak up to say they do not know how to do something or that they think that approach is a dumb idea.

- It is also possible that fear or low confidence triggers the claims that they do not have the skills to perform in the new setting, but have not really pushed themselves too hard to try. Conners suggests that you ask yourself if these people could perform this task if it was a life or death situation. If your answer is yes, then you are not dealing with ability resistance and training will not do much good.

- Sometimes it is very difficult to determine which type of resistance you are facing, and in this case you have to experiment with both solutions to see which one works.

- If you do not know for sure which type of resistance you are dealing with, take Conners' advice and assume you are dealing with willingness resistance. Get the resisters involved in the planning or implementation process. Give them some responsibility, solicit their ideas, and adapt your plan to include their ideas. Offer rewards for participating and for being part of a successful implementation team. If their resistance diminishes and they suddenly discover more skills than they realized they had, you have solved your problem.

---

[19] Daryl Conner, *Managing at the Speed of Change: How Resilient Managers Succeed and Prosper Where Others Fail* (New York: Villard Books, 1993), 127.

- If they still do not know how to perform the tasks, train them or retrain them.

There are many ways to respond to willingness resistance, but in general these strategies fall into two categories. One is finding ways to get people involved in the planning and implementation of the change. If the ideas about how the change is implemented are partially their own ideas, people are usually less resistant. The second way to deal with willingness resistance is rewarding people for their participation in making the change a success. Charles Morgan relates how Acxiom used the second strategy to deal with the resistance that was inevitable when the company moved into the deployment phase of its new technology. Acxiom launched a second 100-Days Project.

Morgan picked up where he left off and explained what happened next with the 100-Days Project.

"Now we had the technology ready for deployment. We were doing a lot of testing with customer data and the results were spectacular, but I knew that anytime you deploy new technology that changes everything, you are going to have resistance. The changes we needed to deploy took processes that were previously a 76-step process and converted them to 12 steps. We had completely redesigned the processes. It was a huge change.

I knew from past experience that resistance is directly proportional to the degree of the change. Small changes trigger a small amount of resistance, and large changes trigger lots of resistance. Change creates the possibility that things could go south, so people resist it. One way you can deal with resistance is with a big stick and beat on people to get them to do it. But that doesn't work. The other way is that you can give incentives that make people want to change. This new technology has an enormous benefit to us and to our customers. It represented tremendous new revenue sources for Acxiom. We needed a scheme—and so the *second* 100 days!

We put up a million dollars of rewards tied to deployment with individual rewards of up to $5,000 per person for people who were a part of a team that had a successful deployment. And we gave them 100 days to do it. We targeted 50 teams to sign up. We had 110 teams join the effort and 70 teams crossed the finish line within the 100 days. Team member awards ranged from $500 to $5,000 a person. And many of the teams exceeded the goals. For example, they were measured on reducing computer time on the core data integration process by 1,500 hours a month. Many of the teams reduced their hours by as much as 2,300 hours. They also found ways to reduce their team size, so we could reassign 150 team members to seed new teams. One of those reassigned people is going out to a customer site to deploy the technology on a project that represents multimillions of dollars in new revenue for Acxiom."

The Acxiom story is a great example of inspiring higher levels of motivation to dissipate the willingness resistance. Not every change a company undertakes will warrant a million-dollar investment to motivate people to change, but the strategy of looking for ways to build in benefits for changing is the right direction to go. In many ways, it is like the simple laws of physics about inertia. When the motivation to change becomes greater than the inertia to remain the same, people opt for change.

APPLYING THIS INFORMATION IN YOUR ORGANIZATION

Below are questions to help you to identify your speed strengths and weaknesses of your current culture and decide what needs to change. Without an organized effort to change the speed of your culture, the status quo will dominate. Just saying you will make decisions and develop products ten times as fast, will not make the culture move faster.

1. Which processes have sped up significantly in your company—product development, service delivery, distribution, or internal processes? If Internet speed is ten times faster than the old pace of business, your operations should be showing the effects of this increase.

2. Is all your current piloting or prototyping done with detailed front-end analysis and long lead times?

3. What needs to be time-boxed for quicker decision-making: meeting formats, key decisions, deployment of new products or processes, or hiring procedures?

4. Do you have rewards and incentives built-in for risk taking whether the risk pays off or not? Are the rewards highly publicized when they are given?

5. Who has the freedom to make independent decisions in your company? Is it only a handful of people? How many sign offs are needed for different types of decisions?

6. How do you currently define consensus in your company? Is it slow and cumbersome? Are there pressure points or milestones for a team to make decisions and move on to the next issue (e.g., FedEx's periodic presentations to management)?

7. Do you ever abandon old products, services, or processes to free up resources to invest in the future? When has this happened recently? What is the decision-making process used to reach the conclusion that abandonment is appropriate?

CHAPTER THREE

Building a Corporate Culture in a Virtual Organization

WHAT IS A VIRTUAL ORGANIZATION?

The term "virtual organization" has entered the vocabulary of almost everyone trying to describe the evolving nature of work and organizational structures found in the new economy. Exactly who coined the term is not certain. HarperCollins has credited Charles Handy, author, consultant, and professor, and William H. Davidow and Michael S. Malone.[1] There are many different definitions of the term virtual organization, but this chapter focuses on the elements that impact corporate culture.

Definition of Virtual Organization

- An organization whose employees do not all work in group settings in corporate offices.

- These employees work out of remote settings, often home offices. In other cases they are mobile, traveling constantly and doing much of their work from cars, airports, and hotels.

---

[1] William H. Davidow and Michael S. Malone, *The Virtual Corporation: Structuring and Revitalizing the Corporation for the 21st Century* (New York: HarperCollins, 1992).

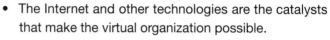

- They can be full-time employees and contract labor.
- The Internet and other technologies are the catalysts that make the virtual organization possible.
- The terms virtual worker, remote worker, and telecommuter are all used to describe people whose work falls within the virtual organization model. For the purposes of considering cultural impact, these three terms are interchangeable.

In some cases the definition of virtual organizations includes alliances created with other organizations, but the focus in this chapter is the employees on the payroll and the impact they have on corporate culture when they are scattered all over the country or the globe. These people spend a large portion of their time working independently away from any work team or functional department. Their communications with their colleagues inside the company take place primarily through technology. There have been virtual workers in small numbers for many years, but the advent of the Internet has made this organization model viable on a much larger scale. It is so common for companies to have at least a minority of their employees working remote that it has become an important issue to consider when building a corporate culture. If 10 percent or more of your employee population are virtual workers, it will affect the culture. In the past when only a handful of people worked remote, they were so outnumbered by the office workers that their impact on the overall culture was too diluted to be an issue worth addressing. The e-business world and its related technologies have changed all that.

Ten million people, or 4.5% of the workforce, characterized themselves as telecommuters in 1998. By 2001, nearly 8% of the workforce could be telecommuters.[2]

---

[2] Robert Barker, "Work à la Modem," *BusinessWeek* (October 4,1999): 174.

The definition of a virtual organization includes contract workers because they often spend enough time working for the company that they have an impact on the way things are done and on the attitudes and the general atmosphere of the organization. Because of this, they affect the culture. Contract employees are hired because they have a specific skill for a specific project. They often have some knowledge of the organization. In some cases the contract employees are former full-time employees of the organization but now may want to work less than full time.

An example of a company that uses the virtual model for large numbers of its employees is Gartner Group, Inc., a technology advisory company. They have more than 700 research analysts worldwide, and many are mobile workers because of their travel schedules or remote workers because they do not have assigned offices at any of the company locations. This is an example of a virtual organization that is very different from a traditional structure of a few years ago. The company uses technology to link the widely distributed workers and to overcome the limitations of distance and time (to some extent). The challenge in this type of organization is how to develop a strong corporate culture when a significant percentage of the employees are no longer in one location.

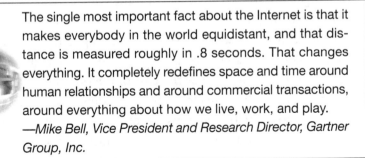

The single most important fact about the Internet is that it makes everybody in the world equidistant, and that distance is measured roughly in .8 seconds. That changes everything. It completely redefines space and time around human relationships and around commercial transactions, around everything about how we live, work, and play.
—*Mike Bell, Vice President and Research Director, Gartner Group, Inc.*

WHY DID WE GO VIRTUAL?

Work is a four-letter word that at one time meant the physical location where you went to earn your paycheck. Work now means what you do regardless of where you are. Is this really new? The concept of performing your job away from a traditional office building is certainly not a new model for sales representatives, who have often worked in territories distant from the corporate offices. Even when they are assigned a desk at the office, sales management often lets the salespeople know that they are not really welcome there unless a meeting has been scheduled because the real work of the sales force is dealing with the customer out in the field.

The recent move to alternate workplaces was triggered primarily by the need to reduce the cost of doing business. IBM was one of the first organizations to take this approach starting in 1989. Its goals were to reduce real estate costs and the amount of time the sales force spent traveling to visit customers. One innovation that IBM used was "hoteling." The sales representatives or systems engineers gave up their desks and cubicles and moved to alternate workplaces, usually in their homes. If the employee needed to do work at a desk or in a meeting room, they would call to make a reservation, just as if it were a hotel. The better run hoteling operations have your file cabinet at your assigned desk, your name tag on the cubicle, and all necessary supplies ready to go.

When companies were considering creating virtual organizations with telecommuting and work at home to reduce the real estate costs, they considered items such as the cost of the offices that they could close or sell, the utility costs to keep the buildings heated, cooled, and lighted and possibly lowering insurance rates and some tax burdens. Also if offices could be closed certain positions associated with staffing the building could be eliminated. If you no longer have a building you will not need security guards, receptionists, cleaning crews, and food service staff.

IBM's virtual structure has saved more than $100 million annually in its North American sales and distributions units.[3] Responding to competitive pressures, AT&T started its alternate workplace program in 1994. This company has also realized substantial cost reductions as a result of its virtual structure. AT&T improved cash flow by $550 million by eliminating offices that were no longer needed.[4]

To decide to create a virtual organization based solely on the potential cost reduction of eliminating office space is too narrow a focus on cost relative to the mission and strategy of the organization. With IBM and AT&T the elimination of offices made strategic sense because it focused on the people whose jobs was spending time out with their customers instead in offices. On the other hand, organizations such as law firms or accounting offices may have no reason to move to a virtual model because their customers want to do business with them in their offices. Historically, there has been a certain comfort in visiting your accountant or lawyer in an office that indicates that they may be around for awhile. We may rapidly be approaching the day when it becomes common practice for businesses like law, accounting, or medical services to be delivered from virtual sites as these professions move into the .com world with their businesses. The key business issue to consider is what impact the virtual structure will have on your customers. If virtual workers will have more contact and better relationships with the customers, then moving to a virtual structure makes good business sense. Other issues impacting the decision of whether to move to a virtual structure are the kinds of work that these employees perform. If their work requires large amounts of time in face-to-face interactions with coworkers or hands-on work with equipment that can only be located in the central computer room, these jobs are not good candidates for virtual work.

---

[3] Mahlon Apgar IV, "The Alternative Workplace: Changing Where and How People Work." *Harvard Business Review* (May-June 1998), 121.

[4] Ibid.

VIRTUAL ORGANIZATIONS ARE USED
TO RECRUIT AND RETAIN EMPLOYEES

Another reason for creating virtual organizations appeared in the late 1990s. In the boom economy of those years, some regions of North America experienced a severe shortage of skilled, qualified workers, and faced with the pressure to keep or hire workers, companies began using creative methods to meet the challenge. In some cases, allowing the person to work at home or even in another city was the solution for recruiting and retaining a skilled workforce.

Many of the first employees to start telecommuting did so because of situations at home, such as new babies or family members to care for, but in recent years retention has become the more common theme. Jill Fallick, for example, is a Project Manager for Morningstar, Inc., a Chicago-based investment-research firm. Fallick's story is becoming a common one as companies struggle to keep good employees. In August 1996, her husband accepted a job in California. Rather than lose a valued employee, her manager asked her to telecommute, and Fallick works out of her home in California. One of her challenges is keeping track of two time zones, Pacific and Central. She keeps two clocks in her office, one set to California time and the other to Chicago time.[5] This story is being repeated all over the world. Rather than lose a key employee, companies are providing alternate workplaces and creating a growing number of virtual organizations.

> One of the most interesting differences between face-to-face and computer-mediated communication (CMC) is in the realm of social cohesion and culture. It may be harder to create relationships when you are entirely virtual, but it is easier to maintain those relationships with e-mail and other forms of CMC. Many people use technology to keep in touch with others once they have established a relationship with them.
>
> —*Nicole Ellison, Ph.D., researcher on communications in virtual organizations*

[5] Robert Barker, "Work a` la Modem," *BusinessWeek* (October 4,1999),174.

BEING A VIRTUAL WORKER
CAN FEEL LIKE BOWLING ALONE

Some individuals liken the isolation of telecommuting to bowling alone. Bowling, like work, has a social dimension and bowling alone, like working alone, lacks this dimension. Moving away from a central location to an alternate workplace can cause employees to feel disconnected from peers and the organization as a whole. No current technology can replace the face-to-face contact provided by the office.

> People ask if I get lonely. Yes, I tell them. They ask... Being alone, do I act weird? No more than before, not counting the time I bought one of those 2.5 gallon jugs of water, set it on a table, drew a cup, and began gossiping with myself.[6]

This feeling of being isolated or disconnected from the organization is defined as "anomie," a sociology term describing a social condition where a breakdown of values results in a sense of alienation of members from their organization. Creating a strong corporate culture that recognizes the peculiarities of the virtual organization goes a long way toward establishing the sense of community and cohesion that helps the employees perform in the limited social interaction of the virtual organization.

TIP   HOW to help virtual workers feel linked to the company and avoid feeling isolated and disconnected.

- When you first hire these workers, have them spend a minimum of several weeks at the corporate offices and other company sites to get to know the people they will be working with from a distance.

- Have corporate or departmental meetings where you bring all of the employees together to get to know

---

[6] Ibid., 170. Robert Baker is a telecommuter and writer for *BusinessWeek*.

TIP

each other and create relationships that can be sustained by remote employees with technology.

- Publish newsletters complete with photos so people can keep up with their peers.

- Have company outings, golf tournaments, and holiday parties and be sure to invite your virtual workers as well as the people from the corporate offices.

- Use the best current video communication tools available to help virtual workers see the colleagues as they converse. This technology is changing constantly, and as it improves it will become much easier to create virtual versions of face-to-face interaction on a regular basis.

- Keep reminding everyone who works in all settings in the company that the virtual workers are out there and are a part of the company. Use e-mails, voice mail, and newsletters to mention the virtual workers and their activities on a regular basis.

EXAMPLES OF STRONG CULTURES SUPPORTING THE ABILITY TO PERFORM WELL IN VIRTUAL SETTINGS

The following two examples of individuals performing well in remote environments with the support of strong cultures—the US Marine Corps and the Roman Empire—both have a military component, but success of this type is not limited to the military. The military does, however, have a history of being exceptionally skilled at taking people from very different backgrounds and transmitting the values, norms, and culture of these organizations. So there is much to learn from how these organizations have dealt with passing on the culture to its members.

In the first example, Thomas E. Ricks was a Pentagon reporter covering the American peacekeeping mission in Mogadishu, Somalia in December 1992. Ricks went on a night patrol with a US Marines squad led by a 22-year-old corporal. Impressed with the confidence the young corporal displayed and his skill in leading others in a hazardous situation, Ricks was determined to study the organization responsible for training the corporal. He wanted to know what type of organization would give so much responsibility to a 22-year-old operating in relative isolation halfway around the world. In Ricks' view the culture of the Marine Corps is responsible: "In a society that seems to have trouble transmitting values, the Marines stand out as a successful and healthy institution that unabashedly teaches values."[7]

To find out how the Marine Corps created this strong culture, Ricks followed a group of young Americans, steeped in the traditions of individualism and consumerism, through their boot camp at Paris Island, South Carolina. Their initial Marine Corps training started at 1:50 a.m. March 15, 1995. Ricks describes that training and outlines the conclusions of his study. He wraps it up with thought: "Marine Corps basic training is more a matter of cultural indoctrination than teaching soldiering."[8]

PASSING ON THE CULTURE THROUGH SOCIALIZATION OF EMPLOYEES

While it is unlikely that you would gather a group of highly skilled knowledge workers together and send them through the rigors of a Marine boot camp, what is important is that the Marines have designed their training to teach the values and culture of the Corps to its newest members. This is not left to chance for the new recruits to figure out on their own. They are told over and over what it means to be a Marine, and then the actions of their officers and the physical training reinforce this message repeatedly through the weeks of their initial training. It works, as you will quickly discover if you ever make the mistake of referring to a retired Marine as an "ex-Marine." There is no such thing—once a Marine, always a Marine. In much the same way, non-military organizations can design orientation and

---

[7] Thomas E. Ricks, *Making the Corps* (New York: Scribner, 1997), 20.
[8] Ibid., 37.

training processes to transmit their culture without a boot camp environment. There are few examples of companies that have a formal program to relay the traditions and culture of their organizations to new members. It is even more important now that many of the employees will work away from corporate offices and have few opportunities for face-to-face interactions with their peers.

Anthony Jay relates another example of the importance of culture in his book, *Management and Machiavelli*. Jay describes how Rome governed its far-flung empire without any modern technology such as telecommunications or computers. "Rome knew that it could not send the wrong man to lead in the remote posts. [Rome] took great care in selecting him. But more than that they made sure that he knew all about Rome and Roman government and the Roman army before he went."[9]

The key to the success of the Roman Empire and the US Marine Corps in socializing their members is that they can identify the values, rules, and behaviors that make them unique and make the effort to see that everyone understands these cultural components. There are examples of organizations that feel that the cultural component of their organizations is so insignificant that they have eliminated it from their new hire orientation. In one example, a New England-based consulting firm left the new hire orientation to an outside firm, so any attempt to transmit the values of the organization was second hand rather than delivered by someone who has actually lived the experience. Contrast that to Acxiom leader, Charles Morgan, who personally does all the orientation training of new leaders from acquired companies. He knows the message must be delivered accurately and that the symbolism of him taking his time to deliver the training is a crucial cultural message.

---

[9] Charles Handy, *Understanding Organizations* (New York: Oxford University Press, 1993), 250; Anthony Jay, *Management and Machiavelli: Discovering a New Science of Management in the Timeless Principles of Statecraft* (Amsterdam: Pfeiffer, 1994).

HOW to transmit your culture to new hires in a way that leaves them equipped to work in remote settings and still feel a part of the culture.

- Invite employees who are excellent role models of the culture to participate in your company orientation of new hires.

- Invite long tenured employees who can tell the new hires the great stories from the companies history.

- Encourage the leaders of the company to attend the orientations or meet with new employees in other settings to talk about the culture of the company and what they expect of people who work for this organization.

- Make recordings of the companies stories on audiotapes or compact disks and send them to all of the employees to reinforce the organization's values.

THE CHALLENGE OF PASSING ON THE CULTURE TO VIRTUAL EMPLOYEES

The virtual workplace makes it more difficult to create and maintain a strong culture. The challenge in the virtual organization is that there is no office and no central point for the employees to gather to transmit the culture. Broadcasting a message, no matter how well developed, by Internet or intranet does not replace informal exchanges at lunch and after work. With the distributed workforce in the virtual organization, transmitting the culture is more important than ever. The corporate culture serves as the glue to hold the pieces together and will give the members a sense of identity and commitment to something greater than their individual jobs.

THE SEVEN STEPS OF THE SOCIALIZATION PROCESS

Various terms such as socialization, enculturation, and indoctrination describe the process of transmitting culture. In some cases, socialization is used in its most basic context to describe the process by which babies learn what they need to know to function. Enculturation is an anthropology term describing the process by which adults acquire an understanding of the rules, models, and context of the organizational culture. Indoctrination is a term that could describe socialization or enculturation taken too far, and the indoctrination process is usually associated with cults not cultures. The most common term, socialization, describes the process of passing on the organization's culture. In some cases, people consider socialization to be a negative process that forces compliance and deprives people of individual freedoms, but that extreme type of socialization is not recommended.

The socialization described here results in a degree of order and consistency but provides flexibility and a range of individual responses. Socialization is the process by which individuals become members of a group, learn the ropes, and learn the standards of "how we do things." Viewing the socialization process[10] as a series of interconnected and overlapping steps is a useful tool for understanding the process and knowing what to do to build a corporate culture (Figure 3.1). When viewing the model, do not think of these steps as sequential. You can work on all seven steps at the same time when building your culture.

The seven steps are:

1. Selecting
2. Conditioning
3. Training
4. Measure and Reward
5. Shared Values
6. Legends and Folklore
7. Role Models.

---

[10] Richard Pascale, "The Paradox of Corporate Culture: Reconciling Ourselves to Socialization," in *The Management of Organizations*, Michael L. Tushman, Charles O'Riley, and David A. Nadler, eds. (New York: Ballinger Publishing Co., 1989), 304-310.

YOU can take action in all seven steps of the socialization process at the same time.

The steps are not necessarily linear or sequential. Other than selection you may act on all of them at the same time or any order that makes sense. Use the seven steps as a blueprint for planning actions to build your culture.

The steps of the socialization process used to develop a strong corporate culture in an organization in the .com world and the traditional business world are the same. The differences are:

- the steps are more difficult to implement because many of your workers are at the end of a data line instead of down the hall.

- creating a strong culture is even more essential as the glue that keeps employees committed to each other and helps them stay focussed on the same goals.

You no longer have many of the traditional methods for controlling or monitoring virtual employees actions, so you must rely more heavily on their belief in the values, goals, and norms of the culture to motivate them to work in concert with the rest of the company.

THESE seven steps in the socialization process should be viewed as ongoing and not a one-time event at new-hire orientation.

The ongoing nature of the process reinforces the values of the organization and helps strengthen the culture.

Figure 3.1: Seven Steps in the Socialization Process

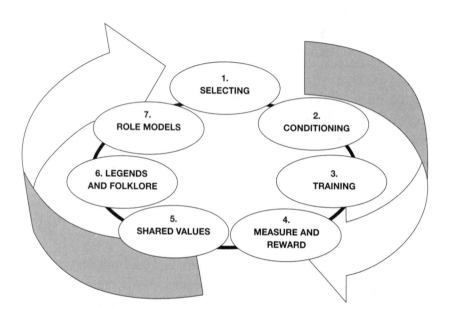

SOURCE: Based on Richard Pascale, "The Paradox of Corporate Culture," in *The Management of Organizations*, Michael L. Tushman, Charles O'Riley, and Donald A. Nadler, eds. (New York: Ballinger Publishing Co., 1989), 304-310.

STEP ONE: SELECTING

Like the Romans selecting the leaders for the remote areas of their empire, a careful selection process for recruiting virtual workers is needed. The goal is to select employees who will "fit." Two kinds of fit are important in a virtual work setting. First, you need to determine if the individuals have adequate skill for working away from coworkers. Can the individuals work remotely? Do they understand the technology requirements (telecommuting, PC skills, etc.)? Do they have the time and project management skills necessary to be productive in a remote environment? Most necessary job skills can be taught, but the aptitude for working in isolation generally cannot be and should be of particular concern in the selection criteria in a virtual organization.

HOW to determine whether a person will be able to tolerate the isolation that goes with being a virtual worker.

- An employee's old work habits tell you a lot about whether they will like virtual work. Get the employee to tell you stories about what they have liked about past jobs and relationships with their colleagues. Listen to the patterns they describe. An employee who has always been the life of the party may not be a likely candidate for becoming a virtual worker.

- If they are the type of person who was always visiting other employees' offices or cubicles rather than using the phone or e-mail, they might miss the interaction.

- If the candidate is the one who always planned the organization's lunches, after-hour gatherings, or the birthday celebrations, they might not be suited for the isolation of working at home.

- On the other hand, if the candidate turned his desk to face the wall, always ate lunch in his office with the door closed, or considered playing solitaire on his personal computer a good way to gather his thoughts, that person may welcome the isolation of the home office.

- There is no fail-safe predictor for how well a person will do in a remote work situation, so discuss with the person that it is a very different experience. If possible leave the option open that she could change her mind and transfer to an office setting if it does not work out. The flexibility may be worth the effort if it will retain a productive, skilled employee.

A second type of fit is particularly important in a virtual setting. Try to hire people who have personalities, values, and habits that match the "way you do things" in your company. You will have much greater success at building a strong culture if you hire people who walk in the door already believing many of the same values the company espouses. For example, if your company values meticulous attention to detail and very high standards of quality, such as a Procter & Gamble culture, try to hire people with a work history focused on exacting standards of attention to detail. If you place great emphasis on frugality like Amazon .com where everyone uses desks made of doors and two-by-fours, look for people who can live without mahogany furniture in their offices. If you are Southwest Airlines, a sense of humor is essential to fit in that company's culture. One myth about Southwest is that you have to tell CEO Herb Kelleher a joke he has not heard in order to be offered a job.

All organizations should pay attention to fit when hiring employees. The difference is that in the traditional work setting new employees will have other employees to use as role models to give them cues of what behavior or attitudes are acceptable in this company's culture. Those working in isolation will not have the role models available on a consistent basis. If the virtual workers do not arrive with many of those behaviors and attitudes, there is much less coaching available for them on a daily basis. Even if everyone in the company works in one building on a daily basis, it is still difficult to take a person whose personality does not match the company culture and try to persuade that person to change. It is even more difficult in the virtual workplace. Start with a fit and build from there. You will have a much greater chance of success.

Recognize that not everyone can handle the isolation of the alternate workplace. Some people need more continuous face-to-face contact with colleagues. Nevertheless, the virtual organization is here to stay, and many people will opt for remote work at times during their careers. The strategies for creating a strong corporate culture in the virtual setting are the same as in any other environment. It just takes some extra effort and attention to make sure the seven steps of the socialization process happen when everyone is not in the same set of buildings.

STEP TWO: CONDITIONING

Author Richard Pascale calls this step humility-inducing to make the new members realize that things have changed and to make them more receptive to the new values and norms.[11] Military basic training is a classic example of this type of conditioning, but in companies humility inducing overstates the case. In corporations, new members must realize that although their past competencies gave them entry into the group, things are different now and new competencies are required. As stated earlier, this is not a recommendation to introduce the rigors of military training in the workplace but that conditioning is an important step to let the new members know how things are done and what standards must be met.

In the military, the conditioning step is truly humility-inducing. It gives new recruits short military haircuts, replaces their civilian clothes with uniforms, and herds them around like cattle. In *Making the Corps*, Thomas Ricks describes the Marine trainees arriving at their training depot at 1:30 a.m. This middle-of-the-night arrival is no mistake. It starts the socialization process. The drill instructors make it clear to the new arrivals that they are no longer in a familiar world. This military training is far more rigorous than anything civilian organizations require, but even there some steps need to be taken to let the new members know that things are different. This conditions them to accept the new values and moves them out of the status quo.

An anonymous high-ranking executive at a prominent Internet start-up company wrote a series of articles for *Fortune* magazine, one of which describes a classic example of the conditioning that he described as "a sort of management torture test that reflects the Silicon Valley's culture of flat hierarchies."[12] Anonymous describes his

[11] Ibid.

[12] Anonymous, "Always Consult Your Employees—Even If You Don't Want To," *Fortune* (December 6, 1999), 320.

entry into the Internet culture, "Two weeks after I arrived at my start-up, my boss asked me to present a product plan to my colleagues. I was shocked." At the large conglomerate where he had previously worked, development of a new product idea would have taken months or years to complete. He describes the meeting where he gave his presentation as a nightmarish experience. "My voice tends to quaver in direct proportion to the amount of bull in my message—I was virtually stammering. I stopped trying to reach for the Coke that some sympathetic soul pushed my way because my hands were shaking too much." He goes on to describe the question and answer portion of the meeting as an "interrogation." The engineers at the meeting used a method of communicating that was "matter-of-fact, nothing personal." They asked questions like, "Do you think our customers are stupid enough to need this?"

Needless to say, this presentation was a humbling experience for the seasoned executive accustomed to a culture where an audience was respectful to a presenter simply because he was a high-ranking executive. In Silicon Valley start-ups, all employees have an equity stake in the company and have given up higher salaries and saner work hours for the chance to become wealthy at these companies. These organizations are dominated by an engineering communication style that puts very little value on tact or subtlety. This executive's experience at that meeting was an initiation rite. At the end of this story, he explains that he learned two important things about his new environment. The engineers did not actually mean to humiliate him. In that culture, "That sucks," does not mean "You suck." And the second lesson he learned about the new culture was to consult colleagues broadly, solicit ideas, and ask for repeated feedback on your ideas. This is how you build a good plan and better teamwork in the .com world he had entered.

TAKE responsibility for your own "conditioning" when you enter a new company.

- If you are new to an organization, consult your colleagues asking for their ideas and listen to what they have to say. This is a very effective way to get yourself oriented to the new company's ways quickly.

- If you are in a leadership position and recruiting new hires into the company, encourage them to take this ask-and-listen approach.

- If you are working in a technology-oriented .com culture, remember the advice from Anonymous about the bluntness of the way engineers communicate. Try not to get insulted by the style and use their directness to your advantage to learn as much as you can about the organization as quickly as possible.

- Never say the words, "The way we did it where I used to work is..." The employees of your new company do not want to hear that information. It is your job to listen to them at this point. Later when you are fully accepted, you can tell them about ideas you bring from other jobs.

Many people accustomed to traditional organizations are not used to open critiques of their work that occur frequently in .com environments and may take attacks on their work as personal attacks. It was previously mentioned that one of the skills necessary in the .com world is sharing, and that is even more important in a virtual organization. The virtual workers have to make a greater effort than office-based workers to exchange information with colleagues. They do not have the benefit of the accidental sharing that goes on around an office when people run into each other or overhear conversations at meetings. The expectation that they will share information should be communicated strongly to new hires and the standards should be as rigorously upheld with virtual workers as for the rest of the company, or a key element of what makes a .com culture function well is lost.

Be careful that you do not leave the socialization to the most negative employees. This is not the type of new hire conditioning you want. In scenes repeated in every organization, traditional or virtual, the new hire is introduced to her peers and a few of the veteran cynics take it upon themselves to tell the new person everything that is wrong with the organization. After a few days of hearing those stories the new hire may have grave doubts about her decision to take this job. There is nothing you can do to completely eliminate this type of cynical indoctrination, but you can make sure that this is not the only message the new hires hear in the first few days and weeks at your company. If the organization does not have a formal process to educate the new employees, there will be nothing for them to contrast to the input about how bad things are going to be.

USE a buddy system for new hires.

This is an approach used by some companies who are particularly concerned about making sure the new hires learn about the company culture in a positive way. Each new hire is assigned a "buddy" who is a long-tenured employee from a similar type of job in the company. These are people who have been asked to take on this role because they are excellent role models of the culture. It is an honor to be asked to perform the role of buddy because it means you are seen as one of the company's best employees. This person spends time with the new person during the first few weeks answering his questions and helping him learn as much about both the formal and informal aspects of the company. This will work equally well with virtual employees. Just assign them more experienced virtual employees to stay in touch with the new hires and help them learn the ropes.

STEP THREE: TRAINING

This training focuses on the skill set necessary to participate in the virtual organization. Technology skills, work process skills, communications skills, and collaboration skills are required.

The technology skills necessary for remote workers are critical. In most cases, telecommunications is the lifeline to the organization. Knowing whom to call when you have a problem with your technology is essential. In some cases, the technology help desk operates on the same clock as the headquarters rather than on extended hours to cover multiple time zones. If this is the case, for the remote workers to remain productive, they must know a "power user" that will serve as their de facto help desk. Just knowing who to call for help with expense reports, medical forms, paychecks, and other related administrative details should be a part of this technical training. Some organizations forget that not all of their employees are located at the corporate headquarters, and they fail to set up sufficient support for remote workers. Deciding how to hook up your computer can be complex. Do you use dial-up services from the phone company, do you ask for a high-capacity ISDN (integrated services digital network) hookup, or does a cable modem make more sense? Organizations with a dispersed workforce must provide training and support for answering these questions.

Training for the technical aspects of operating in an alternate work setting, either mobile or work at home should be designed with the differences in mind. If the remote employees are going to be using laptop computers and dialing into the corporate computer system for their e-mail and Web access, then provide that equipment for the training. It is of little value to talk about dialing into the system remotely but conducting training on a computer that is connected through a local area network. It might help to provide them with a personal trainer for the computer until they are comfortable with the tasks they will need to perform. It will be worth the cost to the company because the productivity rate of these employees will start at a high level if they are not wasting time trying to overcome their technology.

The support for the remote workers may need to change as well. In many cases the remote workers are not on an eight-to-five schedule and may experience technical difficulties after hours. If a sales representative is meeting with customers during the day and checking e-mail in a hotel room at night and experiences a problem, leaving a voice mail message for the technical support person to call the next day is of no value. If remote employees are not adequately connected to the rest of the company and its customers, they cannot participate in any aspect of the organization's life. Technology is the lifeline that creates the connected workplace in a virtual organization, so virtual employees must have the skill to stay connected. In most virtual organizations, they probably require a higher level of technical skill than employees working in the corporate office buildings where there is easier access to technical support. The training and support for remote workers is an added training expense, but it will pay big returns in increased productivity and show that the organization understands that not everyone works out of the corporate office.

Work-process skills deal with the way the organization does business and its standards of performance. An example is the organization's response to customer questions. In some companies, the standard is to return customer calls within two hours while in other organizations it might be within 24 hours. Numerous work processes must be explained to remote workers if they are to meet the expectations and standards and feel a part of the organization. If an organization is starting to create virtual work arrangements they should do a study of all the jobs that they feel are appropriate for this environment and determine what skills will be required and provide the necessary training. One of the best examples of an organization supporting their remote workers was the company that developed a "Yellow Pages" so the employees could figure out where to call to get their questions answered. They encouraged the departments to have some fun dreaming up creative ads to be published in the document. This type of information can also be published on the internal Web pages. If the company does this it must make sure that the numbers are kept current. If the latest phone directory provided to the field still shows that the accounting department is in New York when it really moved to Florida last year then the effort is wasted. Other examples of work-process skills include submitting an expense report, requesting an airline ticket, or having the equipment in your home office repaired. These are not necessarily complex tasks if you can ask the person in the next cubical, but if you are new to the organization and the next cube is 2,000 miles away, they become complex issues.

With a dispersed workforce, training on communication issues is more important than ever. Organizations must develop a communications protocol so that employees will know how to contact each other based on urgency, volume, and level of decision-making authority. As an example, determine which is the best communications method to schedule a meeting with your group. If it's Friday afternoon and your coworkers are located in several different time zones and you want a meeting on Monday morning, do you send e-mail, or do you give everyone a phone mail message? This is a key consideration in communicating with a dispersed workforce in different time zones.

Another communication protocol that must be addressed is time zone differences in a virtual organization. If your company is headquartered in the eastern time zone, a 10 a.m. meeting at headquarters is 7 a.m. in California. It gets even more complex if you have members in other parts of the world. The same New York meeting is 3 a.m. Tuesday in Australia—your coworkers will likely be reluctant to attend a teleconference in the middle of the night.

Unless the knowledge workers in your company are expected to function entirely alone with no contact with fellow employees, collaboration skills are one of the most complex tasks for the dispersed workforce. Thomas Allen, of MIT's media lab, studied the effects of physical layout on the probability of interaction between coworkers.[13] Allen conducted this 1977 study in seven research labs with 512 people working in the labs as his subjects. His question was how often members interacted with coworkers on technical and scientific matters. Allen found that the greater the physical distance between

---

[13] Dorothy Leonard and Walter Swap, *When Sparks Fly: Igniting Creativity in Groups* (Boston: Harvard Business School Press, 1999), 141.

coworkers the less likely they were to interact. Workers that were located ten meters apart found that they interacted with their peers once a week less than 5 percent of the time. For people located 25 meters apart their interactions dropped to zero. Of course Allen conducted his study before the widespread use of e-mail and the Internet, but the findings still seem valid. Physical distance inhibits interaction. In a study in the 1990s, Martha Haywood found that the frequency of collaboration between remote team members was consistent with the Allen study, even with telecommunications.[14]

THE greater the dispersion of the organization, the greater the need for face-to-face meetings. The number and frequency of in-person contact needed may depend on the complexity of the work and longevity of the project, but if possible the group needs to get together at least twice a year.

A pilot project conducted by Gartner Group, Inc. to test methodologies and processes to create collaboration between subject matter experts from various parts of the worldwide research organization was initially conducted with all of the participants working remotely. Technology was provided to allow for sharing of ideas through a software-based program. Additionally weekly conference calls were scheduled to provide input from outside consultants and to continue the project. After several months of struggle the group was brought together to examine the results of the effort. It was concluded that even the most well designed collaborative software had limitations, in some cases the sheer volume of information generated caused the problem. Trying to find a common time to have a teleconference for a worldwide audience was never overcome. The video conference option was not possible because of technology limitations and the time zone problems. An attempt was made to provide audio

---

[14] Martha Haywood, *Managing Virtual Teams: Practical Techniques for High-Technology Project Managers* (Boston: Artech House, 1998), 15.

and videotapes of the various meetings to send to members who were not able to connect. This was an improvement but did not solve the problem. If the members of the project would have met face to face at the start of the project and as often as once a quarter for the remainder, the outcome would have been better. If the members had established relationships in meetings prior to working remotely, they might have been able to overcome the technology limitations.

If organizations created alternate workplaces as a cost reduction measure, there may be resistance to bringing employees together on a frequent basis. This is likely to lead to the organization's inability to socialize its members effectively. There is a need to bring the groups together to sustain the feeling of belonging and help socialize the members. If this is ignored then it may result in increased employee turnover and a loss of productivity that may exceed the cost savings from closing offices. Eventually, we may have video-based technology that will allow people to "meet" in a virtual face-to-face setting, but at the current time physically bringing people together on some regular basis is still necessary.

STEP FOUR: MEASURE AND REWARD

Developing a measurement and reward system requires more attention from managers and human resources departments in a virtual organization. Some specific items that could be measured for employees in the virtual environment are priority setting, quality of results, interpersonal relations, continuous learning, problem solving, communications, conflict management, and decision-making.[15] Designing a measurement system for remote workers is no more difficult than designing a measurement system for employees in the traditional setting. The problem in both situations is that the criteria for measuring employee performance are not always formalized. Experienced managers in traditional organizations may have developed an internal, informal scorecard by which they measure their employees. They may

---

[15] N. Fredrick Crandall and Marce J. Wallace, Jr., *Work and Rewards in the Virtual Workplace: A "New Deal" for Organization and Employee* (New York: Amacom, 1998), 128.

consider behaviors such as enthusiasm, the number of hours spent at the office, and any number of other observable behaviors. The number of hour's worked and other measurements that may have been valid in the traditional setting will not work in the virtual organization.

Creating a valid measurement system for remote workers will require a discipline on the part of managers that may not have been present in the past. The employee's performance must be measured on key behaviors and outcomes. A mobile sales representative can be measured on quota attainment (outcome) and measured on interactions with their customers and coworkers (behaviors). This will require obtaining feedback from the customers and coworkers to measure the behaviors.

 DEVELOPING a valid measurement criteria for remote workers will require a discipline on the part of managers that may have been missing if they traditionally measure performance based on observable behaviors such as enthusiasm or number of hours worked. Measure based on key behaviors such as customer contacts and outcome such as revenue of sales or customer satisfaction evaluations.

Rewards in the virtual workplace may be even more difficult to develop than the measurement system. The reward system must include the normal items like pay increases, bonuses, and other traditional rewards. But informal rewards require special attention and some of the most effective are spontaneous, such as public recognition and acknowledgement. This type of reward is more difficult in a virtual environment, but no less effective. Informal rewards and recognition are very important to the remote worker. Managers should take every opportunity to identify situations where the remote worker performed in a noteworthy fashion and make the results known to coworkers and the management of the organization.

Ace Hardware Corporation gives their employees that go out of the way to help customers a certificate to recognize this behavior. The certificate is signed by the CEO and presented to the employee. It doesn't cost much and there is no monetary reward with the certificate but the employees are proud to receive them and usually frame them for their offices and cubicles. If your organization is moving to a .com environment then the culture needs to reflect the need for speed and flexibility. Rewarding the desired behaviors will help transmit the new values. As the executives travel around the organization they should create opportunities to talk about the need for the new values and recognize employees that have responded to the changes. However, if they talk about the need for speed but continue to reward people that are working in the old ways, the message will get out that the need for speed is only talk.

INFORMAL rewards and recognition are as important to the remote worker as the office-based worker.

- Recognize the effort of a remote worker or team by publishing a note in the company newsletter or Web site.

- Send remote workers e-mail or phone message recognizing some performance they accomplished.

- If you do not know what accomplishments to recognize them for, call them and get an update on what they have been working on recently. The call itself is recognition. Your praise or enthusiasm during the call is the best form of recognition any leader can impart.

- Give small gifts frequently—a pen and pencil set, gift certificate, or a dinner for two at the company expense.

STEP FIVE: SHARED VALUES

This step may be the most important because it involves the transmission of the organization's shared values, which are the compass of the organization. They should be viewed as the organization's core guiding principles and should serve as the basis for commitment to the organization.

These guiding principles define how the organization will respond to a given situation. A famous 1982 product tampering case illustrates this point. The product was Johnson & Johnson's Tylenol, an over-the-counter pain pill. When the altered pills were discovered, the CEO was on vacation and did not have to return to put the company emergency plan into action. Later, when reporters asked why he had not cut short his vacation to handle the matter personally, he responded that the company's guiding principles were so strong that employees knew what to do without him being on site to direct their actions. This is an example of the positive results from making sure everyone in the organization understands the shared values and the guiding principles.

That is exactly what happened. The responsible managers at all levels responded immediately and recalled the products without requiring direction from the top. The company's understanding of these shared values allowed employees to respond without waiting for permission. One of the leaders' responsibilities is constantly to broadcast these guiding principles.

This transmitting of the guiding principles and values is made more difficult by the dispersed nature of virtual organizations. Because of this difficulty the communications effort must be increased. The management team needs to use every medium available—video, newsletters, personal letters, speeches, e-mails, calls to individuals or teams, and showing up unexpectedly at meetings to see how the team is doing and telling them about recent successes in the company that illustrate the values in action. Every time a manager is with a remote employee they should talk about the organization's values and give examples of these values in actions. The universal understanding of these values serves as the compass to keep the organization on course in turbulent times and help build commitment from the employees.

The ability to make sure everyone has internalized the core values is made more difficult in the virtual organization because the transmission methods become less personal. As Johnson & Johnson becomes more virtual they will need to continue to improve on the transmitting of the values to achieve the same results they did in 1982.

Studies on commitment to organizations have identified three types: continuance commitment, normative commitment, and affective commitment.[16] Continuance commitment is the least effective type because the employees continue working for the organization only because they cannot afford to do otherwise. This type of commitment vanishes when individuals feel they can afford to go somewhere else. The clues that an employee is only motivated by continuance commitment are the classic signs of low morale: frequently expressing angry or apathetic opinions at meetings or in communications, never volunteering or expressing enthusiasm about new projects, withdrawing and isolating oneself more than was typical in the past are a few examples of low morale behavior that indicates the person is functioning at the continuance commitment level. We witnessed the effects of relying on this commitment type during the economic boom of the 1990s. When jobs are plentiful and the economy is strong, continuance commitment does not retain talented employees.

Normative commitment works because the employees feel pressure from others to stay and perform. This pressure to commit and support peers is credited with the success of military units in combat. The commitment is to fellow unit members rather than a larger, more abstract idea like nation or the flag. This commitment is the reason that the high-performance teams outperform the others. The team members do not want to let their peers down, and they are willing to do whatever it takes to make sure that all of the team members are successful. This link is harder to build without face-to-face interactions. If you want to build this type of commitment, it helps if you can bring team members together frequently enough that they get to know each other and feel responsible to each other. Between the meetings, communications between peers should be encouraged and

---

[16] Jerold Greenberg and Robert A. Baron, *Behavior in Organizations*, 6th ed. (Englewood Cliffs, NJ, Prentice-Hall, 1997), 192.

the technology provided to assist in this. It is also worthwhile to keep reminding everyone they are in this together and that success is related to everyone's supporting the efforts of their peers.

Affective commitment is also a strong force in bonding individuals to groups. In this case, people are committed to the organization because they agree with the organization's values and goals. Affective commitment and normative commitment are the two types you need to foster in employees to build a strong culture.

In a dispersed organization, leaders must make a conscious effort to communicate the organization's goals and values. This has to be repeated constantly by all the leaders in the organization. Use every opportunity, every form of media, and every face-to-face meeting to communication the values and goals. The employees must view their leader as obsessed when it comes to the core values and goals of the company. The leaders are the most powerful cultural carriers for the organization, and people are paying close attention to all of their words and actions. They must use this power to constantly talk about and reinforce the importance of the core values and goals of the company. This communications effort is more difficult with a dispersed organization, but the step becomes even more important to help ease the isolation felt by remote workers. This level of commitment helps remind employees that they are a part of something larger and helping to create something of value. The eight key leadership activities for building a corporate culture are covered in depth in Chapter 10.

Cyberplex Inc. is a Toronto-based Web site and e-commerce development company that has tripled in size every year since 1994 in both revenues and employees. Its employees are now located in Toronto, Montreal, Halifax, Waterloo, Ontario, and Austin, Texas. The company recognized that it has a cultural challenge in this fast-growing virtual organization: "How to preserve and enhance the corporate culture that it believes was such a key to its success. The idea of a digital archive of Cyberplex's corporate culture was rejected. Drawing on the journalism backgrounds among the staff, the company turned away from the digital life it thrives on to the analog world of ink and paper. Cyberplex published *Ink*, a glossy 48-page full-colour magazine that tells the company's story and introduces its people and what makes them tick." It is not intended for an outside audience but is geared instead toward old and new employees of the company. It captures "the stories, the ideas, and the passion" that are easily lost in the corporate world, especially when a company is growing rapidly.[17]

The Cyberplex story is an example of a .com company using a traditional communications method to transmit its values and guiding principles. Both traditional organizations and .com companies have to be open to using any communications available. Test different communication mediums, both traditional and electronic, to see which ones work best for your company, and be prepared to update and change your approach frequently. To test the effectiveness of a particular communication tool, like a newsletter, identify your target audience and the key messages you are trying to communicate with that medium. For example, you might want to use a newsletter to communicate with front-line employees and with key messages to encourage greater speed, high level of acceptance of new technologies, and greater participation on project teams that are tackling key e-business goals for the company.

Have some front-line employees help you design the format and content of the newsletter. After a few issues have been distributed, go out and ask employees what they remember from the newsletter and ask for their opinions about what they read. If they remember several stories from the newsletters about speed, new technologies, and exciting project teams and want to know how they can get on one of those teams, you have a successful communication tool. If, on the other hand, they do not know what newsletter you are talking about, cannot remember anything they read, or are cynical about the stories they read, that tool is not working. Either have some of those employees help you revamp it or abandon it and use another approach.

---

[17] David Akin, "Web Firm Uses Ink To Tell Story: Digital Archive Rejected: Company Magazine a Vehicle for Selling Corporate Culture," *National Post* (July 7, 1999), C05.

> Too often communication is all over the place. It is becoming more and more important to create filters that enable people to get the information they need when and where they need it. When you ask corporate communication people how they're getting information out, you're likely to hear that they have eight or ten different mechanisms for communicating. Then you ask, "how effective are any of these?" That is one of the problems with all these new mediums. For instance, you may have a Web page, but is anyone going to look at it? Or is it just more garbage? More than ever, we need to measure the effectiveness of our communication so that we don't simply add to the noise.
>
> —Lisa Schenk, Communication Specialist, McKinsey and Company

Jeff Bezos, founder and CEO of Amazon.com, has a reputation as a corporate leader who knows how to communicate the message about who Amazon.com is and what it stands for as a company.[18] The atmosphere inside the company has been described as, "the Cultural Revolution meets Sam Walton." When the energetic Bezos enters one of the company's distribution centers to meet with employees, "You get the feeling that if he wore a tie (he doesn't), it would be flying behind him like a parachute behind a dragster. Even now, as he's supposedly being led on a tour of the warehouse, he's at the front of the line, sailing down a narrow corridor that doglegs and decants into a huge room. For a heartbeat, he's surprised. Seated there, eight to a row in folding chairs, are the latest recruits: 300 employees leap to their feet as the boss on a PA system yells, 'Let's welcome Jeff Bezos!'" He launches into his Six Core Values (customer obsession, ownership, bias for action, frugality, high hiring bar, and innovation) speech, starting with his "watchword" that the customer comes first.

---

[18] Joshua Quittner, "On the Future," *Time* (December 27, 1999), 50.

He says, "Wake up every morning terrified—not of the competition but of our customers." At the end of a long question and answer session, one woman asks the final question, "Can I have your autograph?" The employees encircled Bezos handing him white hardhats, dollar bills, and scraps of paper for his signature. This is a CEO who not only communicates the value message, he is personally a living symbol of the values.

The CEO of a manufacturing company understood the importance of corporate culture and devised a plan to make sure everyone understood the values and goals. He had small credit-card size printouts created that had the company's values and goals on them. They were laminated in plastic so the employees could carry the card with them and refer to it if they had any questions about the values. The cards were mailed to the homes of all employees, but a random survey of those on the shop floor did not locate a single one who was carrying the card. Some of the people remember seeing them in the mail or had heard someone mention the card, but no one had one with them.

In a meeting with the top 80 managers, a consultant asked if any of them had their cards. It turned out that all of the managers had the cards because the CEO asked them about the cards frequently. The attempt to transmit the values was well intentioned, but the CEO had not asked the managers to talk about the cards with the line employees and see if they understood them. A better way to distribute the cards might have been for the managers to present the cards to the employees at work and discuss what they meant. They could be given out at new hire orientation accompanied with a video of the CEO talking about the corporate culture. Any time some one from the corporate staff or senior management made a visit to one of the plant sites they could ask the employees about the cards. If they occasionally rewarded the first employee to produce their card it is more likely that the message would get out.

HOW to inspire commitment to the shared values of the organization.

- Your most powerful cultural carrier is the leader. A leader who is obsessed with the key values and goals of the company and talks about them constantly is your most potent method for inspiring commitment from employees.

- It is essential that the leader's behavior is as obsessed as his words. If a leader talks constantly about the importance of the customers but rarely spends time going out to visit them, the message will lose its power to inspire commitment.

- Use every communication tool available, whether traditional or electronic, to repeat the shared values message over and over. Be sure to test those communication vehicles to be sure they are reaching the target audience and they are getting the intended messages.

STEP SIX: LEGENDS AND FOLKLORE

An organization's legends and folklore are the oral tradition of the culture. These stories reinforce the organization's positive events and accomplishments and provide a sense of history. Even new start-up companies have stories, usually about the founder. Many of the legends of Silicon Valley start-ups revolve around the founders working long hours in someone's garage. At the ROLM telephone company, for example, there was the legend of the founders creating their first computer in a prune shed in Cupertino, California. The legend of Hewlett-Packard, shown in television ads, is that they started in the garage of one of the founders. These stories provide a sense of history for employees.

Nike Corporation developed a corporate storytelling program in the late 1970s. It began with an hour-long session given to new employees when they arrived to sign their tax forms. Today the orientation lasts two days, and the story of Nike's heritage is first on the agenda. Nike also instituted a nine-day Rookie Camp, a Heritage Wall with pictures of the hero's of the corporation at their Eugene, Oregon headquarters. It names its buildings after famous Nike leaders, and tells the company stories to employees of shoe stores who sell Nike products so these people understand the heritage of the Nike products.

> When Nike's leaders tell the story of how Coach [Bill] Bowerman, [one of the founders] after deciding that his team needed better running shoes, went out to his workshop and poured rubber into the family waffle iron, they're not just talking about how Nike's famous "waffle shoe" was born. They're talking about the spirit of innovation. Likewise, when new hires hear tales of (Steve) Prefontaine's battle to make running a professional sport and to attain better-performing equipment, they hear stories of Nike's commitment to helping athletes.[19]

Utility companies have rich histories that are included in their legends. These stories are usually about how the company overcame a disaster such as an earthquake, tornado, or flood to rally and restore electrical power, phone service, natural gas, or whatever their services might be. Southwestern Bell Telephone displays pictures of these extraordinary efforts in its offices. One powerful story, accompanied by a painting, shows two linemen rowing a small boat across a flooded stream to restore telephone service. These stories become part of the organization's fabric. These legends, myths, and folklore define "how we do things around here." These stories are a very powerful tool in the socialization process.

Using storytelling to transmit an organization's norms, values, and beliefs is as old as mankind itself.[20] The tribal elders were responsible

---

[19] Eric Ransdell, "The Nike Story? Just Tell It!," *Fast Company* (Jan/Feb 2000), 44.
[20] Peg C. Neuhauser, *Corporate Legends and Lore: The Power of Storytelling as a Management Tool* (New York: McGraw-Hill, 1993), ix.

for the tribal campfires and the storytelling around them. This is how culture has been passed along throughout history. The storytelling of the organization does not necessarily need to be done by the formal leaders, even though it is an effective leadership tool. The role of tribal elder refers to people who had earned the respect of the members of the group by their past actions and wisdom. Using today's organizational language, they were the informal leaders of the tribe. In the .com virtual organization there are still tribal elders even though many of them may be younger than traditional "elders." What is missing in most organizations is the tribal campfires where the stories are told. This is a particular serious problem in the virtual organization.

DETERMINE who are the "tribal elders" in your organization and encourage them to tell their stories about the company whenever possible. Create virtual campfires where the stories are told.

- Tribal elders are not necessarily old, but they are the individuals who have earned the respect of colleagues and leaders of the organization. Formal leaders might also be elders, but in most cases the people you will identify are informal leaders.

- If you want to know who they are, just ask. If you ask a random sampling of employees in a corporate unit who they respect, are willing to listen to and follow even when the going gets tough, they will name the modern equivalent of the tribal elders. When you hear the same names repeatedly, you have identified your best potential storytellers for passing on the culture.

- These informal leaders do not have to be gifted storytellers. Possessing that skill is an added benefit but not essential. What matters most is their credibility with the audience.

Even though your most effective storytellers are usually the informal leaders who have earned the respect of their colleagues, formal leaders can also use this tool effectively to communicate cultural messages. In fact, one trait of many successful leaders is the ability to tell stories. Skill in delivering this type of message is more important for a formal leader than it is for informal ones. Because of the formal role and the large audience settings of many of their speeches, people expect the formal leaders to be skilled presenters. If you are in a formal leadership role and are not a skilled storyteller, get training. There are a few tips provided in here, but you will need coaching and practice. The best storytellers can connect with their audience. These stories give people a shared identity and a sense of purpose. Herb Kelleher, CEO of Southwest Airlines, is a gifted storyteller and uses this venue to define his organization's culture. Not every leader can match the legendary skill of a Herb Kelleher, but everyone can develop the basic skill.

HOW to tell effective stories. One of the most powerful of tools for cultural transmission is storytelling.[21]

- Keep them short. A minute or less is long enough for most stories in a business setting.

- Catch phrases that create a visual image are excellent versions of stories and are easy to deliver. Here are some examples of famous catch phrases that create a picture. "I have a dream" by Martin Luther King, "destroyyour business.com" by Jack Welch, or "A house divided against itself cannot stand" by Abraham Lincoln.

- Keep it simple. Stick to one plot and no more than three characters. Do not tell a story with subplots or so many characters that people get confused.

- Take a tip from the real tribal elders and end your stories with the word, "And the reason we still tell that

---

[21] Ibid., 34.

story is..." Make sure the audience understands the message you were sending.

- Practice, practice, practice. Even the most experienced speakers who use stories regularly practice timing and fluency. The first telling is rarely as good as the fourth or fifth. If you have not told a story for some time, practice it again to refresh your memory. Most great storytellers sound spontaneous, but they are not. They practice.

- Practice out loud. You will not improve your timing and fluency much by repeating it silently in your head. Tape it and listen to it is even better.

As communication technology becomes more sophisticated, leaders and employees from virtual organizations will be able to use live video and voice systems to tell their stories about the company. Much of the technology available today is difficult to use effectively as conduits for ongoing storytelling because it lacks high quality live voice and visual exchanges among groups of people. It is only a matter of time, however, before new technologies make this type of communication possible. For now, tell the stories using the company newsletter, Web sites, e-mail, and message boards for virtual storytelling. Make video and audio recordings of great company stories and send them out on tape and CDs.

There is no doubt that stories are most effective when delivered face-to-face by one of the veterans of the organization, someone who has "been there." Make sure your company tells its stories whenever you are assembled for meetings or special occasions. If it is not possible to have face-to-face meetings the company should establish a mentoring program and have the more experienced veterans stay in frequent contact with the new members of the organization. This contact can be with e-mail, telephone, or working together as frequently as possible. Make sure to include stories about virtual workers in the company lore. This part of the socialization process is not just for new members. It is also reinforces the values and norms for the more experienced members of the organization. For building and protecting a culture, it is almost impossible to tell too many stories about the company.

STEP SEVEN: ROLE MODELS

Whether your organization is virtual or traditional in structure, role models are an important part of the socialization process. They are the people who display the traits and skills necessary to be successful in the organization. These role models are the people who live by the organization's values. For example, if your organization values customer service, you should identify role models of excellent customer service and recognize these people on a regular basis.

When identifying role models, it is important to make sure they are valid ones. One story from the airline industry pointed out how a discrepancy in measurement criteria might lead to identifying the wrong role model. At a major airline, gate agents were measured on their ability to fill as many seats on each flight as possible and seat the customers so the flight could leave on time. In a management meeting, the gate agent was identified as being the best in the entire airline for getting the passengers on board and seated for an on-time departure. The manager of passenger relations was not impressed because he knew this agent was also named in more passenger complaints than was any other airline employee. It seems that this particular gate agent was rude to the passengers in getting them seated so the aircraft could leave on time. The measurement was inconsistent with a value of good customer service.

Many times in sales organizations, the sales people know whom they think is the best salesperson, but that does not always match the rankings or quotas by which the company tracks performance. Usually the salesforce admires someone who got the most out of their territory or overcame internal barriers to help customers. If the management selects someone else as "best salesperson of the year," it will not have much credibility in the eyes of the sales force. If role models are used to build a culture, make sure that the reasons these people are selected reinforce the desired cultural values and goals. Selecting someone for financial sales numbers alone is not likely to send the broader cultural message you intended.

Some traditional organizations have used the selection of role models with formal programs like "employee of the month." As long as the selection criteria are consistent with the values of the organizations these programs can be one way of identifying role models. One difficulty that companies often run into with a monthly structured program is staleness. It is a very repetitive process and after a few months people begin to lose interest. If you want to institute a formal program, setting up as schedule for choosing the rewards once or twice a year may work better. You can select more than one person to receive awards at any given time, but give them out less frequently. Another approach that has been used in some companies is to select outstanding employees monthly and have their names entered in a random drawing for a substantial financial award at the end of the year. This generates excitement and is fun for the employees. Having your name entered in a drawing for $10,000 is motivating to many workers and generates ongoing interest in the program.

Hospital Corporation of America had an annual award that carried great status in the company. Each of the 400 hospitals in the system would select the winner of their local award. The selection process was a combination of employee nomination and management selection and the criteria for receiving the award was representation of the values of the company. The 400 winners were honored by the company with dinners and prizes, and one person was selected out of that group as the company-wide winner. There was a party to honor the winner, who received monetary awards, and traveled around the company to major events during the next year as the company representative of the best of HCA's values. Informally, winning that award meant you were set for life at HCA with easy access to employment opportunities anywhere in the company.

Start-up .com companies do not have many of these types of formal programs at this point. They are small, new, and most of the employees are so motivated by the project goals and the stock option potential, these kinds of programs are probably not necessary. Traditional companies moving to clicks-and-mortar will have to decide whether this type of program will be well received by employees. Getting employee representatives involved to help you design the program will increase the odds you end up with a success.

Role models are an essential element of any company culture whether the company is a virtual one or located in a building. In a virtual setting, be careful not to have a selection process biased toward people in the central locations, thus overlooking virtual employees that might be excellent role models. To ensure that employees in remote locations are considered, it might be necessary to have two separate selection groups if virtual and office workers do not know each other. Make sure everyone in remote locations is included in the recognition and celebration process that occurs when people are selected as outstanding employees. If you cannot bring people together for the celebration, use your electronic mediums to broadcast the event and run news stories about the people who have received awards.

Informal recognition of role models on a frequent basis is very important in a virtual setting because it is difficult or impossible to bring everyone together for formal award celebrations. Use your traditional communication tools, such as newsletters, and electronic tools, such as e-mail, voice mail, and bulletin boards to broadcast stories about individuals who have done something special that represents the best of the organization's culture. One CEO has field managers notify him of exceptional performances of front-line employees on a regular basis, and he sends these employees personal e-mails letting them know he heard the news and thanking them for their good work.

HOW to recognize role models on a regular basis in a virtual organization.

- Formal recognition programs are one way to do this. Have the employees help design the program so they are enthusiastic about it. Try to avoid setting up a frequently repetitive process that gets stale quickly.

- Be sure you are recognizing the right people. If you select someone that has no credibility with coworkers, it does more harm than good. Ask trusted employees for input in the selection process.

- Use informal recognition methods, both traditional and electronic. Regular e-mails from the CEO thanking outstanding employees for their efforts or stories about employee heroes in the monthly newsletter are as valuable as any formal awards program.

- Be sure that virtual workers are proportionally represented in both formal and informal recognition actions. In some companies you will have to go to the field and ask the people who work remote who should be recognized. Or ask the customers. If high levels of customer service are one of your core values, the customer is your best source of recommendations for employee recognition.

THE DOWNSIDE OF SOCIALIZATION

A company needs to create a strong culture, not a cult. There are many stories in the corporate world of organizations with such strong cultures that they become more important to employees than their personal lives. In Chapter 5 we describe the characteristics of teams that take on temporary cult-like characteristics while working on a project. This type of extreme culture may make sense in a start-up environment when there are relatively few employees who are all functioning like cofounders in terms of their passion for the company. This intense group loyalty may also work well in temporary settings where a team becomes obsessed with its goal for the life of the team. But it is not necessary to develop a cult-like culture in order to accomplish your business strategy. In fact, it might even be detrimental.

A strong culture that emphasizes conformity limits individualism and prevents creativity. In any setting, too much conformity drives out adaptability. It can cause a company to become internally focused, rather than focused on customers and new markets. This is certainly not the type of culture you want to build for moving into the .com world. You need a strong enough culture to generate enthusiasm and a common understanding of the goals and values of the company, but you do not want to go so far as to stifle creativity and variety.

> ... the law of requisite variety... states that for any system to adapt to its external environment, its internal controls must incorporate variety. If one reduces variety inside, a system is unable to cope with variety outside.[22]

A study of firms with strong cultures in the electronics industry identified five possible limitations of a strong culture.[23]

- Makes employees vulnerable to burn out from continuous long hours.
- Makes people unwilling to change what they do.
- Colors the interpretation of information and events.
- Encourages everyone to participate in behaviors that few people do well.
- Encourages ego involvement that heightens the emotionality of events.

---

[22] Richard Tanner Pascale, *Managing on the Edge: How the Smartest Companies use Conflict to Stay Ahead* (New York: Simon and Schuster, 1990), 14.
[23] Harrison M. Trice and Janice M. Beyer, *The Cultures of Work Organizations* (Englewood Cliffs, NJ: Prentice Hall, 1993), 12.

Even IBM, with its famous culture and long history of success, ran into problems by creating a strong culture with too much emphasis on conformity. No one who has had contact with an IBM employee would doubt that they had a strong corporate culture. The ways they dressed, conducted themselves, and did business were manifestations of this culture. One cultural symbol was the IBM dress code. It was so strong prior to 1995 that if a man wore a blue shirt rather than a white one his peers would ask him what time the bus left. Since he had on a blue shirt, he must be a bus driver rather than an IBM employee. In the corporation's folklore, there are many stories of managers sending employees home because they did not have on a white shirt. As the first outsider to become CEO of IBM in 1994, Lou Gerstner remarked on several occasions that he had never seen an organization that was so internally focused. In the past few years, IBM has made great strides in getting its culture back on track, supporting the business strategy and the underlying values of the company. The IBM culture has loosened up on its obsession with following the company rules and is redirecting its attention back to the business strategy and the customer.

The internal focus result in a company that places too much emphasis on making sure everyone follows the rules of "how we do things around here." People forget that the culture and the way things are done are not the goals of the company. The culture is a *means to the end*, not the end itself. The goals are to deliver on the business strategy and the core values that the organization supports. A virtual organization is probably less vulnerable to this danger of over conformity. Because of the employees' physical separation, enforcing a rigid adherence to the rules and procedures of the company would be difficult.

If you find a common belief in the organization that the employees know more than the customer, watch out. You probably have a culture that has become internally focused and stopped listening to feedback from its customers or new markets. If there is no formal process for receiving customer feedback it is very easy to become internally focused.

HOW to know when your company is becoming too internally focused as a culture.

- When organizations start canceling meetings with customers to have internal meeting that is a sign that the focus is internal rather than external.

- When management personnel are "grounded" and not allowed make any more trips to visit customers for the remainder of the quarter because they have been missing too many corporate meetings.

- When your remote workers try to represent the customer to the corporate headquarters people to tell them what customers are upset about and no one wants to hear the news and refuses to take action.

- When customers are never invited into the company to participate in planning meetings or feedback sessions to explain their needs to corporate employees. Or they are invited to these types of meetings, but no action is ever taken to correct the problems the customers describe at the meetings.

- When virtual or office-based employees talk about the customers in derogatory or belittling terms.

Watch for signs that employees have stopped listening to the customer. Make sure that orientation of new employees, coaching, training, ongoing evaluations, and rewards reinforce the importance of listening to the customers and outside markets. Keep the "way we do things around here" flexible so the rules can be easily broken or changed when it benefits the customer or encourages new ideas that may take the company into new markets. In other words, flexibility and listening to your customers need to be two of your key culture characteristics. If you do this, you will have a better chance of avoiding the rigidity and internal focus that trips up many companies as they mature. The virtual workers may be a great resource for reinforcing these characteristics of flexibility and listening. These employees are out in the field close to the customers and markets. They may be the employees who do the best job of listening to the customers and paying attention to what is happening outside the company.

APPLYING THIS INFORMATION IN YOUR ORGANIZATION

Below are questions to help you determine how to ensure that virtual workers are included in the organization's culture. Because of their isolation from the groups of your corporate life, you must make a conscious effort to make them a part of the way you do things in your company.

1. Does your organization use remote or mobile workers today?

2. What is the strategic purpose for creating a virtual workforce? Is it real-estate-related cost reductions, customer service, employee retention, or something else?

3. Does your organization have a commitment to the cultural socialization of employees that goes beyond new hire orientation? Look at all seven steps of the socialization process and see if you can identify examples of actions your company takes that fall within each step.

4. Can employees in your company identify the core values and guiding principles of the organization? How did they learn this information? Do virtual employees have as much exposure to this type of learning as people who work at headquarters or division offices?

5. Do the managers in the organization identify the role models (heroes) that live up to the values of the organization's culture? How are these people rewarded for this behavior?

6. Does your organization make any special effort to make the remote employees feel they are part of the larger organization?

CHAPTER FOUR

Living with Parallel Cultures During the Transition to E-Business

HOW TO GET FROM HERE TO THERE

Most people in business agree on two key points. One is that all companies must figure out how to be a part of the e-business revolution or they will not survive. The degree of involvement in e-business will vary depending on the type of company, but no one can ignore this change. The second point is that eventually there will be no distinction between traditional business and e-business. The companies that survive and prosper will incorporate e-business practices into their operations and e-commerce will become common practice. Venture capitalist Stewart Alsop said, "The e in e-business will soon be irrelevant. In the next wave, businesses will make the e such a core part of their business that the difference between e and everything else will be nonexistent."[1]

On a third key issue, this high level of agreement disappears completely. There are currently dozens of different answers to the question, "How do we get from here to there?" The transition strategy

---

[1] Stewart Alsop. "E or Be Eaten," *Fortune* (November 8, 1999), 86.

for moving a company from a traditional operation to a fully integrated e-enterprise is not clear-cut. Companies are experimenting with many different approaches, and it is too soon to tell which will produce the best results. In this chapter, we look at the way a number of companies are going about it, followed by six decision criteria you can use to help you choose what is the best approach for your company.

> Even though it's still unclear what really works, brick-and-mortar guys are trying all kinds of ambitious ventures. Some companies have put marketers or corporate strategist in charge: others still trust in IT. Some have Internet departments, others e-commerce committees with members from a range of operational departments. Some offer equity to their e-employees, even though colleagues at the brick-and-mortar business don't get stock options. A lot of outfits spin off their Internet businesses into new ventures. Some are willing to cannibalize existing business, while others steer clear of such conflicts. This isn't just evidence of cluelessness (although there's plenty of that). It's also a sign of healthy experimentation. Absent a rule book for e-business, companies are taking steps to uncover the strategies that will work for them.[2]

KEY DIFFERENCES IN TRANSITION STRATEGIES

The most significant difference in the transition strategies is the distinction between a parallel or an integrated approach. In many cases, companies are using a hybrid of both. (See Figure 4.1) Large companies have multiple business units and multiple products, and what works in one area may not work in others. Businesses are setting up separate companies or divisions that are the Internet enterprises and these entities run parallel to the rest of the company that continues to focus on the traditional business operations. In other cases, companies

---

[2] Eryn Brown, " Big Business Meets the e-World," *Fortune* (November 8, 1999), 88.

are making technology changes within each division to bring all elements of their business into the Internet age.

Figure 4.1: Different Strategies for Making the Transition From a Traditional Business Model to an E-Business Model

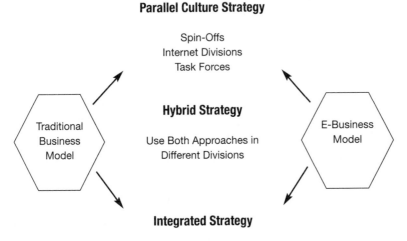

Parallel Culture Strategy

Spin-Offs
Internet Divisions
Task Forces

Traditional
Business
Model

Hybrid Strategy

Use Both Approaches in
Different Divisions

E-Business
Model

Integrated Strategy

Dispersing **IT** to All Divisions
Converting All Business Processes to Internet
Cannibalizing Your Business

TWO key issues to consider when deciding whether to use a parallel or integrated approach. Go back to your business strategy and consider which approach will provide the best chance of success.

- Will your old culture be too slow to change and too hostile to the new business strategy to allow new ideas to take seed and grow? If so, you are more likely to move toward a parallel option.

- Does the business strategy call for all products, services, and processes to be e-enterprises as rapidly as possible. If so, you are more likely to move toward an integrated option.

PARALLEL OPERATIONS CREATE PARALLEL CULTURES

The most extreme versions of the parallel operations are spin-offs. These are separate companies often located far away from the headquarters of the sponsoring company. Bank One's creation of Wingspan, an Internet banking service, or Honeywell's Internet subsidiary called myplant.com are examples of this approach. In other cases the parallel operation is not as extreme as a complete spin-off. A separate Internet division is set up within the organization and given the goal of developing Web business applications. The lowest intensity version of a parallel structure is a task force or think tank made up of a small number of people (less then a dozen in most cases) drawn from many areas of the company and usually from senior-level positions. These groups meet regularly to educate themselves, benchmark against other companies, and explore ideas about Internet applications for the company. In large companies, all three types of parallel operations are often in existence. Author Clayton M. Christensen feels very strongly that it is necessary to set up an aggressively separate company.[3] He believes that the only way the conversion to e-business will work "is if they set up a completely independent organization and let that organization attack the parent. If you try to address this opportunity from inside the mainstream, the probability of success is zero. I've never seen it happen."[4] Although Christensen has a clear-cut opinion, there is little agreement among others. Companies are trying a wide range of transition strategies, and at this point the jury is still out.

It is important to remember that when you set up parallel operations you inevitably create separate cultures with distinctly different characteristics than the mainline operations of the business. In fact, the desire to create a very different kind of organization is often the primary reason for the parallel operation in the first place. This is especially true with the spin-offs. If the predictions that the "e" in

[3] Clayton M. Christensen, *The Innovator's Dilemma: When New Technologies Cause Great Firms to Fail* (Boston: Harvard Business School Press, 1997).
[4] Ravi Kalakota, Ralph A. Oliva, & Bob Donath, "Move over, e-commerce," *Marketing Management* (October 1, 1999) 22.

e-business will fade away and become business as usual are true, companies eventually must blend many of these parallel operations and their cultures together into one unified entity. This blending does not occur easily. It carries the danger of triggering explosive resistance, conflict among divisions, and a mass exodus of valuable talent. Although the verdict is not yet in on how well these options will work, it does seems that parallel operations make a great deal of sense in many situations, even though some perils are involved.

Many people feel that it is important to set up separate Internet operations during the early development stages in traditional companies. RSKCo CEO Bob Kulbick talked about setting up a .com entity within the parent company's CNA insurance environment: "Can you picture it in our company? New people would walk into the big red building in Chicago with blue hair, a ponytail, and a few pierced body parts. They wouldn't survive. What are you going to do, expect them to wear a tie so they blend in? It wouldn't work."

Just because there are dangers in using parallel cultures does not mean that you should avoid this route, but you need to choose carefully; if you choose the parallel route, do not be naive about the implications. You must think through your long-term strategy for integrating the group back into the larger organization, if that is what you will eventually need to do.

IF you decide to use parallel operations, such as spin-offs, Internet divisions, or task forces to execute your e-business strategy, be realistic and acknowledge that you are creating parallel cultures that may not work together easily.

CONVERT ALL OPERATIONS TO THE INTERNET

Companies converting every part of their operations to Internet usage often take the integrated approach. When General Electric CEO Jack Welch told his leadership team to "destroyyourbusiness.com," he sent the message that the entire company was going to transform itself.[5] Welch means that every division within GE will become an e-business operation and will discontinue their old business lines to replace them with Internet driven products and processes. This will be the way the entire GE enterprise will function from this point forward. This represents one approach for integrating the Internet into your operations, often referred to as cannibalizing your own business. Health care executive Jack Lord suggests this approach. He described it as "setting out to create an enterprise that is going to be focused on e-commerce. Think in terms of how you would do the business straight up from there, as opposed to trying to modify your existing business. This allows you to cannibalize your own business. I think those people who are trying to modify or make incremental change don't see all the power and don't see the opportunity in terms of connectivity."

When using the integration strategy, you do not create separate cultures, unless you set up separate operations within each division. By not setting up separate cultures, you avoid the problem of blending them into one operation later, but you do have the immediate danger of triggering a backlash reaction throughout the entire company. If your company has a deeply entrenched traditional culture, the new mind-sets, work habits, and business processes that accompany Internet applications simply may be overwhelmed and stifled before they can take hold. In other words, the dominant corporate culture can squelch the whole effort before it gets a chance to have an impact.

Corporate culture turmoil is likely to surface sooner or later for any traditional company embracing the Internet technologies as an integral part of their business operations and products. No approach allows you to escape the consequences of changing your culture. You can reduce the trouble significantly by anticipating the resistance and laying the groundwork for the changes. Choose the right approach, parallel, or integrated, for what you are trying to accomplish. Once you make your choice, anticipate the turmoil you will encounter and develop a plan for dealing with it.

---

[5] Mark Veverka, "Get Ready for Dow.com," *Barron's* (December 20, 1999): 32.

> In some cases, companies are finding that rather than completely reengineering their business, they can successfully blend their Internet and brick-and-mortar operations. For example, when CD Plus.com merged with Canadian Rock Entertainment, the resulting 100 retail outlets complemented its Internet strategy. Customers can order CDs on-line and then have them delivered to the store nearest them, free of charge.[6]

COMPANY EXAMPLES OF
PARALLEL AND INTEGRATED APPROACHES

The following case examples illustrate the variety of approaches that traditional companies are taking in their efforts to become e-business enterprises. Several companies are using parallel and integrated approaches in different parts of their organizations. After the case descriptions, we identify six criteria to use when choosing the approach that matches your organization's circumstances. In addition to the suggested criteria, read over the cases and draw your own conclusions about what might work in your setting. As *Fortune* writer Eryn Brown pointed out, there is no rule book for e-business. These companies are involved in the grand Internet experiment that is affecting the entire business world, including your own company.

IBM

IBM, under the leadership of Chairman Louis Gerstner, has staked out an aggressive e-business strategy. To get the 225,000-person organization focused on the strategy, Gerstner had to shake it up. He set up the Internet division and appointed Irving Wladawsky-Berger, a respected IBM executive, to head it.[7] This division set the goal of making sure every product in IBM

---

[6] Teri Robinson, "Reinventing The Business Wheel—Ready or Not, Companies Must Be Prepared for a Major Overhaul," *Information Week* (June 21, 1999), S6.

[7] Ira Sager, "Inside IBM: Internet Business Machines," *BusinessWeek* (December 13, 1999), 30.

would work with the Web. Then the staff identified what they call the "white spaces" where the company needed to develop new products.

In an effort to bring the Internet culture into the company, a new design office was set up in Atlanta in 1995. It has become known as Artz Café. There is a billiard table and a Ping-Pong table that doubles as a conference table. Dogs and one iguana camp out with Web designers. The designers are even allowed to work on Macintosh computers! Kerry Kenemer, a Creative Director in Atlanta, said, "to attract the cool, younger people in the Internet business we had to break with the whole IBM culture. We're the only creative bone in the IBM body."[8] This is definitely a different culture. Now IBM is trying to spread the culture throughout the company. It launched Project Springboard and is opening e-business integration centers around the world. Instead of just design services, these centers offer customers a place to work with IBM specialists to set up the next generation of e-business solutions.[9]

By all accounts, IBM has done a remarkable job so far of incorporating the Web into every part of the company's operation—products, practices, and marketing. On-line sales increased nearly 400 percent topping $12 billion in 1999. The company saved $750 million by letting customers find answers to technical questions on its Web site. Internal training over the Net instead of in classrooms saved $120 million. In total, IBM cut nearly $1 billion in costs in 1999 by taking advantage of the Web. On the development side, the company put half of its $5 billion research and development budget into Internet-related areas. Gerstner also created the Institute for Advanced Commerce, a think tank that includes outside consultants and academics as well as 50 IBM scientists to work on e-commerce issues. In the services area, IBM

---

[8] Ibid., 38.
[9] Ibid.

has experienced explosive growth. It now has 130,000 consultants and revenues have surpassed those of its three biggest competitors combined.[10] The verdict is still out on whether IBM, or any traditional company, can move fast enough to take the lead from Internet start-up competition. But many business observers believe that the companies in these case examples are moving in the right direction when it comes to business strategy and creating the culture to support the strategy.

Chapters Inc.

From the very beginning, Chapters Inc., Canada's leading book retailer understood the importance of jumping in with both feet when it came to launching an Internet venture. With the Canadian e-commerce marketplace 18 months behind the US, Chapters had the benefit of looking at the lessons learned by other major retailers about going on-line. "Because many Canadian companies were taking a wait-and-see approach to e-commerce, we recognized we had a tremendous opportunity to become the number one on-line brand in this country," said David Hainline, Executive Vice President, Marketing and Merchandising, Chapters Online Inc. "To accomplish this, we needed to commit to going on-line and deliver on that commitment as decisively as possible." Today Chapters.ca, the Web site that resulted from Chapters's decision to go on-line, is the most popular choice for Canadians shopping on the Internet.

Part of the decision to move quickly and forcefully into e-commerce was to establish a separate e-commerce unit, which would be spun out into a separate company once the new enterprise got to scale and went public. Although the brands of the bricks-and-mortar and on-line operations would be shared along with the ultimate desire to extend and enhance the service delivered to

---

[10] Ibid., 22.

Chapters's existing customers, the company recognized the dramatic differences of the existing and new operations. "Not only did the new division need to work at Internet speed, we needed people with dramatically different skills to get the job done," continues Hainline. "The culture we needed to create to attract and enable the best New Economy talent was something we knew we couldn't create at the head office of the retailing operations. The people who created and built Chapters into the number one brand in Canada needed their work culture preserved as much as the Internet division needed a new culture to foster its development. Blending the two just didn't make sense."

In the newly evolving e-commerce marketplace in Canada, experienced talent was scarce. To create the team of several hundred people required to build this e-commerce engine, Chapters Online, as the division came to be called, set up shop in converted loft space in downtown Toronto, the heart of the city's blossoming new media district. But more than cool office space, great technology and free popcorn and soda, the company developed its culture by listening to its new employees and following their direction. Flexibility soon became the highest law at the new company. For example, because the Chapters.ca Web site never closes, some team members are required to work odd and extended hours. Demanding that everyone work predefined hours would have quickly met with resistance. "If you work until 2 a.m., you shouldn't have to ask permission to come to work late the next day. When you hire the best people, they are going to naturally do a great job. You have to allow them to set their own schedule," says Hainline. "Usually, the only time we have had to intervene is when someone is working too hard and needs a break. We are really big on sending people away for weekends with their partner, or giving teams the day off to play paintball. Its management's role to enable great work and ensure people are taking time to get some balance."

The company also allowed all of its employees to create their own job titles. "A rigid approach to defining one's role was so opposite to the atmosphere of flexibility and creativity we are trying to nurture. The process of allowing people to define their own title, helped enhance the team's sense of empowerment and ownership." Chapters Online employee titles include "retail ambassador," "glitch snitch," and "chief firefighter."

Spinning off the new company and taking it public has resolved many of the potential conflict issues between the two companies. Not only has each company been able to establish and maintain a culture that helps to drive its business forward, the arrangement has also helped the way the companies work together. They companies do cooperate as business partners, drawing off each other's talents to extend a greater service to its joint customers and enhance shareholder value. Chapters owns 70 percent of the on-line company and benefits from its success, and Chapters Online has access to a loyal customer base developed by the bricks-and-mortar company. For example, Chapters advertises extensively in its stores for the Web site because extending an on-line alternative to its customers enhances its credibility and the service it is able to deliver. Chapters Online operates e-commerce kiosks in the bricks-and-mortar stores because it broadens the company's reach and introduces e-commerce to consumers interested in its product categories.

Lucent Technologies

Lucent Technologies' goal is to create a relatively integrated culture focused on a unified company-wide business strategy, but it must start by first acquiring companies with very different cultures and then pulling them all together. Lucent Technologies is attempting to bring together voice and data networks into an integrated set of products and services. Historically, these are two very different technologies, and the engineers in these two fields see themselves as working in completely different worlds. They are known for not getting along with each other. If you ask the data engineers, they will tell you that voice networking is the stodgy, slow-growth field and data is the exciting, fast-moving business. Lucent has the added challenge of dealing with its history as an AT&T company with its traditional culture. *Fortune* writer, Henry Goldblatt describes the Lucent culture as having some of the following traits. "Lucent execs brag about the number of Nobel Prize laureates (12) who have worked in its behemoth, Bell Labs. Lucent's beautifully manicured headquarters in Murray Hill, NJ, looks like an Ivy League campus."[11] On the other hand, Ascend, one of the Silicon Valley start-ups Lucent acquired, is described quite differently. "In the Valley, few people care whether you invent, buy, or borrow the technology that drives your products. They view the Valley as a giant R&D lab. Ascend's campus, linked by outdoor walkways, looks like the high school Brandon and Brenda Walsh attended on Beverly Hills 90210."

To carry out its voice/data business strategy, Lucent acquired several companies with data expertise and opened a Bell Lab in Palo Alto. Now it faces the challenge of bringing these disparate cultures together to create a "Silicon Valley-savvy conglomerate."[12] At the current point in this process, Lucent seems to be succeeding at its goal. It is producing new products, such as the softswitch that links voice and data networks, and this product has been well received in the marketplace.

Much of the credit for making this transition work has been given to Lucent's leadership, especially to CEO Rich McGinn. Goldblatt credits McGinn with having "done a tremendous job melding disparate parts of the old AT&T into a cohesive, powerful unit that is growing at an amazing rate. He has proven to be

---

[11] Henry Goldblatt, "Go West," *Fortune* (November 22, 1999), 336.
[12] Ibid., 335.

a talented manager with a keen sense of the industry's future. Most important to the shareholders, McGinn understands that life doesn't begin and end in Murray Hill, New Jersey." McGinn said, "Lucent's culture is much more open, accepting, and fluid than one might think of a company that had a long parentage before it went public." Goldblatt added, "McGinn's got the lingo down—if his strategy is as on target, Lucent will thrive in the new order of networking."[13]

There is plenty of evidence that the enthusiasm to deliver on an e-business strategy and create the culture to support it extends far beyond the CEO at Lucent. Bruce Brock, who heads the Power Systems Division of Lucent in Mesquite, Texas is taking the old-line business of making batteries and other such products and shifting many of its operations to the net. Brock also created a new unit called Titania to make high-end power systems in partnership with two other companies, all Web connected. The division's revenues are up 25 percent in one year, the cost of processing an order has dropped 30 percent, and Titania is generating $1 million a year per employee.[14] Brock has spent time in Murray Hill teaching senior executives about e-business, and his division's methods are being applied in other areas of the company.

In a different type of application of the new technologies, William T. O'Shea, the Executive Vice President charged with selling corporate client communications equipment, has spent several years building a detailed database with information on 1.5 million customers and 6.5 million potential customers. O'Shea is in the process of connecting the database to the sales team's Web site.

Lucent has to contend with several different cultures, but they seem to have one clear business strategy that ties them together. They are using this unified business strategy to transform themselves

---

[13] Ibid., 336.
[14] Steve Rosenbush, "Rewiring Lucent in a Rush," *BusinessWeek* (December 13, 1999), 46.

into more similar Web-focused cultures. The Silicon Valley operations and the Murray Hill headquarters may never have identical cultures. But if Lucent continues on its present course, over time there very likely will be enough similarities across divisions and enough tolerance for the differences that it can deliver on a company-wide e-business strategy.

Procter & Gamble

Procter & Gamble Co. is moving aggressively into the e-business arena by using parallel cultures and integrated approaches at the same time. P&G has undertaken an initiative called Organization 2005. "Organization 2005 aims to do nothing less than change the Cincinnati company's culture from a conservative, slow-moving, bureaucratic behemoth to that of a modern, fast-moving Internet-savvy organization. Procter & Gamble wants to make faster and better decisions, cut red tape, wring cost out of systems and procedures, fuel innovation, set more-aggressive sales goals, and nearly double its revenues."[15]

In their efforts to integrate information technology (IT) into the company, P&G decentralized it 3,600-person IT department so that 97 percent of those employees now work on individual product, market, or business teams. Or they have been placed in global business services, which support shared services for the P&G units. Only 3 percent of the IT staff remains in corporate IT. The company also has 54 change agents working in the seven global business units. According to CIO Todd Garrett most of these people are from IT and are assigned the job of "leading cultural and business change by helping teams work together more effectively through greater use of IT, in particular real-time collaboration tools."[16] Use of chat rooms and other collaborative

---

[15] Marianne Kolbasuk McGee, "Lessons From A Cultural Revolution," *Information Week* (October 25, 1999), 47.
[16] Ibid., 48.

technologies are a part of the attempt to change the company's polite, conservative, play-it-safe culture to one that encourages employees to be candid and take chances.

Many areas of P&G are affected by the changes. Products are getting to market faster. Linkages to suppliers are improving. Internal communications among employees and with the CEO are carried out through the Web site and e-mail. Retail sales technology is changing, and business-to-consumer marketing is using the Internet to allow P&G "to treat individuals as a consumer market of one as opposed to a mass market," said Vivienne Bechtold, head of Interactive Marketing.[17]

In addition to the efforts to integrate Internet and related technologies into current operations throughout P&G, the company has also started an independent .com company. The spin-off is called Reflect.com and is located in the Silicon Valley, far from the P&G Cincinnati headquarters. It is a partnership with Institutional Venture Partners, a venture capital firm, and is funded with a $50 million joint investment. Its business strategy is to deliver beauty-care products ordered over the Internet, custom-made for each consumer. By every definition of the word, this is a .com company. At this point, Nathan Estruth, marketing director at P&G, said there is no plan to expand this venture to include similar sites for other product lines, but he does not rule that out. "Where we take this will depend on the learnings that come out of it."[18] This is an Internet business-to-consumer application that warrants a parallel culture. And according to P&G, depending on "the learnings that come out of it," it may always remain a separate unit, in a separate location, with a separate culture.

---

[17] Ibid.
[18] Ibid.

Sears and Whirlpool—Companies with Similar Products Take Different Routes

Two companies with somewhat similar product lines have taken two different approaches to implementing e-business strategies. Sears created a new Internet division and located it at the Sears campus in Hoffman Estates, Illinois. Whirlpool created a start-up called brandwise and located it in Silicon Alley in New York City, far from its Michigan headquarters.[19]

Sears' Internet division has approximately 50 people. Their offices have the informal look of other e-commerce businesses with mismatched furniture, boxes piled around, and refrigerators filled with Pepsi and Mountain Dew. The division started by selling appliances and tools on its on-line site and plans to expand into garden accessories, home furnishing, repair service scheduling, and other categories. It is focusing on areas of strength and avoiding bringing products on-line such as apparel, which has struggled in Sears' traditional channels. Even though Sears' approach is certainly not radical, it is a big departure from the old Sears' culture. The company has attracted some Web-savvy employees into the division. Andy Wetmore, who heads the tool products on-line, had quit working for Sears and later came back to join the new division. He said it's like working for a whole different company. "The thing I like is the freedom. This is the most non-Sears in Sears I've ever seen. Sears is all about meetings and status reports. This is a refreshing change."[20] At this point, Sears does not plan to spin-off the on-line business, according to CEO Arthur C. Martinez. This limits its ability to offer the types of stock options that often attract e-types to the start-ups. Martinez is weighing where to

---

[19] Eryn Brown, "Big Business Meets the e-World," *Fortune* (November 8, 1999), 90.
[20] Ibid., 91.

go with this issue. He said he is considering some type of internal carve-out (separate company within a company) where you could offer separate compensation and separate equity.

Whirlpool, on the other hand, created a spin-off. Its business strategy at this point is primarily focused on the business-to-business applications of servicing suppliers and big customers that are mainly other businesses (e.g., Sears). Whirlpool has a 12-person group in its Michigan headquarters that provides the leadership for the e-business initiatives. The company also set up an e-commerce task force of six senior executives, including the head of the e-services unit. This group meets at least once a month to explore e-business opportunities and visit other companies. The ideas do not always complement Whirlpool's larger goals, so at this point, the way it deals with these ideas is to spin them out. Greg Rogers, head of the e-commerce unit said, "If it's core, we bring it in. If it's not core, we spin it out."[21] This is how brandwise, in partnership with the Boston Consulting Group, came about. Brandwise is focused on business-to-consumer on-line sales for appliances and includes competing brands. A primary reason for doing this is to have access to data so it can design future products that more closely match what the customer wants. Sears has signed on as one of the companies whose products are offered through brandwise, even though this spin-off offers the customer an alternative source other than Sears.com. Why did Sears do this? CEO Arthur Martinez answered that question this way, "To not be on brandwise would deny us a chance to reach customers. We went through tortured conversations about it. Would this hurt the appliance portion of Sears.com? But I think the artificial walls, over time, will come down."[22]

---

[21] Ibid., 95.
[22] Ibid., 98.

SCHWAB CHANGED ITS MIND

One of the most intriguing cases of parallel cultures occurred at Charles Schwab and Co. The company changed its mind midstream and redirected its efforts. By all current accounts, the general opinion in business circles seems to be that the Schwab leadership was right to change their minds, and they have managed to redirect the company in its new orientation with great success. Now Charles Schwab and Co. is mentioned regularly as one company that really does "get it" when it comes to implementing the concept of clicks-and-mortar. The company has embraced an integrated business strategy that allows them to serve customers wherever it happens to be—in a store, on the phone, on-line, or off-line in an e-mail program.[23]

The most interesting part of Schwab's story is its change of direction. Originally, the company created a separate e-business called e-Schwab. Later it realized this was the wrong way to go. Customers had to choose between Schwab and e-Schwab. So the Schwab leadership did what many companies find almost impossible to do. They admitted they had made a mistake. It was a painful and expensive transition that involved repricing core products, retraining its employees, and changing its systems. Schwab came out of the experience with what is currently considered the best-positioned retail brokerage in the industry.[24]

As the slower big companies start to "get it," the playing field of applying Internet technology will become more level. So in this next e-wave, every company, big or small, new or old, will try to build physical systems that provide better service to customers. The best companies will now build systems to pick and pack products that are shipped individually, keep track of those shipments, and make sure the stuff gets delivered to our houses or businesses. They'll integrate those systems with the manufacturing,

---

[23] Stewart Alsop, "e or Be Eaten," *Fortune* (November 8, 1999), 87.
[24] Ibid.

distribution, and computer networks already in place. That's not spinning off a Web site or offering some e-variation of a product. That's not so much e-anything as it is figuring out how to use technology to move stuff around efficiently.[25]

SIX CRITERIA TO USE WHEN DETERMINING WHETHER TO GO THE PARALLEL OR INTEGRATION ROUTE

The following criteria should help you decide whether to set up a parallel group or focus on your current structure by integrating Internet technology into your ongoing operations. You also have the option of choosing both. A parallel operation may make sense in some parts of your organization, and at the same time you may launch an initiative to integrate the Internet into every department or division. As technology continues to develop over the coming years, you may make these decisions more than once. There will be waves of changes that will require reorienting your organization from time to time to stay current in your market. Consider the following issues as you make these decisions:

1. Is your dominant, mainline corporate culture likely to be hostile to a .com type of culture?

2. Do you need separate e-business operations for recruiting purposes?

3. Are you changing business-to-business processes or business-to-consumer activities?

4. How clear and unifying is your leadership vision and strategy?

5. Do you have enough resources to create separate parallel operations?

6. Do you have a large number of new employees in your company?

---

[25] Stewart Alsop, "e or Be Eaten," *Fortune* (November 8, 1999), 87.

IS YOUR DOMINANT, MAINLINE CORPORATE CULTURE LIKELY TO BE HOSTILE TO A .COM TYPE OF CULTURE?

The primary reason for setting up parallel operations such as spin-offs or Internet divisions is the fear that the dominant culture will kill the e-business initiative if there is an attempt to integrate it into the traditional organizational structure. If the culture clash is likely to be extreme, as in the case of P&G's or IBM's traditional conservative cultures, you may want to locate the Internet entity at a physical distance. If the cases in this chapter are any indication, a minimum of a thousand miles seems to be in order.

If there is the danger that the dominant culture will interfere with and slow down the new business initiative, setting up a separate entity in the early stages may be warranted. As is evident throughout this book, speed is essential to your strategy. So use parallel operations if this approach promises greater speed.

HOW to decide if you have a culture that would be hostile to a .com culture.

- Use the "blue hair and ponytail" test. If you cannot picture an employee with these traits being accepted in your company or wanting to work there, you may have a problem.

- If you are a company with a history of following an elaborate set of rules, policies, and procedures, .com cultures will either be stymied or disruptive.

- If you are not sure if you are a rules and procedure bound culture, pick two or three of the latest decisions that you or a team you are on made and count the number of times you had to ask permission or get a sign-off to implement the decision.

- If you cannot think of the last time you or a team you are on made a decision that you could implement, your culture would more than likely be a bureaucratic nightmare for any .com culture.

DO YOU NEED SEPARATE E-BUSINESS OPERATIONS FOR RECRUITING PURPOSES?

If you are trying to attract the people .com companies and other start-ups require, you may need to set up separate business entities to attract talented employees. If an unconventional person walks into your organization for an interview and sees wall-to-wall suits, the interview may be over in the lobby. "Are you kidding. I'm out of here," is as far as you are likely to get with that person. The second reason is the need to offer stock options to attract the .com types. Your potential hires can get these kinds of financial incentives in the start-ups, so you may have to offer them to compete. If they are not available in your mainline company, a separate entity is needed to create benefits package that attracts the recruits you need.

 TIP

IF your culture is likely to be hostile and unaccepting of the technology oriented .com types, you may have to create a separate culture in a physically separate setting to attract the talent you need to build an e-business.

ARE YOU CHANGING BUSINESS-TO-BUSINESS PROCESSES OR BUSINESS-TO-CONSUMER ACTIVITIES?

Companies seem to be using different approaches depending on what processes are being changed. If integrating the Internet into all internal and business-to-business processes (e.g., distribution, procurement, communications, and alliances with other businesses), the integrated approach may work better. An example of the integrated approach is P&G breaking up its 3,600-person IT department and dispersing it throughout the organization.

On the other hand, if a company wants to create a business-to-consumer service, it often sets up a separate .com company. This is e-commerce in the classic definition of the term. There are dozens of examples of companies that are setting up .com spin-offs to provide business-to-consumer services. However, there are exceptions.

Sears has kept its .com operation in-house. Or there is Schwab that started down that path of setting up a separate .com Schwab and changed its mind. For Schwab having two separate companies to serve the same client base did not make sense.

It may be important to consider which customers you will serve in the two separate companies. If you are targeting two separate sets of customers with two different types of products, the separate company may make more sense than if you have one customer group with one set of products to sell. How seamless do you want the service to be for the one set of customers? In an interview with Tom Shipley of Gartner Group, he describes an example of seamlessness. "If I buy a book through Barnes & Noble.com, can I return it to a bricks-and-mortar store instead of having to ship it back to the .com company? Or if I'm at one of the stores, are there terminals where I can order a book on-line if that store does not have the book on the shelves?" This is the type of service Charles Schwab created. A customer can go back and forth between live and on-line services seamlessly. If this is what you want, two separate companies could make it more difficult to achieve.

Barnes & Noble has created two separate companies, and this is causing problems with creating seamless service for customers. According to Carrie Johnson, an analyst at Forrester Research Inc., keeping the two businesses separate was a mistake. She believes Barnes & Noble should have advertised their .com counterpart in the retail stories and actively helped shoppers go on-line. The reasons Barnes & Noble decided to keep the two companies separate was to avoid cannibalizing their retail business and to avoid charging sales tax in states where they have retail stories. This extra cost would have put them at a serious disadvantage competing against Amazon.com.[26] As the Barnes & Noble example illustrates, these are not easy choices with clear-cut answers.

---

[26] Diane Brandy, "How Barnes & Noble Misread the Web," *BusinessWeek* (February 7, 2000), 63.

TIP

DETERMINE whether your current business strategy is focused on business-to-business or business-to-consumer (or both).

- If your e-business strategy is a business-to-consumer (e-commerce) plan, it appears that it is often easier and quicker for the company to set up a separate operation or a spin-off. By doing this they can focus on one line of business and one set of technologies. Remember, eventually these companies will probably have to blend the .com and the traditional together and that is not easy, but for the start-up phase, a separate operation seems to be the business-to-consumer choice.

- The exception to the guideline just given is the Schwab example. If you have one customer base that you want to serve with both system-traditional and e-business— parallel may not work. It ends up being confusing or cumbersome to your customers.

- If you are on a fast track business strategy to convert your entire company to Internet operations, then the integrated approach will probably get you there the fastest.

HOW CLEAR AND UNIFYING IS YOUR LEADERSHIP VISION AND STRATEGY?

A clear leadership vision and business strategy is important no matter what approach you take to transitioning to the e-business world. This is discussed in depth in Chapter 10. It does appear, however, that it is even more important if you use the integrated transition approach.

If you convert all functions within the company to Internet usage, there will be a great deal of disruption and fear throughout the organization all at one time. What holds everyone together? What provides the beacon for people to follow to stay on course? Why would they be willing to let these interlopers come into their smooth running departments and make a mess of everything? Employees must understand and believe the leadership message about where the company is going and why it is going there. Without the safety net provided by leaders they trust and a corporate strategy they believe in, the only rational thing for employees to do is to hunker down and defend themselves. When a large percentage of employees become consumed with self-protection, change will slow to a crawl.

WHEN you use the integrated approach, the leadership message for why everyone has to suffer through all this disruption must be very clear.

- Repeat the message over and over and over.
- Use stories, examples from other industries, visitors, and field trips to illustrate to employees at all levels that this is the new reality.
- Learn it yourself. Get personally involved. Join the teams that are working on the transition. Use your presence as a message.

This may not be quite as severe a problem in parallel operations because it may be easier to communicate the new vision and strategy to a smaller group of employees who are excited about being part of a new venture. There is the possibility that the spin-off operation might be small enough and new enough that the leadership vision and strategy is clear to the employees even if the larger company is mired in confusion. This does not mean that you can get away with a blurred, unclear vision and strategy by using parallel cultures. Eventually, the lack of leadership catches up with you, but it might take a little longer if you use parallel operations. Notice that the common thread running through all the case examples is stellar leadership. Nothing can substitute for good leadership, and nothing will save you in the long run if you do not have it.

DO YOU HAVE ENOUGH RESOURCES TO CREATE SEPARATE PARALLEL OPERATIONS?

People from nonprofit or government settings often mentioned the problem of a lack of resources. They simply do not have the money, personnel, or regulatory freedom to set up parallel operations. They had to take the integrated approach and make changes within current organizational structure. They pilot new applications, but they could not set up separate entities to go in new directions.

Will this work? No one knows for sure. Gartner Group's Tom Shipley, who has worked in the IT field for over three decades, reacted to this issue by saying, "They are kidding themselves. It will never work. If they have limited resources, then they need to stop doing some of the old things they have been doing to free up resources." In any case, limited resources clearly limit organizations' options for transition to e-business.

USE Peter Drucker's strategy of organized abandonment, described in Chapter 2.[27] Hold regular management reviews to identify activities that can be stopped to free up resources. Look at revenue issues, business strategy, and cultural values. Identify processes you can stop or change; scale back the resource cost. Use the resources that are freed up to fund your e-business strategy. Depending on your regulatory restrictions, you might or might not be allowed to fund a separate, parallel operation.

Drucker gives an example of a outsourcing services company that held a monthly abandonment meeting at every management level down through the supervisors. Each session examined one part of the business and they rotated which group took each service from one month to the next. They covered every area of the company including processes such as personnel policies. In the course of a year they made three or four major decisions to cut out processes and many decisions about how to do a number of other processes more efficiently. In the process it freed up resources that could be devoted to new developments.

[27] Peter F. Drucker, *Management Challenges for the 21st Century* (New York: HarperCollins, 1999), 79.

DO YOU HAVE A LARGE NUMBER OF NEW EMPLOYEES IN YOUR COMPANY?

Another intriguing criterion is the tenure of your employees. According to some people, the integrated approach might be easier to implement if a large percentage of your employees are new due to a recent high level of turnover or other reasons. The point is that a large number of new employees means you are less likely to have a rigid, entrenched culture that people will fight to maintain.

The basic observation is accurate. It is very likely that a company with many new employees will have a less-entrenched culture. But there is an important question that must be asked to determine whether this situation provides the opportunity to build a new and improved culture: Why did the organization recently experience so much turnover? If some type of restructuring or redirection of the business triggered the turnover, it may not indicate dangerous trouble. But if the mass exodus was because employees were fed up with the organization and its leadership, that is not a good sign, and it will not help with future efforts to change the company. It all depends on the story behind the turnover.

CONSIDER how your company's recent turnover may affect your ability to change the corporate culture quickly.

- If you have had high levels of turnover in the past years (25 percent or more is high from a culture perspective), you may have an easier time using an integrated approach for implementing your e-business strategy. You have a critical mass of new people with no memories of how things used to be, so you can create a new culture almost from scratch. A committed, enthusiastic 25 percent of an employee population can sweep the entire organization along with them because most people do not actively resist. They majority of the population will simply go with the flow.

TIP

If the 25 percent created the momentum toward the new strategy and culture, the majority will go along.

- Is your turnover higher than your industry average? There is no firm guideline for turnover figures, but you can compare yourself within your industry and have a fairly accurate indication whether something is out of sync in your company. If the reasons for high turnover relate to low morale or dissatisfaction with the company leadership, this will not help you with changing the culture.

A PAINFUL CASE OF MOVING FROM PARALLEL CULTURES TO INTEGRATED OPERATIONS

The most dangerous thing a company can do is underestimate the internal resistance that may be triggered by the move to e-business. One of the events likely to trigger the most intense resistance is when it is time to dismantle a parallel operation, such as an Internet division, and merge it into the rest of the company. By the time this merging is needed, a separate culture has probably developed that is quite different from the rest of your organization. If it is a .com type of culture, the members are likely to have developed intense loyalties to each other and their goals. A .com culture tends to be aggressive. Under the best of circumstances, members of a .com culture see outsiders as clueless annoyances. In more extreme cases, outsiders (defined as everyone else in the company) are viewed as the enemy and are treated accordingly. The following case describes a situation where one company unexpectedly triggered a series of corporate culture explosions. The events in this case are not unusual. Many companies get caught in similar tailspins because they did not anticipate and plan for the fallout that occurs when you disrupt corporate cultures.

Integrating Parallel Cultures Leads to Conflict

Alarge research and consulting firm faced the problem of rein-tegrating its separate Internet group. It was clear that the work of this group was no longer a small research and development (R&D) initiative but had grown into a pervasive business issue that needed to be integrated into every division and project team throughout the entire company. Absorption of an R&D team was not a new experience for the company to face. Whenever there were new technologies or business trends, the company has a history of setting up small R&D groups that would function separately in the early stages. Some initiatives would die out and others would grow into company-wide lines of business.

However, there are several differences with the Internet group. The most significant ones were:

1. the extreme importance of the Internet impact on the company's products and services.

2. the speed of the transition from the R&D initiative to the need for practical application throughout the company.

3. the gap between the Internet group and the rest of the company was much greater than usual.

One manager described the gap as a "chasm" and that seemed to be built from both sides. The Internet group had formed a tight-knit team intensely loyal to their group and its goal. This group was very much the type of team described in Chapter 5. They were elitist in their attitudes, thinking no one else in the company would "get it." They were convinced that if other people in the company got involved they would slow down the work or even derail the project entirely. Those working in the other areas of the company were "slow to pick up on the significance of the Internet" at first so they were not paying much attention to this group anyway. Once a large number of people throughout the company did start to catch on to what was happening, they were hesitant to speak up about the work they were beginning to do on Internet-related initiatives. They were afraid of triggering the wrath of the Internet group and being told to stop their work. In other words, the Internet team and the rest of the company were not talking to each other on any regular basis. In fact, the goal was to stay away from each other as much as possible.

Now it was time to stop treating the Internet initiative like a small R&D effort and integrate it into the entire organization. First the company decided to reorganize, splitting the Internet group into two groups that would report to the line managers for areas that needed to integrate this e-business expertise into their product lines. And the explosion occurred. The language used to describe this explosion was colorful to say the least, but suffice it to say, people in the Internet group were upset. This angry reaction triggered a second decision to remerge the Internet group and have it report to a senior manager two levels higher than the line managers the Internet members had been temporarily placed under. This, of course, triggered a new explosion. Now the line managers were upset. In the meantime, a number of other senior management efforts were identifying frontline employees with higher levels of Internet expertise and pulling them into the Internet group or a strategy team. These people quickly became the "chosen people" who were invited regularly to speak at events and received frequent attention from senior management.

By this point, there were large numbers of people upset and a great deal of confusion about who was doing what. There was also a perception of two groups: the chosen people and the second-class citizens. And all this was the result of efforts to integrate the Internet group into the larger company. If anything, the company ended up with a larger chasm and more hostility among the parallel cultures. The reactions to the situation caused a substantial number of people from the Internet group and other parts of the company to quit. These are all highly trained professionals who have no trouble finding work elsewhere or retiring on their stock option wealth from the company's previous history of success. Eventually, there was a complete replacement of senior management, and the company has moved beyond the transition traumas. What can be learned from this case? How can a company make a smoother transition from parallel cultures to integrated operations?

DEVELOPING A GAME PLAN FOR MERGING PARALLEL CULTURES: FOUR CONSIDERATIONS

There are ways to avoid the problems that the research and consulting company encountered, but unfortunately, that scenario is quite common. The good news is that it is not inevitable. There are ways to plan for and implement these types of changes without creating mass confusion and conflict. It is unrealistic to expect people to be happy about the changes or to think you can avoid all explosive reactions, but the transition can be handled in a way that does not derail the whole initiative and cause a mass exodus of your talent.

FOUR Considerations for Merging Parallel Cultures with Traditional Units

1. Plan the Reintegration from the Beginning
2. Involve Members from Both Cultures from the Start
3. Reward Cooperation
4. Expect Emotional Reactions

1. PLAN THE REINTEGRATION FROM THE BEGINNING

The key piece of advice when merging cultures is to develop a plan from the beginning. It is naive to think that you can create parallel cultures and then disband them by leadership edict. The only people who can ensure the development of this plan and its implementation are the organization's leadership. Plan for the eventual merging of the parallel cultures at the time you set up the parallel operations, not shortly before you announce the need for disbanding their operations. When Canadian Tire Acceptance Limited established an alliance with an information technology partner, they knew the ability to merge the two cultures of the organizations was a key element of how well the alliance would function. The company devoted much more time than usual at the beginning of the process bringing people at all levels together to get to know each other and discuss how they would work together in the combined entity. The same type of front-end effort can be made when you are setting up a parallel operation.

2. INVOLVE MEMBERS FROM BOTH CULTURES FROM THE START

Everyone has heard the old truth about human nature. People are more likely to cooperate with a plan they helped develop. On the other hand, if the plan was someone else's idea, people usually feel less obligation or enthusiasm to make it work. This is often referred as the "not invented here" syndrome. At the time the Internet group was set up in the case example, members from that group and from the traditional line divisions should have been having regular discussions led by senior management. These would have addressed how this group would integrate with the larger company if the R&D issue took off. If the company frequently sets up R&D groups and never knows which issue will survive, it needs a general plan for integrating R&D groups quickly no matter which group is involved. In the case of an initiative as significant as the Internet R&D group, the traditional mainline culture may be the one that must change to fit with the new e-business culture.

Health care organizations (hospitals, clinics, laboratory companies) often do a better job than most organizations of getting people at all levels involved early in the discussions and planning of a restructuring that will result in people working in different units with a different group of professionals. The management staff at Henry Ford Health System in Detroit explained that they must take this approach in health care. The professions that play the key roles in health care, such as physicians, nurses, and pharmacists, have cultures that do not respond well to being told what they are required to do. The Henry Ford people point out that this often causes problems when a senior people come into health care from another industry with a different culture. If they are used to making quick, unilateral decisions without involving the people affected, they usually do not last long in health care. The well-known expression "herding cats" is often heard in the health care field, especially in reference to doctors. Leading the highly educated, independent work force of the .com world is very much the same. They must be involved in the planning and decisions if you want their cooperation.

The R&D groups must be reminded regularly that they are temporary units that will be either phased out or merged into the larger company. Both sets of people need to understand the importance of developing relationships with each other from the beginning and staying abreast of what each group is doing. The groups may adopt a hands-off stance toward each other during the time they are functioning separately to avoid interfering with the other's work, but they need to realize that they cannot afford to ignore or hide information from each other.

3. REWARD COOPERATION

From the beginning of the R&D initiatives, reward any efforts to cooperate among the parallel cultures. At the time of the disbanding of the separate group and its merging into the larger organization, reward the individuals and groups that make this process work smoothly. Rewards can come in any form available to you—money, recognition, promotions, and new career or education opportunities. Do whatever it takes to make people glad they cooperated. When Acxiom offered up to $5,000 cash rewards for each team member who pulled off the deployment of their new system on time, they were clearly sending the message that the company wanted well-functioning teams that could produce excellent results. You could not qualify for one of those awards working alone. And no one team was likely to have been successful if they were hostile and uncooperative with the other teams. People are very smart when it comes to figuring out where the payoffs are in a company. If you want cooperation between the groups, put your monetary and nonmonetary rewards behind those expectations and the majority of people will exceed your expectations just as they did at Acxiom.

4. EXPECT EMOTIONAL REACTIONS

No matter what you do, there is always a certain amount of upset when a team is disbanded and people move on to form new groups. Count on it. Be respectful of the pain people are experiencing, but do not change your business strategy to calm them down. If the emotional explosion is intense, as it was in the case example, take this as an indication that your leadership of the implementation process may have been poorly handled, learn from the experience, and handle it better next time using the suggestions in this chapter. But do not go into a knee-jerk reaction and change your business strategy the way they did in the case. That only creates more confusion, anger, and rebellion. If you decide your strategy is flawed, then involve all parties in developing a new one. In the case example, senior management might have decided that the strategy of creating two Internet directions for the company and placing two groups of experts in two line departments was not the right business strategy. In that case, they needed to develop a new strategy with input from all parties in a careful and thoughtful way. Of course, they should have done that in the first place to avoid being caught in this situation.

Why did the leaders in the example change directions at that point and remerge the Internet group to have them report to a higher level of management? Was it really because they decided on a new and better business strategy, or did they just panic at the explosive reaction of Internet group members? Many leaders are just like the rest of the general population. They have allergic reactions to intense conflict and angry emotions. And like most people, they will agree to almost anything to get these tirades to end. Caving in is not

the way to handle emotionally explosive behavior, but otherwise coura-
geous leaders can disintegrate when confronted with tears or yelling.
Distinguish between your business strategy and the implementation
plan. Consider them separately. Extreme emotional reactions may indicate you have botched the implementation plan, but they are less
likely to indicate that you picked the wrong business strategy.

If you decide to change the business strategy, do it for business
reasons. A large service organization merged two very different companies. The CEO spent months on the road going to the 40 field
offices explaining the merger and listening to what people had to say.
He weathered dozens of emotional outburst of varying kinds and
managed to maintain his composure and listen for valid suggestions
and criticisms. After almost every meeting, he could be found on the
phone with staff at the corporate offices telling them to get something
fixed that he had learned about in the meeting. Listening to all that
venting was not pleasant for him, but he did not panic. He just listened and used the information to improve the merger transition plan
wherever he could.

APPLYING THIS INFORMATION IN YOUR ORGANIZATION

Below are questions to assess whether you are currently using parallel cultures to deploy your e-business strategy and whether the
traditional and parallel groups are working together or fighting
each other.

1. Where is the Internet or e-business strategy housed in your
    company? Who is taking the lead? Are you confident that you
    have the right people leading this initiative?

2. Is this leadership located in a parallel operation, such as a spin-
    off or Internet division, or is it integrated into all or most
    departments of the company?

3. If you have parallel groups functioning at this time, do you
    eventually plan to integrate them into the larger organization?

> Have you developed a plan for how you will carry out this transition? Integrating parallel Internet cultures and traditional operations may mean the old culture must adapt to the new e-business culture.
>
> 4. Do the separate operations/parallel cultures cooperate, or at least communicate, with each other regularly?
>
> 5. If you are in any type of leadership role, do you have an allergic reaction to intense conflict or angry emotions? The symptoms of this problem are that you panic and agree to almost anything to make the tirades disappear. This reaction will limit your effectiveness as a leader in an era of turmoil and change.

CHAPTER FIVE

A New Breed of Teams in a .Com Culture

FAST-MOVING, TEMPORARY TEAMS ARE THE NORM

Get in, do it, get out.[1]

Work inside an e-business culture has become project work. People are organized into fast-moving teams brought together to accomplish a specific goal. They rapidly deliver results and disband. In many organizations, at any given time, people may be on as many as seven or eight teams throughout the company and most of these teams are temporary. Each team lasts only as long as it takes to deliver the goal. The old world of a stable organizational chart with divisions, departments, and work units where people live and work day in and day out is fading away. An organizational chart and divisions still may exist, but much of the actual day-to-day work is being done by an ever-changing configuration of teams.

---

[1] Jean Lipman-Blumen and Harold J. Leavitt, *Hot Groups: Seeding Them, Feeding Them, and Using Them to Ignite Your Organization* (New York: Oxford Press, 1999), 58.

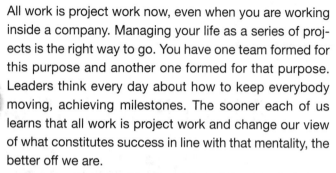

> All work is project work now, even when you are working inside a company. Managing your life as a series of projects is the right way to go. You have one team formed for this purpose and another one formed for that purpose. Leaders think every day about how to keep everybody moving, achieving milestones. The sooner each of us learns that all work is project work and change our view of what constitutes success in line with that mentality, the better off we are.
> —*Christine Malcolm, Vice President of Provider Solutions at Computer Sciences Corporation Healthcare Group*

LEGO TEAMS: AGGREGATE, DISAGGREGATE, REAGGREGATE

Information in the digital world is often described in terms of aggregating and reaggregating. Think of bits of information as Lego pieces that can be assembled, broken apart, and reassembled into completely different objects. This allows rapid customization of products or services. On the Net this often takes the form of self-service, in which customers go on-line and assemble the mix of services or products they want. Then the same metaphor of Lego pieces can be applied to teams in a .com culture. Individuals are assembled into temporary teams for a specific project, and then the team is disbanded. The individuals are reassembled on new teams with different goals.

In his book, *The Digital Estate*, Chuck Martin described how one company approaches teams. Seth Goldstein, the founder of SiteSpecific, an interactive advertising company, described what made his organization different, "We actually assume change is the rule, not the exception." Most companies in the traditional ad agency business are organized into the conventional department structure, but SiteSpecific is not. "SiteSpecific believes in cross-pollinating its talent. Teams are assembled and reassembled according to the particular requirements for a client. Teams are clustered around events, not accounts."[2]

---

[2] Chuck Martin, *The Digital Estate: Strategies for Competing, Surviving, and Thriving in a Internetworked World* (New York: McGraw-Hill, 1997), 1

David Roussain, VP of E-Commerce and Customer Service at FedEx and formerly at Hewlett-Packard, described how these temporary teams functioned at HP. "[HP is a] very strong company on virtual teams. Management layers really don't mean that much at HP. They have individual contributors, managers, section managers, and whatnot, but the real power of the team comes through in the first two layers and its ability to recreate itself in virtual teams very, very quickly. So to be able to connect and form a virtual team and then break it down and disconnect as people get on to other jobs is very, very important."

CHARACTERISTICS OF .COM TEAMS

A number of characteristics typically exist on these temporary .com teams. In traditional companies that are transitioning to the e-business environment or faster paced operations, you find a variety of team structures. Some traditionally organized with an assigned leader, strict reporting relationships, slow decision-making processes, and long life spans. In companies whose entire existence has been in the .com world or high-tech fields, many teams are structured as .com teams. Think of it as a continuum of options that a team can use depending on its purpose and location within a company.

TIP

THERE are five ways in which .com teams differ from traditional teams.

1. Obsessed with Their Goal
2. Creative and Unconventional Style
3. Informal and Democratic
4. Team Member's Feelings or Personalities Are Not Important
5. When the Team is Done, It's Done

1. OBSESSED WITH THEIR GOAL

These groups are intensely committed to accomplishing great things when it comes to their goal. They have very high expectations of each other and the group as a whole. They do not necessarily need charismatic leaders or promises of external rewards. The great idea is the magnetic pull for .com teams. In some cases, their dedication to the team becomes all consuming. They work long hours, put their personal lives on hold, and usually eject any member who does not fit. Fit, in this case, is a combination of intense commitment to the goal and a high level of talent/skills to add value to the group.

> What happens for an individual on the team is that achieving a team result becomes more important than working for the company. So they work for the team rather than the company. The company is the framework in which to engage. The team and the goal are what they are really there for.
> —David Roussain, VP of E-Commerce and Customer Service, FedEx

2. CREATIVE AND UNCONVENTIONAL STYLE

The team members often develop their own unique style reflected in their lingo, manner of dress, behaviors, and office decorations. These are the symbols of their team membership. Humor and antics play a big role in their interactions. Members often can be discovered "partying" on company time, at least that is what it looks like to outsiders. The high performance expectations extend to innovation skills as well as technical ones. As a group, the members often see themselves as special, with a noble mission. Sometimes this attitude spills over into paranoia in which the group sees the rest of the organization as the enemy or at least as a major interference.

Ian Adamson is a founder of Team EcoInternet. The group is an adventure racing team of world-class athletes which combines hiking, biking, paddling, climbing, and running through the wilderness. And the team does this with little equipment; only a compass, a map, and their skills are used. Adamson describes the team mind-set as almost entrepreneurial. "You believe that you can fix any situation with the resources you have on hand. We've got a stick of chewing gum and some string. We're all set! We don't waste time whining because we don't have a hammer."[3]

3. INFORMAL AND DEMOCRATIC

Hierarchy is not the mode of operation for these groups. Jean Lipman-Blumen and Harold J. Leavitt, authors of the book, *Hot Groups*, describe this characteristic in this way. "Communication flows freely, up, down and across those groups. Members treat one another with casual respect, focusing on colleagues' contributions to the task at hand rather than on title or status."[4] Group members tend to be outspoken about their views, and debate is welcome. They rarely argue or engage in personal attacks because the discussions are focused on solving problems and accomplishing the team mission. "Group think" is rarely a problem because opinions are freely aired.

Industrial Light and & Magic (ILM), the company created by George Lucas, produced many of the digitally created shots for movies such as *Titanic, Star Wars,* and *Men in Black.* The ILM team is never late. The company has won 29 Academy Awards during the past 24 years and has a reputation for being fast. Eric Brevig, one of ILM's Special Effects Supervisors, explained one of the team's unwritten rules: Never tell people how to do their jobs. Instead, present them with a challenge and then let them choose the best way to attack it. "Even when I have an idea or a plan, I try to invite people to be part of the problem solving," Brevig said. "That way, they feel like part of the team, and they usually come up with a better idea than mine." Dan Taylor, the team's Animation Supervisor, put it this way,

---

[3] Cheryl Dahle, "Xtreme Teams," *Fast Company* (November 1999), 7.
[4] "How Hot Groups Work: Fast, Focused and Wide Open," *CIO* (November 1, 1999), 78.

"You can't turn people into just a pair of hands. It's always a mistake to dictate how a shot should be done. Doing so completely devalues people and their creative abilities. How can people get excited about being part of that kind of a team?"[5]

4. TEAM MEMBER'S FEELINGS OR PERSONALITIES ARE NOT IMPORTANT

Trust among team members is based primarily on the common commitment to the goal and confidence in each other's technical skills and thinking ability, not on common personal interests or similar personalities. This group is not the type that wants an interpersonal team-building session. Taking personality or social styles surveys does them very little good. They see it as a waste of time, pulling them off task. They get along fairly well and tolerate each other's styles in the passion of pursuing the goal. Friendships may form, but that is secondary to the mission of building a successful company. Often these teams see their mission as crucial to the survival of the company. This is a crisis of sorts. All types of teams tend to pull together and set aside disagreements or personality clashes for the duration of the crisis.

> These teams have hard goals with specific dates. Things have to get accomplished. If you have to get the job done or you don't have a company anymore, it's amazing how well you can get along together. Personality spats emerge when you have spare time.
> —*John Daly, Ph.D. Professor at the University of Texas*

They do take care of each other during the intensity of the team's push toward the goal, covering if someone needs a break. A television commercial for EDS, an information technology services company, captured this spirit of support. In the first scene two people are talking about "crunch time" for a third team member while making him a peanut butter sandwich. When the man finishes making the

---

[5] Cheryl Dahle, "Xtreme Teams," *Fast Company* (November 1999), 7.

sandwich, he squashes it flat as a pancake before taking it down the hall. In the next scene, he knocks on a locked door and slides the flattened sandwich under the door. The last thing you hear is a voice from behind the door saying "Thanks, man."

5. WHEN THE TEAM IS DONE, IT'S DONE

These types of teams disband when the project is complete. The life span is anywhere from one day to a few months, and team cohesion can disintegrate as the project winds down. If the team has been successful, team members are thrilled and proud of their accomplishment, but they know it is time to move on. "Most hot groups don't stay hot for very long. They are, by nature, almost always 'temporary' organizations," said Lipman-Blumen and Leavitt.[6] Sometimes there is a sense of loss or let down for the members as the team ends, but there is not much you can do to change this basic nature of .com teams. They burn bright and die out fast, compared to stable long-lived teams with milder missions and styles. The challenge for companies trying to create a .com culture is to keep finding interesting, challenging projects for their talented employees to tackle. It is more common these days for a technology whiz to leave a company for a new job, because of boredom and lack of new learning, rather than because of demanding work or burn out. This may change over time. The e-business transition is still quite new, and burn out may be more of a problem in the future after several years of participation on .com teams.

Hire.com is a leading talent acquisition and retention application service provider and in many ways a classic fast-growing .com company. Chairman and CEO Jim Hammock described the use of temporary teams, highlighting the speed with which they operate. "You have to build a culture of action, and you do it with four letter words: make, sell, cash. You keep asking, 'Where does it

---

[6] Jean Lipman-Blumen & Harold J. Leavitt, *Hot Groups: Seeding Them, Feeding Them, and Using Them to Ignite Your Organization* (New York: Oxford Press, 1999), 57.

impact making, selling, or cash?' At the implementation level you have lots of task forces to work on the plans. We put a group together in a room, and they stay there until they come out with a total product plan." When asked how long that usually takes, Hammock responded, "They try to do it in one day. It's kind of a failure if they have to come back a second day. If you have the right people with the right mind-set, you can get it the first cut done in that amount of time."

THESE TEAMS ARE NOT A NEW CREATION

The type of teams described as .com teams is not an entirely new phenomenon. Organizations have selectively used these types of teams historically during times of crisis when quick action was needed or for specific projects with an unusually high level of urgency or passion tied to it. In his 1986 book *Peak Performers*, Charles Garfield provided many examples of these types of team efforts, including his own experience as a computer scientist at Grumman Aerospace Corporation (now Northrop Grumman). His first job out of school was at Grumman working on the Apollo 11 lunar earth module (LEM) project, better known to the general public as the "put a man on the moon" project. "I was swept up by the powerful mission of Apollo 11. That was it! I could put my best efforts behind a mission that really mattered."[7] His book is filled with stories of these kinds of peak performing environments in which teams were passionately inspired by their mission.

The difference in the .com environment is that these fast, passionate, temporary teams are becoming much more common. It is the way work is done on a routine basis throughout companies, and these companies are structured to accommodate these teams. In the past they were the exception. Even at Apple in its heyday, these experiences were not viewed as common occurrences. Steve Jobs who put

---

[7] Charles Garfield, *Peak Performers: The New Heroes of American Business* (New York: William Morrow and Company, 1986), 35.

together the team of "A-players" to design and produce the Macintosh computer described the experience. "Opportunities like this don't come along very often. You know somehow it's the start of something... And it's being done by a bunch of incredibly talented people who in most organizations would be working three levels below the impact of the decisions they're making in this organization. It's one of those things you know won't last forever. It's more important than their personal lives right now."[8]

Teams that put a man on the moon or build the Macintoch computer are, of course, exceptional examples of these types of teams in action. Even though a .com team's goal may not seem as dramatic and inspiring to outsiders as Apollo 11, typically the members of that team behave with similar levels of passion and commitment to their mission. They often see themselves as participating in a noble adventure.

.COM TEAMS ARE NOT JUST FOR .COM COMPANIES

Most frequently, you find the .com team environment in start-ups that began their lives as .com companies. But traditional companies moving into e-business are developing their own methods for fostering this type of teamwork. Procter & Gamble is a veteran company with a reputation for a straightlaced, traditional culture. This is not the setting where you expect a hotbed of .com culture to be developing. And yet, as we saw in Chapter 4, P&G established a new venture called Reflect.com with the hope that it will develop into its e-business presence in the marketplace. Marianne Kolbasuk McGee from *Information Week* said, "Procter & Gamble is so eager to encourage cultural change that it's willing to go to great lengths— literally. The company unveiled an e-commerce venture that will be located in Silicon Valley—deliberately physically divorced from the company headquarters in Cincinnati—and will be spun off as a stand alone entity."[9]

---

[8] Ibid., 193.

[9] Marianne Kolbasuk McGee, "Lessons From a Cultural Revolution," *Information Week* (October 25, 1999), 47.

The capacity to tolerate and encourage .com teams is one linch-pin characteristic of a .com culture. Without these teams, it is difficult to move at the speed required or produce the levels of innovation necessary in the e-business world. Like P&G, companies must find ways to seed the growth of these high-performance teams and support them once they have been created.

ENCOURAGING AND SUPPORTING .COM TEAMS

There are a number of ways to support and sustain these teams, five of which are:

- Recruit your most unconventional, irreverent talent in the company to join these teams, especially if you are a traditional company using these types of teams for the first time. Once you recruit a core group to start the team, let the team control its own membership. The members recruit others they need and want to work with on the project.

- Give them a space to work in where they can create a .com environment (messy, games around, dogs under their desks) even if you are not setting up a separate unit with a parallel culture or spin-off. Different teams could use this .com team space over time as the projects change.

- Give them a budget and resources that the team can use without having to ask permission every time they need to make a decision.

- Build in high profile rewards (monetary and recognition) for project success. Provide some rewards for effort and more for success. This is particularly important in traditional companies which are transitioning to this type of team. Employees are watching to see how the company reacts to the teams that do not produce successes. Make sure they are rewarded for effort and treated respectfully, so employees get the message that it is worth the risk to join one of these teams.

- When employees start to ask, "How can I get on one of those teams?" the change to .com teams is starting to take hold in your culture.

WHAT DO .COM TEAMS REQUIRE OF LEADERSHIP?

WHAT YOU DO NOT NEED

Charles Garfield related this story about his experiences with leadership on the Apollo 11 team. "My first manager impressed on his subordinates that his three main values were Arriving Early, Staying Late, and Looking Busy. He was interested in seeing bodies at desks. He worried about having people out of sight doing experiments or research in libraries. We knew he checked the coat rack when he came in to see who had arrived early; I hired a janitor who started work at 6:00 a.m. to hang up my coat so that I could go to the library and work."[10]

That style of leadership does not work well for any type of team—.com or traditional. But it certainly was not appropriate for a team consisting of some of the country's brightest and most creative scientists taking on one of the greatest technological missions in history. Warren Bennis, on the other hand, described a very different model of the type of leader who can succeed in "forming and leading a Great Group. These leaders are almost always pragmatic dreamers. They are people who get things done, but they are people with immortal longings. They are always people with an original vision that inspires the team to work as if the fate of civilization rested on getting its revolutionary new computer out the door."[11]

TWO KINDS OF LEADERS PLAYING DIFFERENT ROLES

In a .com culture, there is not always one clearly defined leader who plays that role on a permanent basis. Even within the short life span of a .com team, the leadership may shift from one person to another as the project progresses. A person who emerges as a leader on one team may not play that role on the next one. In some cases, no one

---

[10] Charles Garfield, *Peak Performers: The New Heroes of American Business* (New York: William Morrow and Company, 1986), 135.

[11] Warren Bennis and Patricia Ward Biederman, *Organizing Genius: The Secrets of Creative Collaboration* (Reading, MA: Addison-Wesley, 1997), 19.

on the team would be able to answer the question, "Who is the leader?" Everyone is simply pitching in and getting the work done. In most cases, however, there are individuals who play leadership roles throughout the life of the team. Two primary types of leaders play valuable roles in helping the team succeed in its mission. These are the hands-on leaders, who actively participate on the team, and the team sponsors who are often remote from the team and sometimes invisible to most team members.

Hands-On Leaders

> Leading a hot group is more like leading a rough-and-tumble political campaign than working at a steady government job. It's much more like leading a military squad in a tough combat situation than managing an ongoing operating unit of a large company. So, to lead them, a leader must think more like a campaign manager than a civil servant, more like an infantry officer than an accountant.[12]

Hands-on leaders live in the trenches with the team as full-fledged members. Subhash Gupta, E-Commerce Business Development Leader at Acxiom described the kinds of people he tries to recruit for teams in his area of responsibility, "We are looking for the ones who get it. There is a mold that I know works. First I want to find the early adopters who have the ideas and are aggressive and confident enough to take the lead in getting started. These people are the risk takers. Then I am also looking for a second category of people. I call them the 'catch em' people. They also have great ideas, but are not necessarily confident enough to dive in and get a team started. But once someone else makes the first move, these people are quick to jump in and join the effort. Then there is the third category and these people are all the followers that will join in later. The

---

[12] Jean Lipman-Blumen and Harold J. Leavitt, *Hot Groups: Seeding Them, Feeding Them, and Using Them to Ignite Your Organization* (New York: Oxford Press, 1999), 99.

ones we are always looking for are the early adopters who get it and the catch em people who will jump in quickly." According to Gupta, the next challenge is keeping these people once you find them. "You can't let the early adopters get bored, or they are gone. Often they will move around a lot from one project to another. They are always looking for the next challenge. There is no loyalty; they are there for the thrill. The business strategy has to challenge them, and you have to keep them working on exciting projects."

David Roussain at FedEx described these leaders in this way. "They have a spark in their eyes that is just unique. I think you can see it in the face of the individual. They'll tell you about their ideas or things that are new or how they want to make a difference. They want to change. They want to make things better. The better ones are able to capture those thoughts and articulate them very clearly." Jim Worth, Director of Electronic Commerce at Phillips Lighting, summed it up as "people looking for solutions and thriving on freedom to do it differently."

Recruiting and retaining these early adopters at this point in the transition to e-business is easier for .com companies because they provide a higher concentration of these challenging project opportunities than most traditional companies do. Research indicates that in the United States approximately 15-20 percent of the general population may fit the early adopter profile.[13] They will not continue to work for companies that do not provide them with the freedom, challenges, and rewards for their efforts.

> **Key Responsibilities of Hands-On Leaders**
>
> As Producer:
>
> - Recruit skills to track down the right players for the team and persuade them to join the effort.
> - Act as an interface with the world outside the team. Finding resources to feed back into the team, selling

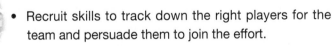

---

[3] Everett M. Rogers, *Diffusion of Innovations* (New York: The Free Press, 1995), 262.

> the team's ideas, and identifying outside competitors to inspire the team are three key external roles a team leader may play.
>
> - Have a high tolerance for work methods that are disordered, ambiguous, and at times near-chaos because .com teams usually do not follow a highly controlled, linear path. [14]
>
> As Catalyst:
>
> - Have a spark or passion that inspires people to get excited about the project. This is a version of charisma, although not necessarily the dramatic or high profile version.
>
> - Be optimistic, resilient, and tenacious enough to bounce back from the inevitable setbacks along the way.

As producer, the hands-on leaders have the most contact with people outside the team. They recruit members to the team at the beginning of the project and as needed along the way. They sell ideas, scavenge, and defend the team, as the circumstances require. The mind-set of a hands-on leader is to do what it takes to keep the project on track.

As catalysts, they inspire and energize the team, which helps the group keep up its momentum during the hard time. Often several people will play this leadership role at the same time on .com teams. This leadership helps create the atmosphere Charles Morgan from Acxiom described when he said their teams had a "take that hill" attitude.

Remember, in .com teams these roles may not be played by one person who is the assigned leader for the duration of the project, but instead they often pass from one person to another as the project progresses. This is not a formalized role in the organization, but a role that people take on because they have the aptitude or enthusiasm to do it.

---

[14] Jean Lipman-Blumen and Harold J. Leavitt, *Hot Groups: Seeding Them, Feeding Them, and Using Them to Ignite Your Organization* (New York: Oxford Press, 1999), 92.

Sponsors of Teams

A sponsor is not necessarily on the team. He or she may be a senior executive who supports the team goal and has the power to help the team succeed. Chapter 10 deals with .com leadership issues in depth, but here the focus is on specific roles that leaders play in relationship to teams. The sponsorship role is essential for a team whether it has a .com or traditional structure. A team within the context of a larger organization cannot survive and succeed if it does not have a sponsor backing it. Even if the organization is so small that it is made up of only one team, there is still a sponsor. In that case, that person will be a part of the team and probably the hands-on leader as well as its sponsor. He or she is most likely the founder of the small company.

Key Responsibilities of Sponsor Leaders

As Messenger:

- Tell the team what you want. Be clear about the goals and the types of teams you will support.
- Tell the truth.

As Facilitator:

- Identify potential hands-on leaders and help them develop.
- Help the hands-on leaders recruit members to their teams.
- Help the team tear down company barriers that slow them down and help them access needed resources.

The Sponsor as Messenger

The first two items in the above box highlight the important role of messenger. The sponsor is primarily responsible for keeping the message clear. Remember the definition of organizational culture from Chapter 1.

Figure 5.1: Sponsor's Role as Culture Messenger

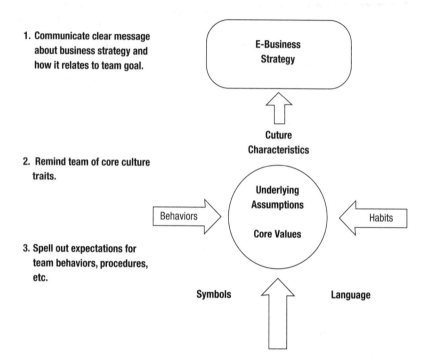

1. Communicate clear message about business strategy and how it relates to team goal.

2. Remind team of core culture traits.

3. Spell out expectations for team behaviors, procedures, etc.

Sponsors communicate the following messages to team members:

- Provide clear messages about the business strategy that tell team members what goals to set for the team to work on with passion. Explain the linkage between the business strategy and the team goals.

- Remind team members of the core traits of the culture, underlying assumptions, and core values. Keep them focused on who you are as a company.

- Spell out the boundaries of how much freedom the team has in decision-making and style. Is .com team behavior acceptable to the sponsor leader or does the team have to stay within more traditional boundaries? If you restrict their freedom, you are not likely to produce high energy .com teams.

Bob Nafius, Director of Culture Development, at Gateway Inc. is a veteran communications expert who has worked with senior executives at GTE, Sony, and Gateway as their speechwriter and advisor on managing the message. He described the role of the leader. "I think a lot of this has less to do with creative inspiration or strategy, than it does with sheer plugging away at it and establishing a rhythm in which you're saying the same thing over and over and over again. I don't care whether it's on-line or whether it's in print or whether it is behind a podium. Those are tactical differences. The crucial strategy is always to say the same thing again and again. It's the marketing principle and it works. You just don't go off message— no matter what. Message discipline is critical."

The Importance of Truth Telling

Nafius also described the importance of telling the truth when communicating the messages. "I am a student of corporate lying. The most dramatic thing a corporation can do is tell the truth to its own people. That's because there is so much lying going on. There are two categories of corporate lies. I call them hard lies and soft lies. Here is an example of how they work. Let's say it is an overcast day. The hard lie is a corporate executive saying, 'The sky is blue.' That's a hard lie. He doesn't want to have any negativity—one of their favorite words—so he will say the sky is blue even though it is overcast. Now, a soft lie is saying, 'The sky is there.' He doesn't have to lie, but he doesn't have to admit that it's overcast. And they are proud of themselves because they haven't told a hard lie. A real leader has to take a third step and say, 'You know what? That sky is overcast. What are we going to do about it?' Soft lies seem to me to be more damaging and insidious than hard lies, because they are less obvious." The messenger must tell the truth to function as a sponsor.

The Sponsor as Facilitator

The other three key traits of sponsor leadership focus on helping the team succeed.

- Identify potential hands-on leaders and help them develop.
- Help the hands-on leaders recruit members to their teams.
- Help the team tear down company barriers that slow them down and help them access needed resources.

These roles are particularly important for traditional companies moving into the e-business arena because the historical culture of the organization is likely to be hostile to the goals and methods of .com teams. Teams in traditional companies need a leader to provide protection and run interference for them even more than teams in a start-up company that had always had a .com culture.

Recruiting .com leaders from the traditional ranks of a company takes insight into untapped potential. A chief information officer of a government agency related one of his experiences of discovering a potential new leader, " I thought he had the ability to capture the imagination of people and make them feel as though they were really part of this project. This was really a transformation for him, because he went from a very stagnant management branch job to being a marketer. He created an alliance with another agency to actually take our whole infrastructure into a regional partnership." A sponsor leader must be looking constantly for the potential team leaders that have not had a chance to surface and give them an opportunity to get involved.

THERE ARE DIFFERENT CHALLENGES FOR .COM AND CONVENTIONAL TEAMS

These fast-moving, temporary teams are extremely effective when high-speed results and exceptional levels of creativity are needed. Teams of this type are better at producing groundbreaking outcomes, but there are the challenges of dealing with the side effects of .com teams. All companies struggle with these issues, but the more traditional ones that are entering the high-speed .com corporate culture probably feel these side effects the most.

The traditional companies must make sure these teams are functioning effectively and also worry about protecting them from interference by the larger company that still functions in the old culture. In a .com start-up company, the second concern of protecting the .com teams from the larger organization does not exist. The entire company is operating within the same cultural framework, so people do not find the.com teams threatening. Besides all the teams are moving too fast and focusing too much on their own goals to waste time or energy interfering with another team's activities.

Five Challenges of Life on .Com Teams

1. Hostile Reactions from the Larger Organization
2. Looks Don't Matter—Results Do
3. Do Not Use Individual Incentives in a Culture of Teamwork
4. Keeping People From Feeling Isolated When They Have No Home Base
5. Burn Out is a Serious Danger for a .Com Team Culture

---

1. HOSTILE REACTIONS FROM THE LARGER ORGANIZATION

Corporations with a well-established culture of "how we do things around here" have a built-in corporate immune system that functions very much like the one in of the human body. Acting like white blood cells that sense the presence of a foreign body, people in the company discover a new idea in their midst, surround it, and kill it immediately. The goal of any immune system is to ensure that foreign bodies are rooted out and destroyed before they gain strength and have a significant impact.[15]

There are several ways to reduce the damage the organization's immune system can cause when .com teams are functioning in a traditional organization. The first and most effective strategy is to teach the

---

[15] Gifford Pinchot III, *Intrapreneuring: Why You Don't Have to Leave the Corporation to Become an Entrepreneur* (New York: Harper & Row, 1985), 189.

team members to keep a low profile in the early stages of a project. The tendency to announce to the world that you are working on an exciting new project is rarely a good idea. Even 3M Corporation, which has one of the most solid and long-running histories as an innovative culture, still runs into problems with the corporate immune system. Bob Adams, Vice President of Technology, said, "If only we could get these intrapreneurs to keep quiet about their ideas until they have developed a more solid position, they would have a better chance."[16]

As we saw in Chapter 4, one of the main reasons some companies start separate e-business units in separate locations is to protect them from the older culture. If the .com teams are to survive in the midst of the traditional company activities, the hands-on leader and the sponsor leader must be especially vigilant about their roles of running interference and interfacing with the outside world. The team as a whole tends to be abrasive to outsiders, especially if it views the non-team members as irrelevant to the team goals. The leaders acting as go-betweens can help to reduce the number of times the team riles outsiders. No matter how these issues are handled, there is likely to be tension between the .com teams and the traditional parts of the organization.

The key here is not to invite unnecessary trouble by the team's own behavior.

- Keep a low profile. Do not broadcast your team's activities or behave flamboyantly or boastfully outside the team environment. Attracting unnecessary attention is the last thing you want to do.

- Ask your sponsors to use their power in the larger organization to tell outsiders to back off and leave the team alone so it can get its work done.

- When there are meetings between the .com teams and traditional groups in the organization, you may want to have a go-between or neutral facilitator to mediate the meeting. It may even be better to send the go-between to the meeting alone to represent the team.

- Some hands-on leaders can play the role of low key, neutral go-between when functioning outside the team environment. This

---

[16] Ibid.

takes a chameleon-like personality to be a passionate team member in one setting and a neutral mediator an hour later in another setting. Many people cannot make the shift, so you may need to rely on your sponsor or other outside help for that role.

- It is likely to take two to three years of regular use of these types of teams before the organization accepts them as normal operating procedure and stops attacking and undermining them.

TIP

IT is important to keep the corporate immune system from attacking your team and its project. This is particularly true during the transition from conventional teams to .com teams. During the initial phase of using .com teams, the immune system is primed to react to the new teams as foreign objects that are threatening the status quo.

2. LOOKS DON'T MATTER—RESULTS DO

Just like any other type of team, .com teams do not always produce the intended results. The fast-moving, temporary team environment does not ensure success. The process may look impressive, but looks do not matter—results do. Team success is either solving the assigned problem or designing a new product that sells. And that does not always happen.

There is a difference between people who look fast and people who are fast. I've seen people come and go at GTE who when you first see them, they blow your hair back. Some of these people were from .com-type companies. You think, "Wow, that's exactly the kind of person we need." And they do move a project along more quickly than we are used to, getting it to market more quickly. But it turns out not to be the right product or wasn't priced in a way to make money. It was quicker, but it wasn't better.
—*Dan Young, AVP-Organization Effectiveness at GTE*

There can be many reasons for why performance does not live up to expectations. One of the most common problems that will produce poor results in a fast-paced team environment is that people are spread too thin on too many teams. Over-scheduling leads to under-performing. Seimens Building Technologies Inc. had this problem when its teams were taking up to six times longer to deliver than estimated at the start of the projects. John Braun, IT Manager of the Enterprise Resource Planning Department in one of the company divisions, said, "We had a lot of over-allocations. We'd want to do a project and knew we needed someone in IS (information systems) to work with someone from manufacturing, engineering, and product marketing, but when we put the plans together, we'd overcommit those people."[17] People were assigned to more than 100 percent of their realistic workload by virtue of membership in several independent project teams.

A team-based, project-oriented company must build into its culture the norm that it is allowable for an employee to say, "No, I don't have time to work on that project." Project management software can aid the managing of staff resources allocation to teams. But software will not solve the problem if the culture makes it a career-shortening gesture to say no to new team assignments when a person is overcommitted. Seimens put in a project management process that resulted in line managers and staff cooperating more effectively on determining what expertise is required and how time-intensive the commitment will be on a new project team. But everyone had to change behaviors and habits to make the new approach work. "We're just learning on this; it's the beginning of this new culture," Braun said. Only a year before, "just doing a time sheet was instant culture shock for the project team members," he recalled. Employees not accustomed to tracking their time had to adjust to a whole set of new habits.

---

[17] "You Overschedule, You Underperform," *CIO Enterprise* (October 15, 1999), 54.

HOW to make sure you are getting results and not just the appearance of speed that is not producing anything useful.

- Do not become enamored with the appearance or rhetoric of speed. Focus on the outcomes and keep asking yourself if those outcomes move the company closer to accomplishing its e-business strategy.

- Allow employees to say no to assignments when they believe they are spread too thin. This is particularly important with your most talented employees. Everyone will want them on teams, so they must have control over their own schedule.

- Use project management systems to help you track and evaluate people's schedules.

- Weed out team projects and other activities that are not essential to the accomplishment of your business strategy. Peter Drucker's strategy of organized abandonment not only frees up monetary and physical resources; it also frees up people's time. And that is your most valuable resource in a .com culture.

3. DO NOT USE INDIVIDUAL INCENTIVES IN A CULTURE OF TEAMWORK

Incentives must change in many traditional companies to successfully create a team-based culture. Accountability and rewards for success must be tied to the team efforts. Teams are the primary vehicle for fast-paced innovation and implementation of their products and services in .com companies. If you are trying to create this type of culture, the single most important action you must take is to change your incentives system, both monetary and recognition. Teams must become the primary route to rewards. This is a major change for most organizations.

In the United States, this team accountability directly conflicts with one of the most intensely held beliefs of the larger national culture—

individualism. Other countries are not quite as extreme in their passion for this particular cultural trait, but it is a core value in many Western cultures. If they are serious about making teams successful on a large scale, most traditional companies must significantly change their compensation systems.

> If one looks at US organizations in general, the clearest indicator of individualism is the sacred cow of individual accountability. No matter how much teamwork is touted in theory, it does not exist in practice until accountability itself is assigned to the whole team and until group pay and reward systems are instituted.[18]

This type of incentive system is easier to accomplish in a small start-up company in which everyone has a financial stake in the company's success. In larger, more traditional companies, a complete rethinking of financial reward systems is required. Most companies historically made eloquent statements on a frequent basis about teamwork, but they still use a system of incentives that is almost entirely focused on the individual. Many companies do better at providing nonmonetary rewards in the form of recognition for successful teams. That is a good start, but it is not enough. Money matters as long as people work for paychecks, bonuses, and stock options. Where a company spends its money is a clear indicator of what it values and what behaviors it wants from those employees.

TIP

REWARD team success more frequently and more generously than individual accomplishments. Individuals team members may receive personal rewards, but it is because they were a part of a successful team. This is the most powerful tool available to an organization that is trying build a culture based on cooperation out of a history that emphasized individualism almost exclusively.

---

[18] Edgar Schein, *The Corporate Culture Survival Guide: Sense and Nonsense about Culture Change* (San Francisco: Jossey-Bass, 1999), 53.

4. KEEPING PEOPLE FROM FEELING ISOLATED WHEN THEY HAVE NO HOME BASE

Is a .com culture a lonelier workplace compared to the old way of working? In the traditional organization, most people worked on a fixed work team in a department with the same people day in and day out. Now the world of temporary teams is becoming more common. If the motto is "get in, do it, and get out," then it seems that no one works with the same people repeatedly. Sometimes team members experience a letdown when an exciting project ends, but does it go beyond that temporary feeling to a broader sense of isolation or loneliness? Is it true that an ongoing network of work friends or colleagues does not exist anymore? If this is the case, what are the implications for people's mental health? If people have few friends or relationships at work and operate in isolation, they are certainly likely to have higher stress levels and be more prone to depression. This is particularly true of people working remote; they spend little time in any type of face-to-face contact with other employees. Issues of isolation and how people deal with it in a virtual organization are addressed in more detail in Chapter 4.

However, isolation and increased loneliness does not seem to be a significant problem for those who spend a large percentage of their time working on project teams. These people find much of their work on teams very rewarding. They are proud of the work they do and feel good about the people they work with on these teams, even if many of the groups are short-lived. Employees do not necessarily lose touch when a team ends, because many people simply use e-mail to stay in touch. In most organizations, people still have a home base; they are a part of a division or department that serves as a base.

5. EMPLOYEES FIND THEIR OWN WAYS TO STAY CONNECTED

People do not feel isolated or lost in revolving team assignments because they devise ingenious methods to keep their connections with the people they liked working with on past teams and ensure that they work with the same people repeatedly. Chris Malcolm of the Computer Sciences Corporation, a global management and technology applications and consulting company, explained, "After a short while, our people learn how the process works. About a month before the end of one project, they start talking to the staffing committee about where they might go next. If they are on a team with people they would like to work with again, they start talking with each other. 'What are you going to tell them? What are you going to do next? What partner is good to work with?' We publish our sales pipeline, so they can see what has a high probability of closure—the projects that are coming down the pike. So they get together. 'Let's both tell them we want this project. We'll tell them that we really like working together and that it's a lot easier for us if we can work together on the next project.' By working the system, some people have been assigned to teams with each other for years."

This repetition of members in teams has many advantages for the organization's culture. It is easier for a new team to get started because it does not have to start from scratch figuring out the ground rules for how they will work together. A core group of members already knows each other and knows the drill. Repetition of team members also creates some group memory of what worked or did not work in the recent past. They already may have even developed a lingo that forms the basis for the team insiders' dialect that every tight team develops as it works together. In short, this repetition increases the team efficiency and allows it to start up more quickly than if the team was an entirely new configuration of people. Malcolm summed it up when asked whether people felt lost or isolated as they moved from team to team. She looked a little surprised and said, "Oh no, they don't feel lost at all."

HOW to help people develop relationships and stay connected within the company when they spend so much time in temporary teams.

- Create a team assignment process that allows individuals to work with the same colleagues repeatedly. This builds relationships, reduces isolation, and creates teams that have a history of working together so they can organize themselves and be productive more quickly.

- For remote workers, use the video and audio technologies you have available to connect them to the teams as frequently as possible

- These technologies are still not adequate substitutes for face-to-face contact. If you have remote workers as team members, you need to bring them in for face-to-face meetings at regular intervals, if you want to foster relationships and reduce isolation. The team may be able to technically do its job without meeting in person, but you risk having your remote workers feel more and more isolated if this is a permanent situation.

- Create a "home base" for people even if it is not the same type structure that existed in the past with rigid departments and work units where people spent all their time. Use the idea of "home room" from school days and create teams of colleagues or functional units where people go for administrative tasks or educational and knowledge sharing gatherings.

Small Teams May Actually Protect Employees from Isolation

Although the fast-paced, temporary team structures that are often used in .com environments may not leave employees feeling as isolated and disenfranchised as some originally thought, there appears to be another source of isolation triggered by the transition to the e-business world. The rapid growth is creating huge, depersonalized corporations often leaving employees with no home base that has any meaning for them. Ironically, using more teams, both conventional and .com, may be a solution to this problem of isolation and loneliness in the workplace.

Gary Aigen, VP of Business Innovation at Arinso International, describes it this way.

"Companies are speeding toward a growth pattern that is just incredible. All these mergers and acquisitions are creating tremendous corporate growth. Because of this, employees are facing a more and more depersonalized work environment. They are becoming part of larger and larger groups. Even if the structures don't change, the scale makes a difference—there is a real change in the properties of large and small groups. I compare it to a drinking straw. If you take a plastic drinking straw and hold it between your fingers and squeeze, it bends easily. There is no strength at all. But if you cut it down to a quarter-inch in length and try to bend it, you can't do it. It will cut right through your fingers before it will bend.

The same is true with organizations. Small groups develop the properties of combat-intensive patrols. The military knows this very well. They have huge structures, but they divide them down into small units because they know that solders will die for their small combat group, not for the Army. They have no feel for the Army at all. They work in a high-pressure situation with a small group and they bond.

In order for companies to have good retention, people need to enjoy working with their fellow workers, build the camaraderie, and feel protected by the group. Companies are growing so fast and becoming so depersonalized that there is no social contract between the corporate world and the employees anymore. The change that is needed right now is for corporations to build that contract into the small group structure."

TIP

IF the divisions or work units within your company are very large, break them into small units and teams where they can develop the camaraderie that allows them to bond with colleagues and feel a part of a unit that matters to them. These teams could be either .com or conventional in structure. It is the smaller size that it important.

6. BURN OUT IS A SERIOUS DANGER FOR A .COM TEAM CULTURE

Rolling from one team to another may not cause loneliness or leave people feeling isolated, but it can leave them exhausted and burnt out. Recruiting and retaining the best talent is one of the greatest challenges every company is facing in today's economy, and turning your talent into burnout casualties at a rapid pace is not a wise business strategy. There is no clear evidence at this point that burnout occurs as a result of intense, high pressure, long hour work cultures. There is some speculation that having exciting, interesting work and a high degree of control over your work is more important to maintaining health than long hours or mental stress and pressure. Others disagree, claiming there is a limit to how far people can push themselves and eventually burnout is inevitable if the pace is relentlessly fast and high pressure. In the .com world it is too soon to tell what the outcome of this debate will be, but it is certainly a concern that is on people's minds.

> We're trying to really come up with graded solutions to burnout caused by exhaustion. We have people who have been at this for four years in our company and we have to figure out a way to get them to learn how to completely refresh themselves in short increments of time.
>
> I've stood at the elevator with people going on vacation and actually taken the laptop and the cell phone out of their hands and said, "Great, now you can actually have a vacation." The only way to truly regenerate yourself enough to be truly creative and inventive again is to be unwired at times in the year and to be in the other part of the world.[19]

One source of burnout can be the letdown effect when a great team ends. Dan Young of GTE said, " I think one of the downsides of fast-paced teams is that people are not used to the emotional ups

---

[19] Judith H. Dobrzynski, "Online Pioneers: The Buzz Never Stops," *The New York Times* (November 21, 1999), Section 3, 14. (quoting Candice Carpenter, CEO of iVillage).

and downs. The project is over. Done. Onto something else. How do you shift gears from mission accomplished to move on to the next project? I think we have small versions of that happening very fast and people are ill-equipped to deal with several of them going on at the same time."

Hugh McColl, Chairman of NationsBank, was attending one of the receptions at the Atlanta Olympics in 1996. NationsBank had been a main sponsor of the Olympics, and a great deal of time, energy, and enthusiasm of a large numbers of NationsBank employees had been poured into the event planning during the previous two years. McColl was asked, "What are you going to do next Monday to keep employee morale up?" McColl responded, "I don't know. I'm really worried about it." He was wise to be worried. The letdown effect can be painful to live through when the entire organization is affected by the same event at the same time.

Allowing themselves a period of coasting is one way individuals often deal with the letdown effect when great team events end. Many people describe a push-cruise pattern of action that seems to work for them. If they purposely can go into a low-energy, low-productivity gear for a time after a high-energy burst of activity, they seem to recover and are soon ready to move on to the next challenge. A fast-paced team culture must allow for cruise time. Without that time for recovery, burnout will happen more often and will be a more serious problem for a .com culture. People do not seem to be mentally capable of moving instantly from one high-energy project to the next over and over without breaks. Managing the scheduling of individuals on high-energy teams may be one of the key skills the leaders in this .com team environment must master to avoid burning out their most talented people. For many organizations, this represents a culture shift away from the old norms of nonstop pressure to produce at peak levels with no recovery time planned into the process. If the norm in the corporate culture equates recovery time with wasting time, you likely will have a high burnout culture that has a difficult time retaining its best talent.

HOW to overcome burnout that may be the result of too much time spent on too many .com teams.

- Let people take breaks and recover. Build in "cruise" time for team members once they complete a project that was a huge effort. Make that one of the rewards for a job well done.

- Give people as much control as possible over which teams they join. Although the jury is still out on how completely satisfying, exciting work will protect people from burnout, there is no doubt that it helps. Working on projects you are personally interested in with team members you respect and enjoy working with will reduce burnout, even if it may not entirely eliminate it.

- Give the teams as much freedom as possible over how they carry out the work of their team. Demanding goals with quick deadlines is a tough enough challenge to tackle without having to deal with the frustration of an organization that interferes with your progress at every turn. Give the team a job and then get out of its way and let it do its work.

- Warn people about the letdown feelings that are normal at the end of an exciting, successful project. Having realistic expectations about the typical reactions helps prepare people for dealing with those reactions if they occur. It is always helpful to know that you are not "crazy" for feeling this way. The letdown syndrome does not usually last very long—a few days or weeks—particularly if people move on to other interesting work after some rest and recovery time.

HAS TRIBAL WARFARE DISAPPEARED?

One of the most enduring problems that organizations struggle with is the never ending turf battles that take place among the departments, professions, and work units within the company.[20] It seems to be one of the basic facts of human nature. When people gather into groups, they develop loyalties to their "tribe" and are leery of and compete with other groups around them. Human beings are as tribal in their behavior as they ever were. In organizations the conflicts usually occur over limited resources. Turf takes the form of competition for budgets, space, people, access to equipment, and any other valuable resource that exists in that environment. Or conflicts will arise because two different groups have different priorities. A typical example occurs in manufacturing when the sales people want a specific product priced low so they can sell it, the finance people want it priced high to maximize profits, and the production people want to run a different product because it is easier for them to make their production numbers. Different goals lead to conflict. Before the advent of the .com world, it appeared that tribal warfare would never disappear from business and professional environments. Now it appears that e-business may be having an effect on tribal warfare in organizations.

On the lighter side of the issue, a new and highly entertaining form of tribal warfare has evolved in the Silicon Valley. This version is carried out using toy guns that shoot rubber bands, Ping-Pong balls, or foam arrows. "Like the dog under the desk, the toy gun is now a workplace trapping no self-respecting tech firm can do without," said Sue Wilson of *Fortune*.[21] When officially asked about this form of workplace play, many companies are skittish about answering, but the employees tell their stories with enthusiasm and glee. According to them, most toy gun play is among friends. "It's actually an affectionate act. You can shoot me, I'll shoot you, and we'll run around and have a little war," said one engineer. There are even battles between departments. To welcome the newly arrived technical-support division, the engineers at one company staged a full-blown raid. "There were a bunch of them, and they came into our area," recalled one of the victims. "And they converged on us and kind of spread out and started shooting. It was great!"

---

[20]Peg C. Neuhauser, *Tribal Warfare in Organizations* (New York: HarperCollins, 1988).
[21] Sue Wilson, "Let's Shoot Foam Arrows at Each Other!" *Fortune* (November 22, 1999): 366.

Ping-Pong balls and rubber bands flying around a company building is a lighthearted form of tribal warfare that is probably akin to football or softball team rivalries that have been around for a long time. But what about the serious side of tribal warfare in which groups of people from different departments or professions get into turf battles that damage the organization's ability to work effectively across functional lines? When employees of a company start identifying other groups in the same company as the adversary, orchestrating the type of teamwork needed for the company to perform at peak levels is more difficult. You cannot tap into the collective IQ of the organization if people spend a substantial portion of their time defending their group's turf instead of cooperating. In answer to the question of whether this kind of tribal warfare still exists in organizations that have moved to a .com culture. The answer seems to be "Yes, tribal warfare still exists, but not as much of it and only under certain circumstances." This is great news. Internal turf battles and lack of cross-functional cooperation takes a significant toll on a company, both financially and in lower morale. At the time *Tribal Warfare in Organizations* was written, managers reported that they spent anywhere from 25 to 60 percent of their working day dealing with conflicts or fallout from people-related problems. Calculating just the salaries of these managers, the cost is huge. Add in the costs of the damage to innovation and quality caused by lack of cooperation, and the price of turf battles is immense. Any improvement in this area is of great value to the company.

WHY WOULD A .COM CULTURE HAVE LESS TRIBAL WARFARE?

One reason is quite simple. Temporary teams with no history are doing much of the work in a .com culture. People keep moving to new tribes, and they do not have the time or inclination to dig in, build up their turf, and develop elaborate rituals for defending that turf. "Get in, do it, get out," is not a ideal setting for tribal warfare. In-fighting is caused by long-running loyalties to the home base and fellow tribal members. If you live and work exclusively in one department or profession for years, it is a basic fact of human nature that the boundaries of that group will become quite dense and rigid. Any change or request to accommodate another group's needs is seen as interference or an attack. If most employees constantly serve on an ever-changing mix of teams, there is not as much opportunity for those rigid boundaries of us versus them to form. People may still be assigned to a home base, but they leave it regularly to do their most intense and important work in temporary teams.

Another reason that tribal warfare may be lessened in a .com culture is that the temporary teams seem more tolerant of the diversity of its members. Lipman-Blumen and Leavitt described this tolerance in *Hot Groups*, "Hot groups don't care about how you look, speak, or dress. They don't even much care if you have an oversized ego. They'll put up with almost any of your less attractive qualities, as long as you contribute to the group's task."[22] As long as team members live up to group standards for the quantity and the quality of their work, members get along with each other. Because of this tolerance of differences, it is easier to put together a cross-functional team from different professions or divisions without bringing the historical tribal warfare of their various groups into the team setting. This tolerance is not the result of more open-minded or highly evolved individuals in these companies. It is simply the result of different priorities. These teams are intensely focused on their goal and if you are a valuable contributor to that goal, they really do not care or pay any attention to your other traits. If these teams existed for long periods of time, this single minded focus would wear thin and difference will start to cause conflict, but on a .com team intense goal focus and short life span leads to a temporarily tolerant environment.

A third reason why .com cultures may produce less tribal warfare is they most likely exist in industries in which the external competition is very intense and real to the employees at all levels. They know who the real adversaries are, and they are outside the organization. Maureen Garrison of GTE described this focus on external competition, "What's happening is employees are starting to realize that

---

[22] Jean Lipman-Blumen and Harold J. Leavitt, *Hot Groups: Seeding Them, Feeding Them, and Using Them to Ignite Your Organization* (New York: Oxford Press, 1999), 219.

their competition is not internal competitors but rather outside the company. If we don't get our internal act together and work collaboratively as a team, they will eat our lunch. At a recent meeting in Florida, regional employees were asked if they knew how many competitors GTE had in their serving area. People shouted out guesses. The answer was over 40. That got everyone's attention."

WHAT TYPE OF TRIBAL WARFARE STILL EXISTS?

Unfortunately, moving to a .com culture is not likely to eliminate all types of tribal warfare. The human tendency to join groups, become loyal to those groups, and then dislike anyone who disagrees or is different from your own group seems to be basic human nature. Any improvement is great news, but there are still areas where the turf battles are occurring.

Clashes between the generations are happening in some companies. There are reports of these types of conflicts at iVillage, a high-profile .com company. Candice Carpenter, one of the founders, recounted in a magazine interview that they had encountered problems with talented young employees constantly coming to her with their latest job offers and demanding more money. At first she was sympathetic, but she finally got fed up. She fired five young, but high-ranking employees and replaced them with "grown-ups." Carpenter said, "These people are smart, but in some ways that can be dangerous. They're so sure they're right. So we kicked some of them out. We felt like we were being held hostage by these twentysomethings."[23] The article triggered resentment within the company among the younger employees. They tried to have a retreat to build cohesion among the staff, but instead it seemed to exacerbate the generational tensions. The age groups were not interested in participating in the same activities together—all night volleyball and skinny-dipping versus traditional team-building exercises.

Crossing divisions still causes some tribal problems in companies using large numbers of temporary teams. Chris Malcolm of CSC

[23] Erik Larson, "Free Money: The Internet I.P.O. that made two women rich, and a lot of people furious," *The New Yorker* (October 8, 1999), 83.

described their struggles with putting together teams of people from multiple divisions within this 55,000-person company. When the team members are drawn from areas that have not worked together before,

"we are still finding that in our virtual world it does not work easily. People coming from different divisions have different standards of professionalism and their own work patterns. For example, some areas work 37.5 hours per week and others work 60 hours per week, or we have the same job titles but they mean different things. I've been sucked into situations a couple of times where I assumed I knew what people meant, because we were using the same words, but I was wrong, and the team just didn't perform the way that I expected. We are working really hard on fixing these problems. We talk about our operating model a lot. We have to make this work seamlessly, because the strength of a company like ours is that we can bring people together from many disciplines to take a project from concept to software to implementation."

"The big lesson for me is to slow down," said Malcolm. "You have to go slowly during the project definition phase. You have to talk through, then write down the actions to be taken, the milestones to hit, the sign-offs, and get clarity on everyone's roles. The consulting teams who are familiar with each other can work more informally. They already know methods, roles, what to expect from each other, and what excellence means. That's not to say that integrating new team members doesn't take time—it is just less onerous. When we are working across divisions, we have to slow down and make sure everyone knows the rules of the road. Once the groundwork is set, each team member or small group can hit the ground and develop their work as fast as possible. We have monthly meetings to make sure everyone knows how we are doing as a team. This helps a lot—as do tough-minded large program managers."

HOW to cope with the tribal warfare that still exists when you bring people together from different divisions to form a team.

- Slow down during the project definition phase when a group from diverse backgrounds is pulled together for the first time.

- The new team needs to establish its own set of rules and standards for behavior within the team, especially concerning how they will treat the customers. Malcolm calls this an operating model.

- Have monthly update meetings of the whole team to help the group stay on track. (Use whatever frequency makes sense for the pace of the team.)

- This is a team that may need a more formal leader than a typical .com team because someone has to be the final arbitrator on what the standards will be.

- Make sure everyone on the team will share in equal portions of the reward if the team is successful. If you are all in this together from a rewards perspective, it will be a great motivator to set aside your differences.

APPLYING THIS INFORMATION IN YOUR ORGANIZATION

Below are questions to help you determine how to use .com teams as one of the key elements for building a .com culture.

1. What types of teams are currently operating in your company? Are they all traditional teams with assigned leaders, bureaucratic procedures, and long timelines? Do you have some that fit the profile of a .com team?

2. What projects need to be tackled right now in your company that could benefit from a fast-paced, temporary team that takes the approach described in this chapter?

3. Who are potential hands-on leaders in your organization that could lead a .com team?

4. Have you recently had any teams in your organization that looked fast and impressive but did not produce the expected results? What do you think went wrong?

5. Is recruiting and retention a problem for your company? If so, are you looking to your team culture to:

   • Create a team environment where people would like to work.

   • Provide team incentives to keep them motivated.

   • Work on ways to protect the employees from the burnout that comes from moving from one high-energy team to another without a break?

6. Where are your biggest tribal warfare battles these days in your company? Are you using temporary teams to reduce the quantity of turf battles that historically have plagued companies?

CHAPTER SIX

Communication Belongs to Everyone in a .Com Culture

COMPANIES LOSE CONTROL
OVER THE DISTRIBUTION OF INFORMATION

Everyone is connected. The Internet and intranets inside companies link people together in ways that are changing everything about how we communicate in the corporate world. And they tell us that we haven't seen anything yet. Engineers developing the new communication systems predict that in a few years today's tools such as e-mail or videoconferencing "will look as primitive as cave paintings."[1] According to Douglas T. Hickey, CEO of Critical Path Inc., a Silicon Valley company that provides communication technology, e-mail soon will include audio, video, and voice mail elements that go far beyond our current capacities. One of the most important aspects of the changes communication technologies are making is that companies are losing control over the distribution of information. Organizations no longer control who has access to the information or the timing of when employees, customers, and the public are given information.

---

[1] Joan O'C. Hamilton, "Like It or Not, You've Got Mail," *BusinessWeek*, (October 4, 1999), 184.

A wired workforce will have access to any public information available about the company, from whatever source.
Want to know what the company president makes? Go to
one of the company's SEC filings. Curious about whether
you're underpaid relative to your peers in other companies? Check out JobSmart, which lists salaries by title,
region, and experience levels. This totally informed workforce will be newly empowered to, if not make, then at
least understand decisions as they're being made.[2]

THE UPSIDES AND DOWNSIDES OF THE WIRED WORKPLACE

Four Key Challenges of Communicating in a .Com Culture

The following are key concerns that companies are struggling with during their transition to the e-business environment. The problems that must be solved in these four
areas are quite different than the ones traditional companies dealt with in the past. This chapter describes the
strategies some companies are taking to adapt to the new
world of Internet-based communications.

1. **Dealing with Cyberspace Name-Calling**

    Deciding how to respond to the annoying and even
    illegal use of net communication and finding con-
    structive uses of these new communication tools.

2. **Coping with E-Mail Hell**

    Being overwhelmed by a random mix of valuable and
    worthless e-mail in very ever increasing quantities.

3. **Changing from Push to Pull Communications**

    The old system was based on management pushing
    information out to employees in their efforts to get

---

[2] Chuck Martin, *Net Future* (New York: McGraw-Hill, 1999), 55.

the right information to the right people. The new systems rely on employees pulling in information as they need it.

4. Moving from Hoarding to Sharing Information

In-house competition is one of the fundamental cultural characteristics of many organizations. E-business relies heavily on collaboration as the basis for forging alliances inside and outside the company. Making that shift is a major cultural change.

There is a great deal of good news for companies in the form of improved capacity to communicate inside and outside the company. If Lou Gerstner, Chairman of IBM, wants to communicate news quickly to the company's 266,000 employees in 165 countries, he can get the word out almost instantly. Dow Chemical Co. installed document-sharing software for 30,000 employees that allows work groups of as many as 25 people to view a document at the same time from any of their 120 sites worldwide.[3] Computer Sciences Corporation (CSC) can set up global special interest groups for the sharing of knowledge on specific topics and had 400 employees from all over the world sign on to attend a two-hour virtual meeting to discuss an issue.

However, it is equally true that employees can use the technology for unofficial Web sites that are not a welcome addition from a management perspective. Borders Books' employees who were trying to organize a union, set up a Web site where employees could sign on for the latest news on the organizing campaign.[4] Disgruntled employees who are living through mergers or restructuring often use company Web sites as a place to air their grievances, spreading both accurate and inaccurate news about the company. According to Boston attorney Charles L. Solomont, Partner at the Boston law firm Bingham Dana LLP, the problem is not just limited to "cyberspace

---

[3] Ibid., 54.
[4] Ibid., 55.

name-calling." Solomont elaborated, "Trade secrets are being disclosed, anonymously of course, over the Internet. Stocks are being illegally manipulated through mass dissemination of false information."[5]

> We've gone out and seen something published on the Web associated with our company that was very surprising in terms of some of the insights that people had of things that were actually happening within the company that were not widely known. The majority of it was speculation, but there was some very good speculation out there. I think it is important to really understand what is happening rather than trying to combat it. You must know that it does exist.
>
> —*Bob Sells, CIO of Brunswick Corporation*

1. DEALING WITH CYBERSPACE NAME-CALLING

At the beginning of the book we saw the example of corporate graffiti moving to the Web to illustrate one of the frustrations facing traditional organizations in their efforts to learn to live with and benefit from the new technologies of the connected workplace. These kinds of public rumor mills and gripe sessions are new experiences for companies used to the Old World. There has always been a rumor mill and disgruntled employees ready to expound their views, but they have never had such a public forum for these discussions. Now these discussions take place in public arenas such as Yahoo or Raging Bull Web sites where customers and competitors can see the running dialogue as it occurs. And the participants can remain anonymous. So the old restraints of being careful about what you say because it may come back to haunt you have been diluted dramatically. People believe that using aliases when they sign on protects them from detection. In Chapter 1, we left Bob Kulbick, CEO of RSKCo, a company that had recently gone through a difficult merger and

---

[5] Charles Solomont, "Scared Straight," *CIO Web Business*, (October 1, 1999), 34.

received its share of employee bashing on the Net during the transition, wondering how to handle this situation.

Coping with Corporate Graffiti on the Web

Kulbick is a CEO who puts a high value on communicating with employees on a regular basis. During the merger transition he traveled to 40 field offices and met with all 2,500 employees to explain what was going on and listen to their concerns and ideas about how to improve the company. He encouraged his senior staff to do the same. Now that the transition period is behind them, the RSKCo leadership team continues its campaign of staying in touch with the employees. Kulbick and the senior staff continue to travel to offices every month, have telephone conference calls with other offices each month, have special e-mail addresses for employees to access the leaders directly, and use regular voice-mail calls to communicate with all employees. This is a leadership team with an unusually intense interest in talking with employees. So how do they handle the Web chat?

"My perspective has changed over the past few months," said Kulbick. " I read the Web everyday because I want the additional information. I want to see any information I can about the company, and the Web is one of my sources. I don't have to believe it or accept it, but I want to see it to spot trends or issues. I may see new people appearing on the site or new issues coming up, so it is very important to pay attention. What has changed for me in the last six months is my view about whether to join it or fight it or ignore it. Before, I was considering signing on and joining the conversation, but now I am leaning toward ignoring it. Read it everyday, but beyond that don't do anything." The reason for the change is the content he has been reading on the Web site. "It's losing all credibility," Kulbick said. "It's the same people all the time. Other people have dropped out because they are tired of the same tirades. If the people signing on continue to have a negative approach to every issue that comes up, people start ignoring them and saying they're nuts."

The question that interests Kulbick at this point is how to tap into the Web in a different way that produces something positive for

RSKCo. He is "struggling with how we can structure a Web site so that we can have an interactive communication mechanism with all of the employees in the company. We would want a site that is actually used to communicate back and forth, not just to disseminate company propaganda. For example, we might set up a company chat room and announce that every Tuesday and Thursday between 2:00 and 4:00 p.m. the CEO is going to be in the chat room." At this point he is considering what might work and what to try next. He laughed and said that he does have one dilemma if he decides to sign on to chat. "I type like a snail," admits Kulbick. "I would drive people crazy with how slow I'd be typing my responses."

TIP

IGNORE the annoying cyberspace name-calling on the Web, and look for constructive ways to set up Web sites for employee communication with each other and with leaders. Take action if the chat behavior is illegal (e.g., libel, disclosure of trade secrets, or SEC violations).

When Chat Crosses the Line into Illegal Actions

Sometimes on-line discussions cross the line into actions that are illegal, and this is a different issue for companies to consider. These on-line transgressions can go in several directions, according to Charles Solomont, and sometimes they take the form of libel and defamation. Solomont, who specializes in Internet and intellectual property law, described one situation where "the chairman of one client, Talk Visual Corporation, faced an on-line barrage of falsehoods accusing him of violating SEC and other laws." In another case a senior corporate executive was accused of being "a lesbian and a whore who sleeps with other employees." In another type of violation, Raytheon Co. took action against employees for disclosing trade secrets on-line. In other cases, stock manipulators holding short positions are posting false reports of corporate doom and gloom to drive down stock prices.[6]

---

[6] Ibid.

Companies are investigating what they can do about these situations when they occur. According to Solomont, under the Communications Decency Act of 1996, Web site operators, Internet access providers, and on-line service providers are virtually immune from liability for content transmitted on or through their services and systems by third parties.[7] Internet service providers can screen and remove offensive material but are not required to do so. Solomont explained that it is possible to identify message posters and serve legal process upon them. Internet access providers are not immune from the discovery process in civil lawsuits. When a lawsuit is filed, on-line networks can be subpoenaed for information concerning the defendants' true identities.

Even if the posters were not required to register with their real names, they usually leave an Internet portal (IP) address. Using the IP to trace through the service provider usually can produce at least the telephone number or e-mail address of the posters. Once the poster is identified, the offenses generally stop immediately. Solomont recounted in one case "months of offensive and defamatory messages about our client permanently ceased the day after we filed a complaint which was delivered to the defendant on the very message boards on which they had been posting their defamatory messages about the client." Damages can be pursued, but Solomont pointed out that "the mere filing of a lawsuit can scare them straight."

Every Company Needs a Trooper Brown

Trooper Brown is a riffed employee (reduction-in-force) who worked for GTE for more than 20 years. He took this experience and used it to create what is reported to be one of the most useful employee Web sites around (www.trooperbrown.org). This opinion was expressed by management people working for GTE, who would have been in a position to resent the site.

---

[7] Ibid., 36.

Here is his story in his own words.

"I had been with GTE for twenty-plus years, and it turned out my last administrative task was to coordinate the reduction-in-force for my organization. A large chunk of the organization was eliminated, including me. So I was working through that process knowing I was on the list. I discovered that there was a lot of information that I didn't understand. Stuff about pensions and retiree benefits. GTE has an 800 number for employees to call with questions, but the language was new to me and didn't make sense. I found myself asking questions and getting answers that made less sense. So I started asking questions on the message board associated with Yahoo's GTE stock quote because I knew a lot of GTE employees and retirees were watching the board. After a few questions, I found I was monopolizing the board, and that wasn't fair. So I went out and opened a free message board, and a bunch of people followed me over. Within the first two or three months, I had around 100,000 hits on the site. I was flabbergasted—no advertising, just word of mouth. I knew there were some questions out there that needed to be answered. But I didn't realize. You know, I saw some serious pain."

Trooper went on to explain, "My basic premise for the whole thing is an anonymous exchange of information and a place for information that people may not be able to get through the company. Things that allow them to get better information and make better decisions because they are more informed." At the time Trooper set up the Web site, he established *Trooper's Rules of Order*. He explained "That was one of my basic requirements for people that join the process. I had seen a lot of the nonsense that goes on out there in some of the chat rooms and message boards. They can get really nasty, really mean-spirited and unproductive, and in some cases borderline illegal. So I set up the basic ground rules."

Trooper Brown
Scout for the Corporate Downtrodden

I've been trying to codify what we've called "Trooper's Rules of Order" and came up with two versions: the short form (the letter of the law) and the long form (the spirit of the law).

The Short Form

1. No personal attacks on anyone living or dead, born or unborn, evolved or not evolved.

2. No direct attacks on the company by inference, innuendo, or shorting the stock.

3. No inter-post bickering, sniping, or rude gestures (you're on the honor system with that one).

4. No posting of company confidential information (including the Wednesday Special in the Cafeteria).

5. No whining about the rules.

Pretty simple, huh? And the best part is—I get to enforce them! Be nice to me, OK.

The long form is the poem "Desiderata" that begins, "Go placidly amid the noise and haste." The name of his message board is Trooper Brown's SAFE Message Board.

When asked how he monitors the board since he refuses to block anyone from participating, Trooper responded, "No, I won't block them, but I can delete a post." (Remove that specific message.) Or he can do what he did in the case of an angry poster. Trooper described what happened, "We had a couple of exchanges on the board. Finally, I asked him if he wanted to be constructive and abide by the responsible rules that we play by there. If not, he needed to find another venue where he might be a little more appreciated or get more value for what he wants to do. He left for a while. I have found that it is a self-enforcing environment and I don't have to be the cop all the time. The regular posters police it themselves. If someone posts something they don't like, it draws fire from the regulars, 'This is not something we want to hear about.'" The following is a sample of one of Trooper's responses to an irate poster. Trooper is responding to a poster who has stepped over the line in the language the poster is using to criticize someone in GTE management.

> **Easy, ...**
>
> You're certainly entitled to your opinion and I have no wish to be Draconian in my Pollyanna-ish attitudes but go easy on the name-calling. What any of us were or are is a product of our histories and experiences. However Tom [the person being attacked] got to where he is, I think he deserves credit for the good he did. You pretty much wound up in the same place with your post so I don't think we disagree.
>
> Regardless, it's good to see you back in Trooper-land. Everyone needs a good devil's advocate to keep them honest. Thanks tb

When asked what advice he would have for companies or employees trying to use these communication tools in similar ways, Trooper said. "There are different ways to go about it. You have to focus on your intent. Do you want to get good information or are you just looking to have a pity session?" The second piece of advice he offered concerned the independence of the site. "I think one of the reasons this site works is that it is independent of the company. It gives it credibility. It's a safe place to be. Unless a company has a very open information culture, I think they would probably want to out-source something like this to an independent third party [human resources or public relations firms]. They could set up the ground rules and send out a memo letting employees know about the site with a published policy statement. The executives could sign the memo saying that this will be a hands-off area unless it gets into a legal situation. Regardless of how they do it, it has to be personal—that's crucial. Someone has to be the 'voice' of the board. I've seen a direct relationship between the activity on the board and my level of involvement." Trooper's third piece of advice is related to the format of the site. "I kept it fairly simple, no flashy bells and whistles or graphics. This is the cracker barrel where everyone sits around and talks about what they heard today. I think that has real value."

2. COPING WITH E-MAIL HELL

If you think you are getting a lot of e-mails today, listen to this prediction. The quantity of e-mail is "likely to grow tenfold in the next ten years, upping the average person's inbox to more than 1,000 messages a day," predicted Michael L. Dertouzos, Director of the Laboratory of Computer Sciences at MIT.[8] In 1998, the volume of e-mail in the United States surpassed the volume of hand-delivered mail. Many people are concerned about the problem of dealing with an ever-increasing quantity of e-mail, not to mention voice mail and all the paper that still comes at them on a daily basis. They described the various strategies they use to control the volume.

Individual Strategies for Dealing with E-Mail

Much of what people currently do to handle the onslaught of electronic communication is unique to an individual or a work team. The following comments are not intended as advice that you should necessarily adopt, but as examples that may trigger a few useful ideas for your own e-mail survival kit.

- I have more than one e-mail address and give out different addresses to different sets of people. Some e-mails are the ones you check every few hours, and the others are the "when I get to it" sites.
- I have unlisted e-mail addresses that I give out very selectively. Not on my business card.

---

[8] Joan O'C. Hamilton, "Like It or Not, You've Got Mail," *BusinessWeek*, (October 4, 1999), 184.

- Don't copy anyone on an e-mail unless they really need to see the information. And if you copy them and they only need to read one paragraph of the document you are sending, tell them at the beginning of the e-mail which paragraph it is. Don't make everyone you copy read the whole document when there is no need for them to do so.

- If someone needs a quick answer, no one in our company (a small .com company) uses e-mail. We go find the person and deal with it face-to-face.

- If we have two exchanges by e-mail and there is still a misunderstanding or confusion, pick up the phone.

- No e-mails longer than a paragraph. If it's more than that, call me or come find me. I'll go blind staring at the screen reading lots of long e-mails.

- Proofread your e-mail before you send it to make sure it makes sense. No stream-of-consciousness e-mails. They never make sense.

- I start at the bottom and work up. Often a later message cancels out an earlier one.

- As far as I'm concerned "Administrator" is Latin for "delete." I never read those e-mails.

- I delete everything except messages where some action is required.

- Don't send me an e-mail or voice mail thanking me for my e-mail or voice mail. If there isn't a content response, don't respond.

- Limit yourself to one topic per e-mail.

- Archiving them into categories doesn't work for me. I never go back to read them later.

- Agree on different usages for the different mediums. The more you need immediate feedback, the more you move toward face-to-face communication (or telephone in a virtual environment). If the message is one directional and more uniform, use the bulletin board or e-mail. Stop to think and use the right medium for the message you are sending.

Is It Possible to Develop Company Protocol for Using E-Mail?

The broader question about e-mail and other communication vehicles is whether it is realistic to develop a company-wide protocol for e-mail etiquette that people will follow. There are two points of view on this issue that seem to come from organizations with two different types of cultures.

One stance seems to fit more unstructured, looser environments. According to this perspective, it is not possible to mandate or formally adopt a list of ground rules and make them stick. The belief in this case is that people will simply ignore the rules and do whatever they want. The only way to end up with a generally accepted set of communication ground rules is by universal suffering. When almost everyone in the company is sufficiently fed up with a particular e-mail offense, the group then arrives at an informal but lasting agreement to stop that behavior. In cultural terms, a new norm is established by general group agreement. If someone breaks a rule, the group demands that the person stop the outlawed behavior.

A second point of view maintains that it is possible to develop more formal rules, announce them, and make them stick. This approach seems to work better in organizations with a history of more hierarchical control and a willingness to follow rules. Even in such a case it is not a simple matter of issuing orders. A key to making this approach work relies on who makes up the rules. If the CEO or an informal leader with high credibility on the subject (e.g., a respected techie) sends out the word on the new ground rules, they are more likely to be followed. It is also important that the new rules make sense to people. Even though the group may not have to reach the point of universal suffering, employees still have to react to the new rule with basic agreement, or compliance will not last. The last factor that seems to be important with this approach is that the people who sponsor the new rule, the CEO or the respected techie, must set the example by following their own rules with impeccable consistency. If they make up a rule for everyone else in the organization except themselves, no one takes the rule seriously.

TIP WORK on developing e-mail protocols for the company or your division. Depending on your culture, you can do this by informal group agreement or by mandate from leaders. If you are a leader, be sure you follow the protocol rules unerringly.

The following communication guidelines come from Southwest Airlines. CIO Ross Holman explained that these guidelines were developed and communicated by Herb Kelleher, the CEO of the company. Kelleher is a CEO who is renowned for his passion about his company's culture. The communication bias in the Southwest Airlines culture is toward the more interpersonal mediums (i.e., the top portion of the chart in Figure 6.1). This protocol fits the broader culture at Southwest that emphasizes informal, friendly, humorous interactions among employees and with customers. E-mail and intranet broadcasts are not the company's preferred mode of communicating.

Figure 6.1: Communication Choices

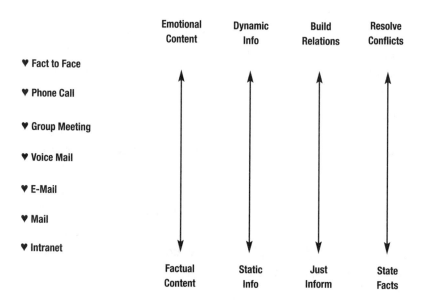

3. CHANGING FROM PUSH TO PULL COMMUNICATIONS

The Internet is changing the way companies communicate and sell to their customers. The same type of change can be brought in-house and used by employees at all levels to simplify how they communicate with each other. In Internet lingo, this change is often described as a shift from push communication to pull communication. Here is how it works on the Internet with customers. In the Old World, a company pushed advertising or product offers out to passive customers and hoped to attract their attention and trigger them to buy. Most messages or offers were generic, mass-market messages. The same offer was pushed out to everyone. Now on the Internet, active customers come to a company's Web site and pull the specific information and products they want. Each customer pulls only what he or she wants, so each customer ends up with a customized product. The company can use electronic filtering to track the customer's previous selections and use the information to customize special offers to that individual in the future, increasing the odds of future sales.

What if communications inside companies worked the same way? No more *push* in the form of broadcasting information or e-mails sent back and forth trying to provide or track down missing information. Instead, the company relies on the *pull* of active employees who go and get information when needed. For example, one company with large numbers of field offices has a frequent problem with the "why wasn't I told that?" syndrome. When the corporate staff arrive at a field office, they are often told about company information that should have been given to them earlier. It puts them in an embarrassing position of arriving from headquarters and being told by people in the field what is happening back at the central offices. For example, if there has been a policy update from accounting that impacts how the system is used, it damages the corporate person's credibility if the field people have been notified about the change, but he has not gotten the word. At this point the e-mails and voice mails start flying, according to the people who work for the company. "Why wasn't I told that?" And "whose fault is this?" are the usual messages.

Notice that the assumption underlying the statement "why was-n't I told that?" is passive employees waiting for information to be pushed out to them. If the employees have Web sites and other communication tools where they could pull information when needed, much of the problem is eliminated. Now if the corporate employee arrives at the field office without the correct information, it is that person's fault for not having gotten the information before the visit. That employee would know to check for updates before arriving at the field office, instead of assuming that it is someone else's responsibility to let them know if anything changes. And in many cases it would not be much of a problem anyway; that corporate employee can just turn to a terminal at the field office and pull up the needed information on the spot. By switching to a pull method of disseminating information and placing the responsibility with employees to go to the intranet to pull up what they need when they need it, many of the "why wasn't I told that?" e-mails and voice mails can be eliminated. All those messages looking for the missing information and complaining about not being "kept in the loop" never need to be sent.

If a company decides to switch to a pull method of communicating internally, there are problems to address. One is the same issue companies face on the Internet. The information sites must be updated and edited frequently or they are useless, and this function is labor-intensive. Another problem is cultural habit. If employees are used to waiting to be told, switching to the active role of retrieving information may come as a jolt. The accountability for staying informed shifts to the individual—there is no one to blame anymore. Companies also must decide whether to make a complete shift to pull rather than push. Traditional companies might decide that certain types of information still need to be broadcast using the push method. One reason for this might be traditional employees would be insulted if no one sent them a message about certain company news (e.g., the hiring of a new CEO). Another reason for retaining the broadcast approach for some topics might be that the company wants to retain control of getting a piece of information in front of each employee rather than relying on the employee to go get the information if she is interested. It is certainly possible for a company to use a mixture of push and pull communication methods, but there is no technological or cultural reason that restricts a company from converting entirely to pull communications inside the organization.

GUIDELINES for types of information that might be disseminated more effectively using the pull method of communication.

- Most information in a company could be disseminated by the pull method as long as all employees have the equipment to access the information easily and the Web sites, databases, and directories are kept current and are easy to use.
- Exceptions would be unpredictable information that no one would know had happened—a merger, a death, a retirement or resignation, a special celebration, a favorable article in a major journal.
- Broadcasting stories and messages from leaders about the core values and business strategy.

GETTING THE RIGHT INFORMATION TO THE RIGHT PEOPLE

The key challenge for large companies is linking the employees who have information and skills with those who need those resources and doing this in a timely manner. In a slower and more structured time, this practice was much easier. Because department structures and individual job assignments remained stable for long time periods, it was a relatively simple matter to figure out who knew what and where they were. Now everyone is on the move, and the organizational chart does not give a clear picture of where resources are located. This situation may not present too much of a problem in a small .com company with 100 people or less, because they informally can keep track by getting to know everyone in the company personally. But if there are hundreds or thousands of employees, the informal knowledge people carry around in their heads is not adequate. The organization needs to create dozens of ways for people to find each other and the information they need at the moment they need it.

In Chapter 7, we look at the current efforts to capture knowledge, share it, and keep it constantly updated, but here we focus on efforts by companies to link the people who need to communicate with each other. This includes examples of meeting structures, directories, and personal strategies for staying connected in the fast-moving workplace.

Acxiom Corporation is building a system to capture associates' competencies which Pete Hoelscher and Cindy Childers defined as a broader category than just skills. "Competencies include not only what people know, but how they behave. It is our intention to have these living resumes about every person at Acxiom that are accessible to every human at Acxiom." Hoelscher and Childers gave several examples of how people might use this new system. "Let's say Pete has a question about a particular kind of database, a particular industry, or a database billed in a particular industry. He would be able to query the system and identify the names of seven people at Acxiom who have been in that place recently, with their e-mail addresses and phone extensions so he can call them to get information from them. Or a team wants to install a new market database for a new customer and we can go to the system to find that a similar database was installed in another part of the company last year. We can find out their projected costs and how they sold it."

Procter and Gamble has historically made good use of collaborative technology and was one of the first to implement a company-wide e-mail system. P&G uses this technology externally to introduce and ship new products around the world faster. The company also uses the technology internally to help the various product groups develop ideas more quickly for new products. They are replacing their old "hodgepodge of e-mail systems" with a standardized Lotus Notes system that will be rolled out to 93,000 users. P&G has launched an on-line library that allows employees to look at proposed advertising copy over the Internet instead of having to ship the materials from office to office. The company has also launched what it calls "collaboration rooms" that use desktop videoconferencing technology to allow virtual teams to meet electronically. The result has been "a 50 percent reduction in new-product concept development time, better sharing of tacit knowledge, quicker business decisions, and reduced travel expenses."[9]

Intel Corporation has protocols for meetings that help ensure that the right people are there and the right topics are discussed. Those who call the meeting are responsible for assessing whether it is necessary. They e-mail ideas to a few people for comments and suggestions, draft an agenda, and distribute it to a wider audience for revisions. The result is a one-pager containing the meeting's purpose and goals, subtopics with time frames for each one, a list of attendees, and what each should bring to the table. After the meeting, participants can contribute to the minutes that are posted on an internal Web page within 24 hours. The company also conducts an annual culture survey at the business unit level to assess how well it executes action plans.[10]

Company Intranets Become an Important Tool for Internal Communication

Intranets are the internal Web networks that many companies have installed to help them share information efficiently with employees. Intranets use initially was confined for the most part to broadcasting information about human resources benefits, job postings, training programs, and company news, but now intranets are providing employees with information that helps them generate business or improve service to customers.[11] FleetBoston uses its intranet to let employees download software, reset passwords, and access financial data they need for their jobs. Charles Schwab and Co. uses its intranet—called Schweb—to provide broad access to databases and

---

[9] Marianne Kolbasuk McGee, "Lessons From a Cultural Revolution," *Information Week* (October 25, 1999), 52.

[10] Karen Carney, "Making Meetings Work," *Harvard Management Update* (October 1999), 7.

[11] Bob Violino, "The Leaders of E-Business: Innovative Users of Internet Tools Take Charge of the New Economy," *Information Week* (December 13, 1999), 226.

a browser-neutral platform to let employees publish content that can be shared throughout the company. Insight, a computer reseller, considers its intranet its most important tool and uses the network to conduct employee opinion polls on a variety of topics twice a week.[12]

General Kostelnik, Commander of the Air Armament Center at Eglin Air Force Base, pointed out a situation when virtual communication is not the best choice for communicating a message.

> "The virtual world is not the best medium for delivering very good news or bad news. We tend to carry too much of our personal message in our facial expressions and in the nuances of our verbal delivery. It is much too easy to misinterpret what exactly an individual is trying to communicate in a written e-mail message. In order to overcome this shortcoming in our 'virtual' management approach, we have incorporated a personal video teleconferencing (VTC) capability on each key manager's computer. With this enhancement, supervisors can not only review large databases of management information on-line, they are able to discuss the more serious issues with subordinates in 'virtual person' through individual desk top VTCs. This complete 'virtual' approach improves our management efficiency greatly, and allows our supervisors more time to conduct the most important management functions, such as mentoring and counseling, which we still do in person."

4. MOVING FROM HOARDING TO SHARING INFORMATION

The e-business environment is triggering massive numbers of new alliances and partnerships among companies that were once fierce competitors or had no contact with each other at all. This is no way to own every element of the business process in any industry and maintain the speed to market that is necessary, so companies are linking up with other companies to collaborate in ways that would have been unimaginable a few years ago. This means that the people who work in these companies must be skilled in the art of collaborative communications with colleagues inside and outside of the company,

---

[12] Ibid.

but this is not the case in many companies. Sharing information, joint problem solving, and collaborative negotiations are not the norm in many companies. Competition, hoarding, and survival of the fittest are the key culture traits that drive the communication strategies within these companies.

Dean Wold, a partner at Ernst & Young LLP, describes the importance of moving to an information sharing culture.

> "Information used to be very compartmentalized. From a traditional management control model, that made a lot of sense. They would tell you what you needed to know to do your job and give you enough information to help you bond with the company in a newsletter of some kind. It was reasonably effective in a world where people had relatively static functions.
>
> In the new world, that kind of model will crush you. The reason is that every job changes all the time, and the relationships between functions are highly dynamic. You need to understand what else is going on in the world at large so that you can build new relationships between functions quickly. You have to have a communications program in place that encourages and incentivizes everyone to tell each other what is going on and to learn as much as possible about the rest of the organization.
>
> For example, the guy in the warehouse needs to understand what is happening on the retail side. He needs to know what effects his actions have on the rest of the company. If he does or doesn't accept delivery on a partial shipment, what are the issues? What risks should he take? He has to be able to make judgment calls. The more information he has, the better the calls will be."

If a company historically has a culture that emphasizes hoarding, structures and strategies are not powerful enough to overcome the culture. If good intentions contradict the culture, the culture wins. People may go through the motions, but they never can make the new approaches work effectively. You will find that you are fixing the same communication problems over and over. They just do not stay fixed. As soon as you stop paying attention, everything seems to slip right back to the way it was before. This retreat to the status quo is one of the clearest examples of the culture's power and its control over the patterns and habits of life in an organization.

> Trust, teams, and technology in that order. Culture comes first, and then technology. If you reverse them, you're in trouble.[13]
> —Carol Anne Ogdin, Founder of Deep Woods Technology Inc. in Santa Clara, California

The following cultural habits are some of the most deadly to a company's ability to share information. These are typical descriptions of a culture that is low on internal collaboration and high on internal competition and survival of the fittest.

- Hoarding information so you can show up at a meeting as the sole source of that particular information. This behavior enhances your status in the company as an expert, especially if you repeat this behavior on a routine basis.

- Rugged individualism of the "cowboy management" variety is favored in your company, complete with "shoot-outs" to see who survives and rises to the top.[14]

- Failing or taking a risk that did not produce the desired results is a blot on a person's record. If possible, employees hide a failure by burying it away to be forgotten or by distorting the report to make it sound like a success.

- In-fighting between individuals, departments, or teams is tolerated with no effort to stop it or hold the perpetrators accountable for their actions.

- Collaboration skills are not taught or built into meeting structures. The language and habits of the organization are clearly geared toward competition among employees and work units instead of collaboration.

---

[13] Bill Roberts, "Making Beautiful Music," *CIO* (December 15, 1999-January 1, 2000), 108.

[14] Rosabeth Moss Kanter, *When Giants Learn to Dance* (New York: Simon & Schuster, 1989), 70.

We need to make a distinction here between two varieties of competition: wars and races. In wars, the goal is to destroy the enemy. We can't think of many circumstances under which intraorganizational warfare can produce net positive results. In races, the purpose is not to destroy, but rather to outperform others and also, at least as much, to outperform ourselves, to exceed our personal best. In organizations, races can be productive, if they can be kept safely within that category.[15]

A CASE STUDY OF CONFLICT

This type of competitive, survival-of-the-fittest culture becomes so pervasive throughout the enterprise that it becomes second nature to the participants. You hear that famous culture identifier, "What do you mean? That's just the way we do things around here." This statement means that these cultural traits have become such ingrained habits that they are invisible. When presented with the suggestion that their approach needs changing, people in an ingrained culture often react with confusion. They may understand what you are saying, but they cannot think of any alternative actions to their usual behavior. Or if they do think of alternatives, those actions do not seem practical or reasonable to them.

A few years ago, a large medical center experienced one of these entrenched reactions while trying to resolve some conflict between two divisions. The source of the conflict was the relationship between the two division heads. To be perfectly candid, they detested each other. No amount of negotiating or persuading produced any changes in either person's position. In the many hours spent in discussions

---

[15] Jean Lipman-Blumen and Harold J. Leavitt, *Hot Groups: Seeding Them, Feeding Them, and Using Them to Ignite Your Organization* (New York: Oxford University Press 1999), 139.

with each party, the only suggestion that either person offered to improve the situation was to fire the other person. Both division heads were making six-figure salaries while costing the medical center substantial revenue by creating a situation in which the two divisions could not work together effectively to provide service and expand their operation.

The Chief Operating Officer (COO) received the recommendation to take the advice of the two division heads and fire both of them. The COO agreed that the situation was hopeless with the current people in place and the fallout from the conflict was damaging the organization as a whole. But he hesitated to act. No management person at that institution had ever lost a job for this type of behavior. Sitting in a meeting with his board chairman, he wondered out loud if firing the division heads for this situation might send a bad message to the rest of the management staff. He suggested that if he decided to proceed, maybe he should not tell people the real reason for the termination. The chairman of the board, who was a seasoned veteran with decades of business leadership as the founder of a major company, spoke up. "Of course, you tell them. That's exactly the message you want to send. They *should* be worried if they act like that. You should treat that kind of behavior just like you'd treat fraud. They are stealing from the company. And especially at that level, you have a right to expect people to figure out how to get along with each other." The COO had great respect for the chairman's opinion, so he took the advice and terminated the two division heads with a clear explanation for the reasons. The two employees were surprised, and shock waves rippled through the management ranks. The message that long-running, damaging conflict would not be tolerated signaled a change in the culture. Of course, the words had been said before, but definitive action had not ever been taken.

WHAT IS THE COST OF IN-HOUSE COMPETITION?

Rosabeth Moss Kanter, a leading authority on business management and organizational change, pointed out the drawbacks of a culture based on internal competition. "There is a twofold rationale for competition, a rationale embedded in American mythology as well as in management philosophies. Competition is supposedly a spur to performance, and it theoretically stimulates the development of alternatives. But more often, in-house competition has the opposite effect: depressing performance and decreasing alternatives."[16] Kanter listed five negative effects that are signs of a culture with high degrees of internal competition. She said this type of culture depresses performance and inhibits the development of alternatives for the following reasons:

1. Employees pay more attention to beating their rivals than performing the task well. They see the task as an instrument for winning. The winning becomes more important than the task itself.

2. Friendly competition among people who respect each other is replaced with mistrust, suspicion, and scorn.

3. Fear of missing out on some strategy or action of the internal rival causes people to focus on spying and copying rather than on searching for creative new options. Imitation drives out innovation.

4. The weaker parties give up because the goal has become winning or dominating the rival. If they cannot win, why bother to continue to fight? You lose the value the weaker parties might bring to a cooperative effort.

5. The stronger parties begin to feel invincible. Pride spills over into arrogance, and they begin to believe that they can rest easy and do not need to continue to drive themselves for high standards. They have already won, so they grow lazy and complacent.[17]

---

[16] Rosabeth Moss Kanter, *When Giants Learn to Dance* (New York: Simon & Schuster, 1989), 70.
[17] Ibid, 81.

CHANGING FROM A CULTURE OF HOARDING, CONFLICT, AND COMPETITION TO COLLABORATION

There are number of specific actions to take that will move your company away from a culture of hoarding to one that use more collaborative communication behaviors. The following six actions will help to trigger that kind of change in your culture:

1. When there is long standing, repeated conflict between two key people whose functional areas need to work well together, bring in a mediator to try to resolve it. If they are not willing to cooperate, terminate them. Make sure people in the organization know why they were let go. This sends a strong cultural message about what is not allowed in this company.

2. When recruiting new personnel pay close attention to what they say about their skills and attitudes toward collaboration. Have them tell you stories of successes in other jobs and listen for whether cooperation or competition was the strategy used to achieve success. Ask the person "What would you do in this situation?" And then give them a scenario that involves a conflict that needs to be resolved between team colleagues or with partners from another company.

3. Find teams and work groups that have made special efforts to work cooperatively with another team or have resolved an old conflict between the two groups, and reward the team members for their effort. Public recognition and praise is a powerful reward that is always available to use. If you have other resources such as monetary rewards or the ability to make assignment to high status projects use those resources to reward the collaborators.

4. Train people on the use of collaborative negotiation skills if they have not already had this training. Training alone will not change your culture, but if people lack the skill they will not be able to perform in the new way even if they want to do so.

5. If you promote or financially reward even one person who has a reputation for using cutthroat, competitive tactics with colleagues, your campaign to change your culture is dead. That action will carry far greater significance than words.

6. Introduce symbols and language that have a cooperative, sharing theme. Language helps create momentum in the right direction. Create a new slogan that carries the new message. Bob Nafius, currently with Gateway Inc. has helped Gateway and other companies develop some of the following phrases to capture the company for the work force: Gateway's *Keeping it personal, making it simple,* Sony's *Lighting Up Screens Around the World,* or GTE's *Easiest Company to Do Business With.* Using language in quick, catchy phrases that stick in people's memory is very helpful in creating momentum. If people remember the phrase, they remember the message. Notice that all three phrases have a theme of linkages. These are all companies that understand that the connected workplace requires linkages inside and outside their companies.

LAUGHTER IS A SIGN OF A COLLABORATIVE CULTURE

Laughter may be the most important indication of all that you want a culture in which people collaborate and share information. The amount of laughter in an organization is one of the most reliable indicators of high morale and a willingness to cooperate with each other. Jeff Bezos, Amazon.com's high-energy, enthusiastic CEO, is a well-known proponent of the value of the laughter as he leads one of the .com world's star companies. His famous laugh has been described as "a rapid honk that sounds like a flock of Canadian geese on nitrous oxide."[18]

> On a recent sunny morning in Seattle, high on a hill overlooking Puget Sound, Amazon's competitors and mounting losses are the last things on Jeff Bezos' mind. He's trying to crank open one of the old-fashioned windows at his new headquarters, the former Pacific Medical building. "This is great—I love being able to open the window," he burst out cheerfully. A boat horn sounds in the distance and he laughs—an infectious, gulp-from-the-throat laugh that he is known for. It's almost impossible to be in the same room with Bezos and not have a good time. He's

[18] Joshua Quittner, "On the Future," *Time* (December 27, 1999), 50.

relaxed, he's funny, and he's disarmingly humble. "Nobody is more surprised than me by what has happened over the last four years," says the man who in that span has amassed $9 billion.'[19]

APPLYING THIS INFORMATION IN YOUR ORGANIZATION

Below are questions to assess your company's current progress in making the transition to an open book corporation. How are you handling the new communication challenges that exist in the wired workplace?

1. How has access to information changed in your company in recent years? Has technology made it easier and quicker to find out what is happening with the company?

2. Is your company experimenting with new ways to use chat rooms, message boards, and Web sites to link employees and managers so they can share information more easily? If so, what are the new methods and how well are they working at this point?

3. What are your strategies for keeping your e-mail under control?

4. What e-mail protocols have developed in your company—the dos and don'ts of e-mail behavior? Did they develop through universal suffering or by mandate from leaders?

5. Do you have any pull communication mechanisms in place for employees where they can go to a source to retrieve information when they need it instead of having all company information broadcast or sent to them (push mechanisms)?

5. Do you have a "cowboy" culture of rugged individualism and "shoot-out" competitions to see who survives? Look for hoarding of information, low risk-taking tolerance, in-fighting

[19] Katrina Brooker, "Amazon vs. Everybody," *Fortune* (November 8, 1999), 123.

among divisions, and competitive language as indicators of this type of culture.

6. Do the key leaders, formal and informal, value collaboration or competition inside the company? Watch their behavior and listen to their words.

7. How much do people laugh in your company? It is highly unlikely that there are high levels of creative collaboration occurring if there is not a lot of laughter. The two go together.

CHAPTER SEVEN

Knowledge Management is Managing People's Brain Power

I n today's marketplace, knowledge management is essential. Knowledge and information drive the economy today, whether a company is in a .com business or an old-line producer of goods or services. To be effective, companies must manage the knowledge and information that drive them in order to maximize resources. Companies must constantly fine-tune their processes. Burgeoning .com companies are built almost exclusively on knowledge and information. Sound knowledge management techniques must reflect the reality that huge sectors of the economy and many entire industries are based almost solely on knowledge. And even those companies that are not engaged solely in knowledge businesses must adopt knowledge management models in order to succeed or in some cases to survive in a world constantly changing.

WHAT IS KNOWLEDGE MANAGEMENT?

Organizations in the corporate sector as well as non-profits and government agencies have developed complex knowledge-gathering techniques and systems to enhance business processes. Knowledge management consultants and company information technology (IT) groups have created a small industry in response to these economic shifts.

In a formal, academic sense, knowledge management is an involved, detailed process, often dominated by consultants and specialists who try to help companies distinguish between such terms as wisdom, knowledge, know-how, intelligence, information, facts, and data. Next, the consultants work with IT groups to install knowledge management technology systems that capture the elements of these types of knowledge that are of value to the company. The goal of these efforts is to establish criteria that combine management skills with technology-based systems to catalog, preserve, and store information. The objective is to provide a tool so that employees can benefit from the company's collective skill base and have adequate tools at their disposal.

The limitation of these complex technology-driven knowledge management processes and systems is that they can take several years to create and implement. They are also very expensive, frequently ranging in cost from tens to hundreds of thousands of dollars in consulting fees and hundreds of thousands to millions of dollars for computer hardware and software. Unfortunately these kinds of knowledge management systems and processes don't work particularly well in a .com world where business and product conception, development, production, and marketing operate at warp speed. More to the point, in a .com world you are not likely to have time to undertake all the differentiation and analysis of the terminology of formal knowledge management processes.

DON'T worry about the distinctions that some people make among and between data, information, knowledge and wisdom. The key thing to do is to get people to share what they know about their work and the best ways of getting it done. This includes:

• "How to get things done around here."

- Know-how about their specific work.
- How they make decisions, how they improve things.
- What works and does not work.
- Who else in the organization knows these kinds of things.
- When "rules of thumb" operate in their work.

You also might not have staff resources and money to implement complex technological knowledge management processes. What you need to do is to move fast, with a straightforward definition of knowledge management and then foster an informal knowledge sharing culture in your company. The overarching characteristic of operating in a .com environment is that much collaboration must occur. In the frenetic warp speed of the .com world, employees must take time to reflect, think, and solve problems about how their work gets done.

WE KNOW IT WHEN WE SEE IT

This chapter uses a simple, easily understood definition that you can apply to knowledge management and sharing in your company.

Knowledge Management

is managing people's brain power and the company's collective memory.

The primary purpose in this chapter is to provide illustrations to facilitate recognition of what can be a fairly elusive concept. Managing brain power is not a task that can be easily quantified or measured. Nonetheless, in the .com world, it is one of the most important elements of culture to refine. The examples will demonstrate the attributes of a good knowledge management environment.

Effective knowledge management requires both high tech and high touch solutions. Many aspects of the high tech side of the equation—

the systems, databases, and storage elements of knowledge management—are beyond the scope of this book, so this chapter is principally (but not exclusively) about the high touch side of the equation, focusing on the human interactions and problem-solving mechanisms that facilitate good knowledge management.

The goal of effective knowledge management is to create an environment where each worker has access to all the tools needed for success. In the .com world, the goal is to succeed as quickly and resoundingly as warp speed will allow. Likewise, the days when hoarding knowledge was perceived as creating power are gone. Today, knowledge is indeed power, but only when everyone has access to it.

IS SHARING AN UNNATURAL HUMAN ACT?

Leading experts in knowledge management discipline differ in their answer to this question. Some claim that it is unnatural to share knowledge, especially when employees believe that their power derives from hoarding knowledge. Others say that it is quite a natural act and that people do it informally all the time. Knowledge sharing does become an unnatural corporate act when negative cultures or rigid organizational structures get in the way. On the other hand, companies that succeed in getting their people to share information waste less time re-creating things or resolving problems. They make fewer mistakes and get things done faster.

The cultural habit of sharing information with ease is critical for any organization operating in a .com world. At a fundamental level, an organization has a better chance of making good decisions when many points of view are considered in the course of a project. Sharing information also becomes a critical success factor because it raises the level of quality thinking. The sharing process flushs out more detail and more specificity among team members. It facilitates troubleshooting and identification of soft spots and vulnerabilities. As basic as it sounds, knowledge sharing accelerates the speed at which projects can be completed. In both traditional and .com companies, the quantity of information and the speed with which it changes means that no individual can function alone. The employees' skills and knowledge must be linked for a company to move at warp speed in the e-business environment.

Catherine Ballantyne, a marketing manager in a Silicon Valley hardware company, stated the imperative of sharing: "Today's markets require adroit maneuvering at warp speed. The right people accessing the right information at the right time makes or breaks companies here every day. You have to fly. And you have to fly because you don't have six months to get a new product to market."

Describing an informal cultural norm in her company, she said, "People need to know. You'd never *not* tell anybody. No longer can we sit in ivory towers and cart blanche ascribe to the old adage, 'Information on a need to know basis' that plagues security minded people buried in minimizing the risk of distributing information and knowledge. The risk of sharing is a factor that has to be managed, but no longer can we be so arrogant as to presume that those with whom we work don't 'need to know' something that may affect their ability to build our company. When we subscribe to such thinking, we limit our company's ability to compete."

Several characteristics of information and knowledge make it difficult to create effective linkages. One stumbling block is the *decay* factor. In any organizational setting, whether bricks-and-mortar or e-business, the longer that data, information, or knowledge has been around, the less valuable most of it is. The knowledge may be stale, out of date, obsolete, superseded, or even wrong. Because of the speed at which business processes and decisions occur in the e-business environment, this decay can happen very quickly. A second stumbling block is the difficulty many people have when trying to verbalize or write what they know. So much of information is personalized in the process of becoming knowledge and it simply does not necessarily occur to a worker that a particular piece of information might be important to share. He or she will assume that what is obvious or known to them is common knowledge: "I thought everybody knew that." In this case, employees do not intentionally withhold information. It simply does not occur to them that there is any value in sharing it.

ONE simple but useful way of generating the habit of sharing is to encourage workers with a simple inquiry: "What do you think?" This question invites sharing and can be a particularly direct way to encourage creativity and identify concerns.

Ballantyne identified the "What do you think?" model played out in an international company she worked for. She describes how the use of this question enables information and knowledge sharing; and in so doing, increases the effectiveness of on-the-fly decision-making. At her company, many decisions were simply made in the hallway. If the decision dictated a change of direction for a project or team, minutes after conception, the prospective decision was e-mailed to people potentially affected. The e-mails generally triggered either an emotional or a content concerned response. As they read their e-mail they would get angry, "freak out," challenge the correctness of the decision, have verbal and e-mail conversations with others, and send their own perspectives back to the originator of the e-mail. When everyone had been heard from, and this was usually within 40 hours; most decisions, with adjustments if needed, could move to an implementation phase.

Note the amount of knowledge sharing and the rapid exchange of information that occurs in this setting: e-mails were sent, recipients would have conversations, challenge one another, assert the correctness of their own points of view, create solutions to concerns raised by others and then communicate all of it. The context for this full-fledged knowledge sharing is an expression of the norm that "you'd never *not* tell anybody."

People do need to know and they need to know what others know. When employees capture the knowledge they have and share it with each other they are able to do their jobs better and a knowledge sharing culture is fostered. "Sharing is a practice that is in everyone's best interest. When my people, the company, and I share information and knowledge relevant to the success of the business, we tap into a collective intelligence that is significantly greater in value than the sum of its parts. With this as an asset, we have a far greater chance of building a successful company.

LOOKING FOR EXAMPLES OF KNOWLEDGE SHARING

Unfortunately, most organizations, even those filled with so-called "knowledge workers," are not very good at effective knowledge utilization. They do not do a very good job leveraging their people's knowledge in order to improve business processes and practices. Interviews and searches of the literature revealed only a few "war stories" of managers who had really given much thought to the "hows" of getting people to share. They could identify the benefits of sharing knowledge and list many positive and negative characteristics of organizations that did and did not manage knowledge and get people to share their brain power. Their lists are useful and provide good pointers for managers.

The following case describes the actual experiences of a highly specialized corporate lawyer who carried out the role of knowledge worker in two different companies with three different managers. Two of her experiences provide excellent examples of knowledge management at its best. The third was a frustrating failure. This case illustrates that you can have the same person with the same skills in different situations and have success in one setting and failure in another. It takes a knowledge-sharing culture to allow individuals to use their skills. In a culture dominated by egos and hoarding of information, employees are powerless to make the organization function the way that they know it should. The attorney in this case is called KW (knowledge worker). After the case descriptions, the key characteristics of these three settings that contributed to the successes and failure are identified.

THE FIELD MARSHAL CASE:
A STUDY IN ANCIENT HISTORY, THE EIGHTIES

In 1978, a national accounting and consulting firm decided to expand its practice in Washington DC by providing "government affairs" services to its clients across the nation and around the world. The new government affairs practice was to provide information and technical assistance in the highly specialized area of federal income taxation. The firm would assist clients in their various interactions with the legislative activities and regulatory agencies of Congress and the Executive Branch of the US federal government. The government affairs practice would develop its client base from referrals from the firm's worldwide offices.

To head the operation, the firm appointed one of its senior tax partners (the "Field Marshal" [FM]). He had never lived in Washington, never attended a Congressional hearing, and never visited the IRS. One of his first hires was KW, who had worked for several years as tax counsel and policy advisor to a senior member of the Senate Finance Committee. She was to serve as the firm's "eyes and ears" as Congress went through the laborious, highly competitive, and high-stakes process of creating winners and losers as tax laws changed. She and FM then had to figure out how to disseminate that information throughout the firm, and to its client base. KW and FM also had to determine how to provide Congress with practical, real-life, and real-time information to demonstrate how proposed tax law changes would affect whole industries as well as particular companies. In short, KW was a lobbyist, and the best lobbyists are actively engaged in the knowledge business. This is much more important to their success than influence peddling and fund raising.

THE FIELD MARSHALL AND THE KNOWLEDGE WORKER: A DISASTER IN THE MAKING?

It sounds like an invitation to disaster. FM knew nothing about Washington and its arcane ways. And KW, the Washington insider, knew nothing about the intricacies, technicalities, and practicalities of business taxation or about the firm and its resources. In fact, it turned out to be anything but a disaster. By 1986, KW and FM had built an organization with approximately 20 tax law specialists, and the government affairs activity was effective enough to move from being an overhead function to generating revenue.

Their great success came because each day, when KW returned from Capitol Hill, FM asked her three simple questions:

1. *Who* needs to know?
2. *What* do they need to know?
3. *How* can we share that knowledge?

In that world without PCs, e-mail, or broadcast faxes, FM developed a list of people to contact. FM and KW identified every shred of useful information from that day's congressional visits and hearings. KW got on the phone, time zone by time zone, for as long as it took.

The people on the "who-needs-to-know" list fell into two categories. First, they were the experts within the firm who needed information. The second category included people who could help KW develop her technical understanding of the changes being made so that she could more effectively make her case to the congressional legislative attorneys or congressmen. As the government affairs staff expanded, FM kept repeating the mantra: "Who needs to know?" "What do they need to know?" "How can we share that knowledge?" Eventually, the mantra became habit and sharing information was the dominant characteristic of the culture in the government affairs organization.

OLD VEEP AND NEW VEEP: DOING AND UNDOING

In 1997, KW was working as a tax legislation lobbyist for a mature organization in the not-for-profit trade association world, as the senior advisor in a 40-person government affairs operation. That year, Congress proposed a tax law change that would increase taxes on the industry the association represented and on investors who purchased the industry's products. A team had to be mobilized to prevent the proposal's enactment.

The group in which KW worked included a variety of professionals. Some had strong subject matter expertise on industry programs at various federal agencies, while others had political acumen and contacts with congressmen and senators. Still others were skilled field and grassroots operatives. A senior Vice President for Government Affairs managed the group. We call her Old Veep. She knew that a full-bore operation had to be mounted. For every percentage point of taxes involved in the proposal, there was literally a billion dollars at stake for the industry.

Old Veep marshaled her troops in an "all hands on deck" manner. Each evening at 6 p.m., the full group convened. Absentees called in from wherever they were at the Capitol or in the field. The staff had varying tenures and varying degrees of experience in major legislative campaigns. At the meeting, the political and field staff described the contacts they had made that day and listed all the questions or challenges presented to them. The group then developed the tactics for the next day's operations.

KW was responsible for developing answers to each question, preparing talking points for each, training the political and field staff about the proposal, and teaching them to respond to the questions.

KW met regularly with the congressional legislative attorneys and with private-sector attorneys also opposed to the tax increase proposal. Otherwise, she remained at the office to field calls from the trade association's members, senior management, volunteer leaders of the organization, White House officials, and the press. Old Veep kept in constant communication with each functional area of the staff throughout the day. Old Veep and KW periodically summarized new developments and distributed them through voice mail and e-mail to the government affairs group, senior management, and others with a stake in the debate.

Old Veep never dictated the strategy or tactics for the operation. Rather, she used the 6 p.m. meeting to generate ideas, based on that day's operations, from the entire group. There were often heated disagreements about particular tactics, so she facilitated consensus. While there was not always total agreement, there was a shared basis for each decision. At the conclusion of each meeting, Old Veep summarized the plan for the next day, made assignments, and gave a word of encouragement. In the end the original tax increase proposal was not defeated but a less onerous version was enacted.

THE NEW VEEP (AND HIS EGO) ARRIVES ON THE SCENE

A year later, Old Veep left the organization and was replaced by New Veep. New Veep had an impressive resume of positions and contacts. When he arrived, he made sure the staff was aware of his many contacts and the political appointments he had held over the years. He clearly believed that his resume and contacts were his primary value to the organization. He made no effort to learn about the staff's duties or expertise or find out who their contacts were or what they knew. He had little subject-matter expertise in the issues of concern to the trade association's membership and made little effort to acquire it.

Because he believed that his contacts and prior political positions were his primary asset, he set about to reinforce those contacts with the objective of strengthening the organization's profile in the legislative arena. He maintained an active meeting schedule on Capitol Hill but did not share his schedule with his deputies or the rest of the staff. After his meetings on Capitol Hill, he did not meet with the staff or tell them what he had been doing and what he had learned. His leadership style was to share nothing and want to know nothing from the staff. He hoarded information in the belief that it made him more powerful.

In 1999, another tax bill came under active consideration. If an important new provision could be included in the bill, a substantial win for the organization and its members was a good possibility. Following the model they had learned from KW and Old Veep, the staff met regularly to develop and implement a plan to get the provision in the bill. New Veep did not attend those meetings, but instead requested briefings from the staff about their progress. He assured the staff that he also was working with congressional leaders to secure enactment of the new provision. New Veep maintained his practice of meeting with members of Congress without briefing the staff on his own progress.

The provision that the organization fought for was not included in the new tax bill. Some of the reasons why were well beyond the control of the trade association or the New Veep, but there is no doubt that his behavior was a contributing factor. It is also worth noting that during New Veep's tenure staff turnover tripled.

LEARNING FROM THE CASE: WHAT WAS THE DIFFERENCE BETWEEN THE SUCCESSES AND THE FAILURES?

Use the Journalist's Creed

The Field Marshall and Old Veep are both exemplars of using the journalistic model of:

- Know how.
- Know why.
- Know who.
- Know what.
- Know where.
- Know when.

TIP

CONSIDER developing a knowledge sharing formal rule and a cultural norm in your company that says all knowledge in the company must be shared unless there is a government regulation, internal security, or alliance/partnership security reason not to.

FM's great achievement was developing a culture in a new operation in which those pre-eminent questions were:

1. Who needs to know?
2. What do they need to know?
3. How can we share that knowledge?

By focusing repeatedly on those questions, FM set in motion the processes that answered the rest of the journalistic questions. Because of his long experience as a tax practitioner in the firm, he had great mastery of the "who," "where," and "what" elements of this equation and thus could guide the young lawyer. He steered her to the places where her new information on legislation would be valued and to those individuals who could expand her own knowledge base.

Because KW had never been a tax practitioner, she often did not always know how to frame questions that could develop the information she needed. In those situations, FM helped her by quickly providing an overview of business consequences of a particular proposal and then assisting her to prepare a checklist of information she needed. At some point, her own intellectual curiosity took over, so the "why" part of the equation was also solved. During the eighties in the emerging new government affairs operation, the "when" question was no less urgent than it is today in the .com world. The answer then and now is almost always the same: yesterday.

 KNOWLEDGE management has strong social elements. You can have an effective knowledge management culture without technology but not without a strong knowledge sharing environment.

FM was trying to create a new division within a mature, competitive organization. Old Veep was operating within a mature, fully staffed organization as she tried to solve the problem of thwarting a potentially burdensome new law. Her 6 p.m. staff meeting operated almost exclusively on the journalist's questions model. The objective of each meeting was to share so every staff person could answer the who-what-why-where-when-how questions. She would dismiss the meeting only when all the tactics had been agreed to (i.e., those questions were answered) and there was a shared goal for the next day's activities.

Both FM and Old Veep provided significant leadership in knowledge management. They mobilized as much organizational brain power as they possibly could under the circumstances to solve a problem. Their processes were collaborative within the group and with outside experts. No elaborate technology was required; in fact, the knowledge was shared just as effectively (though not as efficiently) in the relatively simple technology environment of the eighties as it is in the more sophisticated, but more complex communications environment of the nineties and the new century.

HOW DID THE NEW VEEP GO WRONG?

The existing knowledge management structures were disbanded by the New Veep's behavior. He did not identify the resources that already existed in the organization when he arrived. His behavior appeared to be based on the assumption that neither the staff nor their knowledge had value and that the organization was "about" him. By failing to maintain the existing knowledge culture within the staff, he quickly destroyed it. There was simply no incentive for them to continue to share. Their morale quickly and seriously eroded.

When New Veep first arrived, the staff attempted to continue Old Veep's knowledge sharing process that had served them well. But their efforts were futile because management did not value their knowledge, nor were they given any encouragement that they were headed in an "acceptable" direction to achieve the division's goals. There was certainly no incentive or reward for having or sharing knowledge. The hallmarks of a sound knowledge management culture were missing in the New Veep-led organization.

Hallmarks of a Knowledge Management Culture

- Shared history (the staff's experience under the Old Veep)
- Shared purpose (legislative victories)
- Shared values (talk to each other and agree on the direction of tactics)
- Shared context (we're all in this together)

With the FM and Old Veep, these hallmark characteristics were "the way we do things" in those organizations. Even though the employees had differing specialties and differing perceptions of internal and external politics and power, they ultimately had the sense that everyone was better off with the maximum amount of information.

HOW DOES YOUR COMPANY COMPARE?
THE KNOWLEDGE AUDIT

The case study illustrates knowledge management at its best and worst. You may have recognized some qualities of your own organization. If your organization veered sharply to either the strong or weak side of KW's experiences, you may want to undertake what is called a knowledge audit. A knowledge audit is a tool that will give you important information and clues about the status of knowledge management in your company. Since so much of your success in the .com world depends on your ability to tap into the best from your workers, an assessment of where you are today is prudent.

Some organizations have acquired bad habits that must be identified and eliminated. Others wish to confirm their perceptions about what is working and where. Still others have made a conscious decision to enhance their knowledge culture and therefore need some data to formalize their starting point. The knowledge audit can take different forms. The case study suggests one type of analysis. Other knowledge audit techniques are described later in the chapter.

The Field Marshall's techniques for knowledge management resemble an audit based largely on factual determinations. As suggested in the case study analysis, it resembles the journalist's inquiry of Who, What, Why, Where, When, and How. It might ask such questions as:

- What explicit knowledge exists?
- Where it is stored?
- How it gets physically transferred from place to place?
- How often does it get used and how it is used?

An audit provides raw data. The process is painstaking. It's not a "back of the envelope" sort of endeavor. It requires some thought, because it's certainly arguable that much of your company's success will depend on how well you foster a quick, sleek, efficient knowledge culture. The "Journalist's Creed" audit method is an inventory-style inquiry that is valuable for making an assessment of where things stand now. The table below includes the types of questions that can identify strengths and weaknesses in your company's knowledge culture.

KINDS OF INQUIRY FOR AN INVENTORY-STYLE KNOWLEDGE AUDIT

Who:	uses knowledge?
	owns the knowledge?
What:	knowledge exists in the organization?
	is the form of the knowledge?
	knowledge do people need to do their jobs?
	systems and processes exist (not just technology)?
	gaps exist?
	barriers exist?
	opportunities can be found?
	strengths and weaknesses are present?
Where:	does the knowledge exist?
When:	is the knowledge used by people doing their work?
Why:	is the knowledge used?
How:	is the knowledge acquired and created?
	is the knowledge stored and transmitted (and how fast)?
	is the knowledge used?
	is knowledge management fostered, encouraged, and supported?
	is knowledge being used to improve work processes, services, and products?

This inventory will provide you with insights about the health of your company's knowledge sharing culture. You can use it to identify the changes you want and need to make in your culture. You can identify the most immediate needs and begin to plan for the transitions needed to make progress toward faster, more efficient and effective knowledge sharing.

TACIT KNOWLEDGE AND EXPLICIT KNOWLEDGE

As you begin to make assessments about your knowledge culture, you may find it useful to make a distinction often made by knowledge management experts. They differentiate between two separate but essential types of knowledge: tacit and explicit. In a thriving knowledge management culture, both types are valued, rewarded, and nurtured.

Tacit knowledge is what is inside people's heads and the knowledge generated between people as they talk with each other about the business of the company. John Seeley Brown, Director and chief scientist at Xerox's PARC (Palo Alto Research Center) describes tacit knowledge this way: "In a conversation, I say something, and we will scaffold this thinking into something neither of us understood before. In that participation something new comes into being."[1] Tacit knowledge resides in individuals and is enhanced when they interact and something new emerges.

Tacit knowledge can also be thought of as people's knowledge about the content of their work and about how they do it. The manager must help workers recognize this knowledge and to feel confident that the knowledge is a form of capital at least as valuable as the stock of the company or the computers and tools they work with. When the value of that brain power or capital is readily valued and freely available, the task of fostering a positive corporate culture in which employees will share what they know—their brain power. Technology can play an important role in facilitating sharing of knowledge,[2] but tacit knowledge sharing can occur without information technology (IT).

---

[1] Steve Barth, "Function of X: Is there more to life than documents? Xerox bets the company that the future revolves around knowledge" *Knowledge Management* (February 2000), 33.

[2] See the series of two-page illustrated "K-Maps" that appeared monthly in the September 1999 through February 2000 issues of *Knowledge Management*. The "K-Maps" graphically illustrate how technology aids knowledge sharing and management.

Explicit knowledge can be thought of as the organization's collective memory. It is comprised of the knowledge and information that can be found in documents stashed in an employee's desk or file cabinets and data and information found in databases and other storage areas. The manager has two chores in dealing with explicit knowledge. First, workers have to be able to find the knowledge and information. The challenge is to create a process for people to put their documents and knowledge into the company's knowledge management storage areas in ways that people can readily access it. This endeavor often revolves around information technology (IT) systems. Since systems creation and management is its own specialty, and since it's not related to the human, interactive aspects of culture, data management is not our primary concern here.

The second chore is managing explicit knowledge in a .com world is to expand the company's collective memory with what's inside the employees' heads in ways that everyone:

- Puts their explicit knowledge, when appropriate, into the company's knowledge management storage areas.
- Has easy access to knowledge.
- Shares their tacit brain power knowledge.
- Uses the collective memory knowledge and the brain power to improve their work.

The relationship between of tacit knowledge—employee brain power—and corporate culture in a .com world is important. Whether knowledge sharing flourishes or flounders depends on the extent and amount of conflict among and between employees and organizational units. Paul Strassmann notes that he has "seen very smart people with very smart ideas producing no economic value. Similarly, some average, even mediocre, organizations have continued to prosper. It was the diversion of managerial efforts into energy-absorbing 'civil wars' that explained the results."[3] If the corporate culture does not support information sharing and collaboration among employees, it will be difficult

---

[3] Paul Strassmann, "Response to a Letter to the Editor," *Knowledge Management* (February 2000), 10.

to build a knowledge management system that actually works. Sophisticated technology cannot offset the cultural barriers.

 EMERGING technology companies exploring the future to exploit changing market conditions can enhance their knowledge sharing cultures by giving employees time to think, converse with others, and enter their knowledge into formal knowledge management systems. These companies must also reward risk taking.

THE KINDS OF WORK THAT WORKERS DO AFFECT THE KNOWLEDGE CULTURE

Another way of looking at a corporate knowledge sharing culture is to consider the work that people do. You can look at your company and determine whether your workers spend their time principally doing structured, routine work (i.e., using their explicit knowledge) or unstructured knowledge work (i.e., using their tacit knowledge). Structured, routine work is comprised of tasks that are repeatable, standardized, and specified in detail. Like an assembly line, explicit knowledge work is fairly predictable, can often be automated, and frequently can be written down or diagrammed. It might include activities such as processing mail, reporting expenses, scheduling meetings, generating payrolls, and handling inventory. Most people have the information and knowledge they need to do their structured, routine work. Nevertheless, the organization must have clear channels of formal and informal communications and adequate technology and information systems to support it.

EXAMPLES OF EXPLICIT KNOWLEDGE MANAGEMENT SYSTEMS FOR ROUTINE, STRUCTURED WORK

Toward the end of 1999, Lucent Technologies acknowledged the need for an explicit knowledge management system when it announced plans to share data among its 150,000 employees through the use of computer servers. Lucent's corporate intelligence databases previously had been confined within single business units or to one activity such as sales or marketing. With the new system, all 150,000 employees gain access to all information in each unit. For example, just one of these databases, based on information about more than one million customers, is available company-wide. The expectation is that "Lucent will be able to pinpoint obscure buying patterns or unearth hidden market opportunities that no one has detected before."[4]

Do not fall into the trap of thinking that this type of explicit knowledge work does not need knowledge management. This is the work that lays the foundation for the day-to-day environment in the company. If, for example, a team finds it a constant challenge to get their meetings scheduled or has little confidence that the meeting setup will be adequate or correct, the team is less likely to meet. Similarly, patterns of lost mail can be infuriating and demoralizing. The employees assigned to these "routine" tasks know what would make them work better and how these routine functions can be operated more efficiently in the organization.

Managers disregard these routine operations at their peril. At one large warehouse operation of a large membership organization, the workers were charged with fulfilling orders for pamphlets requested by members. A study of work done at this fulfillment center showed that the workers in this so-called "routine" structured work spent from 10 to 20 percent of their time looking for the information to do their jobs. The lead supervisors were asked simple questions 10 to 20 times a day. The questions could have been answered by the workers themselves if the operation had two key elements of an effective knowledge management system: a culture of encouraging the workers to talk to each other and sufficient technology and infrastructure to give the workers the information they needed.

This problem was compounded at this organization because the lead supervisors also were not given the tools they needed. The study showed that these supervisors had to spend 30 to 40 percent of their time looking for information and knowledge to do their jobs. The

---

[4] Steve Rosenbush, "Rewiring Lucent in a Rush," *BusinessWeek* (December 13, 1997), 50.

higher up the management chain in the operation, the greater the inefficiency. And this was all because workers were not provided tools or encouraged to share information. In the .com world, where efficiency and speed are all-important, even the most rudimentary tools and information are critical at every level. If no one knows who has the paper clips or where to get more, the operation will fall short. In the membership organization, the managers could have improved the operation if they had provided a forum for the workers to classify and suggest solutions for the problems they had. Rather than conduct periodic problem-solving sessions so that everyone could perform better, the supervisors simply permitted inefficiencies to cascade up the management chain.

Buckman Laboratories uses methods that provide a sharp contrast to the membership organization. Buckman is a global chemical company with 1,200 employees in 80 countries. The workers have round-the-clock access through laptops to a company intranet that includes electronic forums, bulletin boards, knowledge bases, on-line libraries, virtual conference rooms, and e-mail. A Buckman salesperson attempting to land a sale of its products and services in Indonesia needed know-how to handle the problem of pitch control, which is used to remove stickiness in making paper. To solve this assembly line, explicit-knowledge problem, Dennis Dalton, Managing Director of Asian activity, used the company's intranet with his laptop to call for help. Within three hours, he received a suggestion from a Memphis employee about a specific Buckman chemical and a reference to a master's thesis by an Indonesian student at North Carolina State University. In a few more hours, Dalton had 11 suggestions and advice from Buckman employees in six different countries. Most of the ideas were concrete and useful. The result was a $6 million order from the Indonesian pulp mill.[5]

---

[5] Shan L. Pan and Harry Scarbourgh, "A Socio-Technical View of Knowledge Management," *Journal of Knowledge Management* (Vol. 2, No. 1, September 1998), 58. See also Bruce Cuthbertson, "Buckman Labs International: Chemical Company Proves that Top-Down KM Works," *Knowledge Management* (January 2000), 24.

In another era, or under a different model, Dalton might have been criticized for not appearing to have all the answers and for distracting the other workers. Similarly, the individuals who responded to his call for help might have been worried about being perceived as underemployed and having too much time on their hands when they answered the request. In reality, Buckman is known in management and leadership circles for its positive knowledge-sharing culture. Both the formal sharing processes and the culture insisted that workers both ask questions and answer them. Questions and answers are simply part of their job. This Buckman model is the antithesis of the old model of hoarding information and knowledge. The model is not an indicator that the employees have nothing to do or that answering questions distracts them from their job. At Buckman the way to get recognition is to share knowledge.

Another strategy has features that could be used in combination with Buckman's techniques. A real estate board in Northern California holds regular "Have/Need/Want" meetings for sales agents from all the board's local member companies to share routine listing information. At these meetings, realtors from agencies in one county gather for breakfast once a week. Sales agents who have clients who want to buy a new home with particular requirements describe the type of property desired. Agents who have listings that meet those criteria identify themselves, and these agents collaborate after the meeting. Even though home-sales listing database services are kept up-to-date, the personal exchange of information on routine characteristics of homebuyers presents new opportunities for the agents, purchasers, and sellers. The "Have/Need/Want" metaphor extends naturally into many disciplines.

TACIT KNOWLEDGE MANAGEMENT SYSTEMS FOR UNSTRUCTURED WORK

The second kind of work that poses different challenges for managers is unstructured work with unpredictable or few (if any) specifications. This work is more unique than routine and often focuses on defining and solving problems because it involves the part of the organization where things are created, learned, or changed. Examples of these tasks include conducting research, negotiating and conflict resolution, planning, new product creation, and coaching. Problems arise in these unstructured or tacit knowledge areas when the employees have sufficient content or subject matter knowledge to do their jobs, but they do not have adequate context for their knowledge. What's often missing for them is some sense of purpose, goals, or a mission.

Knowledge sharing problems also occur when the corporate culture is earmarked by conflict, has norms that discourage sharing, or when trust among employees is low. Three cases explore both the positive and negative sides of tacit knowledge sharing cultures.

Xerox's service workers provide an example of tacit knowledge sharing and an excellent knowledge management culture. Xerox knowledge sharing began informally when a dozen or so technicians began to meet at the end of the day after they serviced clients' copy machines. "They would get together to exchange tales of how they had helped to solve the clients' problems... they found these meetings much more useful than Xerox's service manuals."[6] Xerox leaders saw the value of the knowledge brain power held in their service technicians' minds and expanded the sharing throughout its service operations. Wisely, they also provided the technicians with an electronic system into which the technicians could enter their tips. "Today, there are thousands of tips stored in the Web-based system."[7] Service employees worldwide use the process. Xerox reduced their cost of service by 10 percent by taking advantage of the brain power of their service technicians.

This case of knowledge sharing illustrates the power of stories in corporate culture. These tales are the basis of tacit knowledge. The shared stories described how the technicians did their work and solved problems that could not be solved with the explicit knowledge found in the company's service manuals. Xerox capitalized on the shared experiences by encouraging the technicians to meet. Xerox

---

[6] Michelle Delio, "Grass Roots Are Greener: Knowledge initiatives advance from bottom-up successes, not by executive fiat," *Knowledge Management* (February 2000), 49.
[7] Ibid.

then fostered the process by providing electronic tools so that hundreds of their worldwide employees could add their own tips and also benefit from the knowledge that had once only been in the heads of a few employees.

What might be the motivation for an individual to answer questions and share aside from the general idea that it's expected? Xerox showcased this team as a group of winners. People like to identify with a winning team, and this Xerox winning team was one where questions were asked and knowledge was shared. Moreover, people do not like to be on the wrong side of informal group norms. At Xerox, the team was expected both to contribute to the database and to use it. People were more comfortable being in synch with the norm.

WHAT is the individual's motivation to answer questions and share, aside from the general idea that it's expected of them?

- People don't like making mistakes. If they can learn from others, there is a better chance they can avoid mistakes.
- People like to identify with winning teams.
- People don't want to be on the wrong side of informal group norms. When these informal norms are readily perceived, most people find it appealing to be in synch with them.
- Some respond because they see compliance as a barter system. They anticipate reciprocity when they are looking for answers themselves.
- Some workers have altruism. They simply like to help others.
- Some are motivated because they gain a reputation as being a contributor and an expert.
- The wish for success is sufficiently powerful that people conform to the norms of sharing and receiving.

In another case, tacit knowledge was not shared in a nonprofit organization. This organization attempted three times to enter into joint ventures with book publishers to write, publish, and market books for its members and the general public. Each of the joint ventures failed for a number of good reasons, but the sad story is that the odds of achieving success for second and third attempts might have increased if the knowledge about the first effort had been shared.

Unfortunately, the corporate culture of this nonprofit had norms of hoarding knowledge and of not asking other employees what knowledge they have that might be useful. It was a situation of "not-invented-here." The employees who undertook the second and third tries had the attitude that, " I didn't participate the first time. I'm inventing the new joint book publishing venture now, and no one could possibly help me. They failed before so what could they possibly provide me." It's not surprising that the second and third joint ventures failed. There was a cycle of reinvention, mistakes were repeated, much staff time was wasted, and no books were published.

Years later, the story about the joint ventures was finally told. One employee remembered what had happened during each attempt. She had formally participated in the first venture. While she was not asked to work on the subsequent ventures, she had carefully observed what happened in them. She did not volunteer her insights, mostly because no one bothered to ask her what she knew about the failed ventures, and because she felt no incentive to help others. There was nothing in the non profit's culture that encouraged or (informally, at least) even permitted seasoned employees to share their experience and knowledge. There was no expectation that sharing behaviors would be accepted or rewarded. Significantly, too, there was no expectation or practice for employees to seek out others for advice. In a hoarding culture, you just don't go to other employees either to share or to ask for advice, information, or knowledge. A good knowledge sharing culture encourages a natural curiosity on the part of employees undertaking new projects to ask, "What do you think?" Seasoned employees should be able expect that their experiences and knowledge can and should be offered.

The third case is a more successful example of shared tacit knowledge. British Petroleum use of technology to create "Virtual Teamwork stations."[8] In 1995, drilling production at a North Sea mobile ship site was halted when critical equipment failed. Thanks to the virtual teamwork process, an engineer hauled the piece of faulty equipment to a small video camera attached to the teamwork station. The TV signal was transmitted by satellite to an employee based hundreds of miles away who was familiar with the problem. Looking at the TV screen and talking to the on-site engineer, the employee "quickly diagnosed the problem and guided them through the necessary repairs. In the past a shutdown of this kind would have necessitated flying an expert out by helicopter or sending the ship (leased at a cost of $150,000 a day) back to port and out of commission for several days. This shutdown lasted only a few hours."[9]

This was a case of technology married to the know-how that was in the mind of an expert who was able to share his expertise. But, more than that, British Petroleum had a culture in which knowledge was highly valued, sharing was encouraged, and technology was in place to facilitate problem-solving.

 YOU can enhance knowledge sharing cultural behaviors by spotlighting employees who share knowledge and by establishing mentoring programs in which longer-tenure employees can help shorter-tenure employees.

A CASE OF KNOWLEDGE MISMANAGEMENT: THE SATURN PROJECT FOR THE APOLLO MISSIONS

The need to carefully manage both explicit and tacit knowledge is illustrated by a dispiriting story from one of the United States' great triumphs: the Saturn rockets that propelled the Apollo missions to the moon. The story about knowledge management derived from

---

[8] Thomas H. Davenport and Laurence Prusak, *Working Knowledge: How Organizations Manage What They Know* (Boston: Harvard Business School Press, 1998), 21.
[9] Ibid.

the Saturn project is an example of successful and careful overall project management that had no concurrent knowledge management goals or plan.

The irony of this story is that the National Aeronautics and Space Administration (NASA) had a strong knowledge management culture. A significant cultural norm was to archive millions of pages of plans, specifications, reports, notes, correspondence, and test results. Huge amounts of this explicit knowledge were dutifully preserved on microfiche. Unfortunately, as the Saturn project unfolded no plan was developed for how the microfiches were to be organized, nor was any automated system developed for retrieval. It gets worse. In our throwaway culture, the blueprints for the Saturn booster were thrown away after the final Apollo 17 mission in 1972. No other blueprints have ever been found. The Saturn booster was the only rocket with enough thrust to send a manned operation to the moon.

One writer in the knowledge management field, Geof Petch, said it this way. "A few miles from Mission Control in Houston stands a warehouse the size of a stadium. There, like the crated relics consigned to history in the last scene of *Raiders of the Lost Ark*, the documents of the Apollo mission wait for eternity."[10] Even if the documents are ever retrieved, they will be mostly useless because they lack meaning and context, Petch concluded. He believes that even if we wanted to, "Today we can no longer put a man on the moon," because the blueprints have been lost and the task of retrieval of other data and information would be "too difficult and costly."[11]

But that's only half of the story of a flawed knowledge management culture. The documents and blueprints represent data and information or explicit knowledge that is archived. Only about 22 percent of it represents what Petch calls enterprise knowledge. The other 78 percent of the enterprise knowledge has also disappeared for all practical purposes, probably forever. No one at NASA ever dealt with the tacit knowledge that was in the heads of the Apollo

---

[10] Geof Petch, "The Cost of Lost Knowledge," *Knowledge Management*, (October 1998), as appearing at http://enterprise.supersites.net/kmmagn2/km199810/fb1.htm., unpaged.
[11] Ibid.

workforce, including the astronauts. Petch concluded, "Even if we could launch the Saturn again, we wouldn't remember how to fly it."[12]

YOU'VE GOT ALL THIS TECHNOLOGY: USE IT!

Significant barriers arise when employees do not know who the "players" are for their task—who else in the organization might be engaged in similar activities or who in the organization needs the work done. The key for helping employees develop a context for their efforts is to return to the journalist's questions. As two of the tacit knowledge cases illustrated, sometimes a little technology helps, too.

The Xerox Palo Alto Research Center (PARC) has a culture that promotes knowledge sharing by providing many whiteboards throughout their facility, some going from floor to ceiling. Researchers freely record knowledge about things they are working on in hope that colleagues will stop, review what has been recorded on the board, and scrawl ideas that come to them. John Seely Brown, Director and chief scientist at PARC, said, "We're looking for a way to support a constantly evolving conversation in a way that we don't have to reset it each time someone comes along."[13] The organization provides the tools that foster informal interchanges just like the ones that take place at water coolers and coffeepots but more effectively and efficiently. The whiteboards preserve this information so that the conversation can involve significant numbers of people. Barbara Waugh, Hewlett-Packard Laboratories (HPL) Manager of Worldwide Organizational Development said about the need for facilitating knowledge conversations, "There's a hunger for diversity of perspectives—and for a chance to bring them to bear on people's research questions."[14]

Another global company, Nortel Networks, uses a talk show format with company executives hosting a monthly program, "Virtual Leadership Academy"[15] for 2,000 Latin American and Caribbean

---

[12] Ibid.
[13] Paul Rober, "Live From Your Office!" *Fast Company* (October 1999), 168.
[14] Ibid., 170.
[15] Ibid., 152.

employees in 46 different countries. The program is an opportunity to have real-time corporate conversations between the employees and the executives. Employees are comfortable with the talk show format, which tends to break down barriers found in large multinational companies operating across geographic and cultural boundaries. The advantage comes from the fact that talk shows are popular in most of those countries. They accommodate people saying what they have on their minds because that is what people do on talk shows.

Nortel is not the only company moving to this form of interactive communication. HPL, Home Depot, IDEO Product Development, and Xerox's PARC have all been successful using this "edutainment" format.[16] Besides breaking down barriers, the talk show format enhances the transmission of company knowledge because the medium focuses on conversation, arguably the best way to foster transmission and understanding of knowledge. The format also builds rapport and interpersonal communications between management and employees. Substantial benefit accrues to the company as well when the edutainment activities result in informal, unstaged local follow-up conversations. These unstructured conversations seem to provide employees who participate with greater understanding and certainly provide a most effective means of transferring culture.

TECHNOLOGY IS NOT ALWAYS THE ANSWER

Systems and technologies are not always the answer. At one large trade association senior management had the worthy goal of enhancing member awareness and customer service on the part of the association's staff. To implement the objective, the CEO had the IT staff develop a database with separate profiles for tens of thousands of members. Database fields within each member entry provided the member's name, address, phone number, and company affiliation. Other fields identified services that the member had used or purchased in the past. All staff were supposed to keep the database open

---

[16] Ibid., 160.

all day, and, when a member called, pull up that member's profile, fill in any missing pieces of the profile and then add new information, based on the conversation. Staff resisted because they were embarrassed to ask callers to spell their names. Members resisted providing profile information, possibly because of "Big Brother" concerns, and because in many cases they were calling for relatively simple information and did not want to spend time responding to questions. There also were no incentives or rewards to encourage the behaviors the senior staff wanted. Nor were there any sanctions developed to deal with those who resisted the initiative.

Some experts argue that knowledge management requires a great deal of high-tech software and that information technology should drive knowledge management. Recognize that the information technology people in your organization may want to control and drive a knowledge management effort. If that happens, the technology emphasis could hinder rather than enhance effective sharing and a great deal of money could be wasted. The reality is that knowledge management requires both high tech and high touch. "Today's leaders must pay attention to environments rather than rules, coach rather than tell; ask the right questions rather than provide the right answers. The result is a more distributed decision-making system in which all members can and must participate."[17]

A CULTURAL CHARACTERISTICS AUDIT FOR KNOWLEDGE MANAGEMENT

Corporate knowledge cultures will vary by the types of work that they do, the mix of explicit and tacit knowledge endeavors and the extent and practicality of technology solutions to the variety of tasks in an organization. Earlier in the chapter one model of knowledge audit followed an inventory model to help managers describe their organizations in order to identify strengths and weaknesses.

---

[17] Wendi R. Bukowitz and Ruth L. Williams, "Looking Through the Knowledge Glass," *CIO Enterprise* (October 15, 1999), 78.

Another type of audit helps managers gather more impressions and data about the company and about the environment that has been created for sharing both the explicit and tacit knowledge of the organization. This audit focuses on cultural characteristics on a continuum so that you can assess not only where you are (as in the inventory model), but also where you might want to go. The continuum is designed to provoke your thinking about whether you need to create and manage transitions from negative to positive cultural characteristics. Some of the "how-to" techniques will become self-evident when you have identified where you are. Others will require extensive planning and many incremental steps. Sometimes managers will want to involve many employees from several units to make these assessments.

In this type of audit, you might be seeking answers to questions that include:

- Why or why not is knowledge shared?
- What barriers get in the way of sharing?
- What gets shared? When and why?
- What effect do incentives and rewards have on sharing, collaboration, and teamwork?
- What are the informal rules and norms for employees in sharing or not sharing knowledge?
- How do power and status affect sharing?
- What are the levels of collaboration, teamwork, and sharing?

As you undertake a cultural characteristics audit, you'll discover whether your corporate culture enhances or detracts from knowledge sharing in your company. As has been noted all along, your future success depends on the skill and speed with which employees gain confidence in their own knowledge levels and share them.

A CULTURAL CHARACTERISTICS AUDIT

If your knowledge management culture has this characteristic	You need to move here to be successful
Your people do not have much power to make decisions.	Decisions are decentralized and collaboration takes place.
Your people mostly do what they are told.	Curious people are willing to take risks, show initiative, and decisiveness. There is autonomy with clear guidelines.
Ideas and wisdom come mostly from the top.	Contributions come from all parts of the organization.
Good ideas are ignored, ridiculed, smothered by bureaucracy.	Good ideas are taken seriously and people are willing to test ideas out on others.
Your people do not know what is going on.	People know a great deal about what is going on through formal and informal channels.
Your people do not challenge assumptions.	People are free to explore and challenge.
There are few or no incentives and rewards for sharing knowledge.	People and their knowledge are valued, recognized, and rewarded.
Your people do not know what to contribute to a knowledge base or share with others.	People know what they know, others know what they know, and much giving and receiving takes place.
The norm in your organization is "don't rock the boat."	A strong common bond encourages people to work together to identify problems, solve problems, and move in new directions.
There is lots of "rugged individualism."	Teamwork and collaboration predominates.
There are few informal networks and "communities of practice."	There are many open and easily identified informal communities.
There is little talking in the hallways, at coffee machines, and water coolers. There are few facilities for people to informally converse.	Collaboration zones exist in all parts of the organization's facilities, and lots of problems are discussed and sharing takes place in halls and at the coffeee machines and water coolers.
You have a rigid hierarchical organization, and your people hesitate to cross authority lines and boundaries.	There is organizational flexibility with limited hierarchy. Communications flow across and through boundaries.

A "COMMUNITY OF PRACTICE" CANNOT BE APPOINTED

Although each employee knows a very great deal about the work of the organization, the knowledge has little utility until workers come together to share the information. In the end, knowledge management has a strong social, high touch component. Many knowledge management experts focus on that social element by pointing to the so-called "community of practice" as a primary solution to enhance knowledge sharing. The conundrum of the community of practice is that it absolutely cannot be *formally* organized; yet it is a very structured type of entity that can set the pace for information-sharing and knowledge management.

The roughest equivalent to the community of practice might be thought of as a 1950s-style water cooler or coffee break crowd. It is a group of people, sometimes from different areas but with similar functions, who have joined together for some common purpose and then remained bound by their trust relationships and the sense of purpose in either working toward a new solution or having solved a particular problem. In the "olden days" of hard wall offices, it was the group that won the XYZ account and kept getting together in the same team member's office to try out solutions to another problem. This group continued to meet even if no one from the XYZ account days was working together any longer. A community of practice is not made up of the office gossips. It is the group of associates who, when they get together, have conversations built around phrases like "Have you ever... ?" or "Do you think you could... ?" or "Is it possible to...?"

 THE water cooler metaphor works. The manager can create break rooms that are actually inviting or have lunch brought in for a problem-solving session.

The community of practice is a place where knowledge management is already occurring. Its members are the exemplars that a manager wishes everyone would emulate; yet the manager cannot "appoint" a community of practice. It simply cannot be institutional-ized. The manager can, however, facilitate creation of communities of practice. David Roussain of FedEx goes so far as to say that when project groups meet, "It has to be fun." Roussain goes further and notes that every room should be equipped with whiteboards and over-head projectors and that every employee should have access to cell phones, broadcast voice mail, and home access to e-mail. Roussain believes that all these modes of communication are essential so that "whenever you have the right frame of mind, you can engage."

The critical challenge for a manager is to figure out how to gen-erate a community of practice without appointing or organizing it. Probably the first step, even in the rush of the .com world, is for the manager to impress on people that their daily rhythm needs to include informal communication and/or reflection about how work gets done and goals get accomplished. In addition, managers and employees both need to have celebrations when a particular problem has been solved, a goal achieved or a project completed. These rein-forcements enhance the sense of sharing in the group. This social contact can facilitate creation of communities of practice.

TIP

THE most powerful way to get people to share knowledge is to tell stories about successful sharing.

Stories are powerful because employees identify more with stories that are connected to them than they do with cold facts or appeals. Stories help employees relate to what is familiar to them.

Another essential how-to is recognition that a community of practice needs areas that are open, yet private. Hence, the water cool-er metaphor. People do gossip at the water cooler but they also do some of their communications and problem-solving work there. Often what they are doing is updating an informal knowledge base. They transfer valuable knowledge about how to do things, tell who has left the company (so you cannot rely on that person any longer!), or identify who has transferred to a new project (so they might be more or less useful to what you are doing). The coffee machine or water cooler is also the place where informal socialization of new employees takes place. The new folks on the job can observe how people behave and listen to stories that give them valuable insights into "how things are done around here." Notably, design firms are now beginning to develop specialties in moving beyond the geometry of cubicles to create more space that is both open and private.

TIP

KNOWLEDGE sharing conversations help employees to understand their own as well as the perceptions, assumptions, and beliefs of others.

Conversations that include these factors are particularly valuable because they move the company's culture from an authority, command and control model to one involving many people in work processes and decision-making.

The cultural issue here is trust. Management must provide open and/or informal space for people to naturally congregate and management should not attempt to suppress gossip. Just as soon as managers squelch any kind of informal employee communications by telling folks to get back to work, sharing will stop. The organization needs to use all possible channels of communication. Informal communication can be more accurate and rich simply because it isn't screened or filtered. Workers can usually develop their own informal screening techniques to figure out who simply wants to gossip and tell stories and who uses informal communication to further project or group goals. The worst thing management can do is institute a rigid "Everybody back to work" environment that suppresses informal exchange.

Over time the group develops norms for doing things. A community of practice does require a maturation period. The group becomes more than a network that has relationships or a clique. Its fundamental characteristic, and the one that is most valuable to the organization, is that the groups that comprise communities of practice in the organization identify with the organization and its needs. These communities are valuable to the organization because they understand the issues a company faces and the leaders trust them to explore issues and focus on achieving company goals. The community becomes bound by its tacit knowledge and becomes a living organism. The group has stories of its own and develops its own norms. The more communities of practice in an organization, the more effective this process can be for a company.[18]

COMMUNITIES OF PRACTICE GO TO CYBERSPACE

The rise of e-mail, intranet, extranet, and Internet communications has created an offshoot of communities of practice called virtual communities. Some companies have found that e-mails and chat rooms are ways to "manage information within the enterprise."[19] Companies such as BP, Amoco, Ford, Kaiser Permanente, and Monsanto used the virtual community setting to integrate complete strangers into their knowledge management activities.

Fostering a positive knowledge management culture in virtual communities requires encouraging a diversity of opinion and recognizing the needs and requirements of the community participants. Most importantly, the sponsors must give up much control because people involved soon claim the virtual community as their own even though the sponsor still owns the hardware and software that runs it. Author Stacy Horn, said, "...it means they've invested in it, but as a business person you have to realize you can't dictate to them."[20]

Hallmark Cards is an early adopter of on-line virtual community knowledge management. The company created a pilot extranet for some of its independent storeowners to share experiences and tips for

---

[18] Wendi R. Bukowitz and Ruth L. Williams, "Looking Through the Knowledge Glass," *CIO Enterprise* (October 15, 1999), 78.

[19] Daintry Duffy, "It Takes an E-Village," *CIO Enterprise* (October 1999), Section 2, 40.

[20] Stacy Horn, *Cyberville: Clicks, Culture, and the Creation of an On-Line Town* (New York: Warner Books, 1998), 40.

such things as promotions and selling. Hallmark wisely asked the first participants to tell the company what would meet their needs. This began a knowledge management culture of sharing that has led to increased profits for some stores. Hallmark hopes to expand this pilot extranet to eventually include most of its 8,000 affiliated retail stores as well as consumers.

Kaiser Permanente has discovered that building a positive knowledge management culture is easier when they sponsor virtual communities and find participants willing to act as hosts for on-line discussions. Anna-Lisa Silvestre, general manager of Kaiser's National Member Technology Group, said, "It's like having a host at a party. They welcome people and tweak conversations. If sites don't have active hosts, they die. You can't just leave them unattended."[21]

According to John McElfresh, Director of Electronic Business and Communications at Schneider Automation in Andover, Massachusetts, an open culture on the company's extranet allows people to vent. He says, "we try to use it as an opportunity to find the root cause of the problem and fix it."[22] McElfresh believes that it is also crucial that someone in the company culls suggestions and ideas and forwards them to those in the company who can act upon them. This sharing of knowledge moves idle chatter to action.

A GOOD KNOWLEDGE MANAGEMENT CULTURE THROUGH RECRUITMENT AND RETENTION

Scient Corporation, an e-commerce firm based in San Francisco, only hires employees "who want to share knowledge" says Doug Kalish, Chief Knowledge Officer. At each recruiting interview, managers at Scient "emphasize knowledge sharing."[23] They follow up this recruiting emphasis by using performance management criteria for evaluations, raises, and promotions that include "how many training

---

[21] Ibid.,44.

[22] Ibid.,46.

[23] Rick Whiting, "Knowledge Management: Myths and Realities," *Informationweek.com* (November 22, 1999), 48.

courses people have designed or taught, documents or white papers they have written, and new employees they have mentored."[24]

It is also a good idea to reframe your traditional recruiting practices. Adjust requirement criteria and practices so that the specific skills you enumerate include the knowledge sharing skills and mind set that you want prospective employees to bring to the organization. For example, you might develop job descriptions that include such standards as:

- Uses knowledge in business processes or activities and describes how that knowledge is used.
- Enters knowledge into the company's formal knowledge management system.
- Identifies where in the company the knowledge needed to do work resides.
- Informally shares knowledge with colleagues.

Once the criteria have been added to the skill mix for a particular position, interview questions must be developed that will reveal the candidate's familiarity with and attitudes toward knowledge management. You have to do that because sharing knowledge runs counter to the way workers of all ages have been taught in school and the way they traditionally have been rewarded at work. "In school, students are taught to compete rather than collaborate. In business, fast-track employees typically have been rewarded for what and who they know, not for who they shared knowledge with."[25]

TIP

QUESTIONS About Knowledge Sharing to Ask a Potential Employee

1. In the last place you worked how much knowledge sharing took place?

2. Give me some examples of how you shared knowledge with your colleagues. What happened in high pressure situations?

---

[24] Ibid.

[25] Dr. Edward Wakin, "Teaching Employees to Share Knowledge, *Beyond Computing* (January/February 2000), 54.

TIP

3. Did that company have formal knowledge sharing processes? If so, please describe them and give me some examples of how and what you contributed to that process, and how you used it to obtain knowledge you needed.

4. Did you use any informal methods to acquire knowledge you needed to do your work or to share your knowledge with them? If so, please tell me about it and what were the results?

5. What articles or books have you read lately outside your work and your specialty? What did you learn or what interested or amused you?

Laurie J. Flynn, writing in *Knowledge Management* magazine, says that retention of key knowledge workers requires that companies "must also make strategic investments in information technologies, foster a supportive relationship between management and employee work groups, and develop a culturally integrated work environment across geographic boundaries."[26] If you have people leaving your organization, whether quitting or being fired, you are probably allowing their valuable knowledge to walk out the door with them.

Incentives and rewards in managing a knowledge sharing culture must shift emphasis from traditional systems focusing on individual achievement to focusing on rewarding team efforts and knowledge sharing. Knowledge management experts recommend rewarding both the sharer of knowledge and the receiver when the knowledge is reused or when the receiver adds to the knowledge. *Knowledge Management* magazine suggests, "One of the best ways to increase the value of knowledge and the likelihood that it will be used is to link it to a real person."[27] In other words, give credit by naming the knowledge and the person who has it. Punitive disincentives when people do not

---

[26] Laurie J. Flynn, "Brain Drain," *Knowledge Management* (November 1998) as appearing at http//enterprise.supersites.net/kmmag2km199811/fb1.htm.,unpaged.

[27] "Sharing Knowledge and Other Unnatural Acts," *Knowledge Management* (January 2000), 79.

share can be very powerful ways to apply pressure. One Silicon Valley company hires individuals on a three-month provisional basis. During that period, the employee's "fit" with the organization is assessed. At the end of the three-month period or at any time during it, the company can terminate the employee without providing any cause. Another reality of the .com workplace is that coworkers informally punish people who do not share by failing to include them on project teams. Over time, the employees who do not get "picked" have little value-added to show for their tenure, so their performance-based objectives cannot be met.

Interspersed in this chapter are references to an inventory knowledge audit that helps you assess where you are today and an in-depth cultural characteristics audit that helps you look at your knowledge culture on a continuum so that you can determine where your culture needs to be. You absolutely have to keep making evaluations of your status and progress. The following quick and easy knowledge audit is a middle ground that combines features of both approaches and is a cost effective way to conduct continuing evaluations.

A QUICK AND EASY KNOWLEDGE AUDIT

1. What do you know about power and people relationships in your organization?
2. How much trust, honesty, and openness exist now in your organization?
3. How much top management support exists for sharing information?
4. How often are mistakes repeated, and how often does work get duplicated in your organization?
5. Is your organization dependent on a few key people to get things done right and to solve problems?
6. Can you identify when the knowledge that is needed for people to do their jobs is used?
7. Can people in your organization tell how they use information and knowledge in their work?

8. Is your management culture one of control or one of coaching, advising, facilitating, and sharing?

9. Do the disciplines and specialties (the "tribes" in your company) in your company suffer from organizational knowledge sharing rigidity because they tend to screen knowledge out if it does not relate to their discipline or specialty? Are there paradigms and mental models limiting the view of the future, especially when things seem to be working well right now?

10. Does your reward and incentive system support or hinder knowledge sharing?

11. What's included in your organization's performance management system about sharing knowledge?

12. What positive and negative values and norms exist in your company's knowledge sharing culture?

13. How good are the people in your organization at sharing with each other the things they do best? Why and how?

14. Is the primary emphasis in your organization on individuals or teams?

15. Which of the following characteristics (traits, attributes) do your team members exhibit that will help them to effectively develop and manage knowledge and then share that knowledge? Can you say that your employees:

   - are flexible
   - are willing to learn from others
   - are continuous learners
   - collaborate easily
   - are interdependent with others
   - are networkers
   - have the ability to bridge between thinking and action

16. The development of shared knowledge usually comes through conversations as people interact in their work practices (more about this in the next chapter). What have you done to promote conversations?

17. If the knowledge that people need to do their jobs exists somewhere in the organization, can it be found? Is it ignored?

18. Which of the following in your company are supported by knowledge sharing?
   * decision-making
   * improving business processes
   * creativity and innovation

AT THE END OF THE DAY: YOU'D NEVER *NOT* ASK

Obtaining intelligence and insights about the health of your company's knowledge sharing culture is only the first step in making improvements you want to implement. Use what you now know to identify the changes in your culture that you want to make. The table on page 237 describing the cultural characteristics audit should give you some ideas about what you need to change. Sometimes it will be prudent to start small, with small groups or with narrowly defined objectives. A crucial determinant of success will be to secure sponsorship for the idea.

HOW to get started on the development of your company's knowledge management initiatives.

* Start small in your knowledge management initiatives. Conduct pilot projects, especially when some informal knowledge sharing is going on and find ways to replicate the sharing conditions and culture.
* Have patience but be vigilant all of the time. You make progress in knowledge sharing slowly with hard work.
* Be sure you can identify the people in your organization who stand to lose the most in the short and long run if you start some knowledge sharing projects. You must identify them and get them on your side, or you must deal with their resistances to change.

Gary Aigen, VP of Business Innovation at Arinso International, notes that a major difficulty in knowledge management is securing the kind of sponsorship that leads to real organizational change. He said, "You've got to assign people, allocate resources, put in processes and programs to capture what's been learned, promote and reward sharing what's learned, so that people can and want to use what the company knows." The follow-up for this kind of endeavor is to reiterate and imbue as habit with workers the need to ask questions and to seek constantly for ways to implement the "What do you think?" and who, what, where, why, when, and how inquiries that foster a strong knowledge management culture

The company that is committed to managing people's brain power has recognized two things: first, knowledge management is essential to success in today's business environment, and second, when you know what you know, you can begin to learn. You must continually assess your knowledge management strengths and weakness through audits, reward valued behaviors and celebrate successes. If you do these things consistently, you send clear messages to your workers and colleagues that sharing knowledge matters and that it will make projects move faster and more effectively. The learning can begin, and the processes and qualities described in this chapter can be implemented.

APPLYING THIS INFORMATION IN YOUR ORGANIZATION

These questions will get you started in thinking about the current state of your organization's knowledge management processes. If you are ready to work through a more detailed knowledge management audit after answering these broader questions, there are versions of short audits in this chapter.

1. Does your organization have any success stories about how employees shared knowledge to get something done better or quicker?

2. If so, how many people in your organization know the stories?

3. Is your organization's approach to sharing knowledge an emphasis on high tech to manage the organization's database and file cabinet explicit knowledge, an emphasis on facilitating the transfer of tacit knowledge existing in the minds of your employees, or a blend of both?

4. What behaviors about knowledge sharing do you expect and how does that differ from how your employee's actually behave?

5. What role does technology play in your organization's efforts to share knowledge?

6. Do you have an organizational environment where employees feel they can grow and thrive?

CHAPTER EIGHT

The New Corporate IQ and Getting Smart

I n a .com world your company must be smart, have smart employees, and learn faster than your competitors. In fact, companies with high corporate IQs are the ones with significant collective intelligence. They are the most likely to survive and prosper in the increasingly turbulent environment of the twenty-first century. In Chapter 7, we were concerned primarily with unleashing the individual employee's knowledge and brain power. At some point, all this brain power coalesces and takes on a life of its own within the company and becomes a symbolic entity, called corporate IQ.

Corporate IQ

The collective ability to accurately understand the company's internal competencies and external markets, and the ability to rally resources to respond to the challenges that are identified.

Worldwide, corporate IQ is a key determinant of success, as discovered in studies conducted by Stanford University, McKinsey & Company, and the University of Augsburg in Germany. This study of 2,000 managers from 164 business units of Asian, European, and U.S. high-tech firms and drew three primary conclusions. Companies with high corporate IQs are:

1. more likely to survive in the Information Age
2. make greater profits than their industry average
3. outperform their counterparts during business downturns.[1]

In this chapter we describe the kinds of brain power your company needs to be smart and how companies are increasing this collective intelligence through new kinds of learning. This is particularly important in the technology-driven business world where speed is a given. Using the metaphor from physics of the "half-life"[2] of radioactive decay, Ed Michaels, a McKinsey & Co. director says, "The half-life of technology is growing shorter all the time."[3] By that he means that technology becomes obsolete at a rapidly increasing rate. The obvious corollary to this is that the half-life of knowledge and skills is decreasing rapidly as well. Everyone needs to learn more and learn faster to keep pace and contribute. For an organization to survive and thrive it requires a corporate culture that places a high value on being a smart company.

How can a team of committed managers with individual IQs above 120 have a collective IQ of 63? The discipline of team learning confronts this paradox. We know that teams can learn; in sports, in the performing arts, in science, and even, occasionally, in business, there are striking examples where intelligence of the team exceeds the intelligence of the individuals in the team, and where teams develop extraordinary capacities for coordinated action.[4]

---

[1] Haim Mendelson and Johannes Ziegler, *Survival of the Smartest: Managing Information for Rapid Action and World-Class Performance* (New York: John Wiley and Sons, 1999), 5-8.

[2] Half-life is the time required for one half the atoms of radioactive substance to disintegrate.

[3] John Byrne, "The Search for the Young and Gifted: Why Talent Counts," *BusinessWeek* (October 4, 1999), 108.

[4] Peter Senge, *The Fifth Discipline: The Art and Practice of the Learning Organization*, (New York: Doubleday/Currency, 1990), 10

The first part of this chapter gives you some broad principles to apply as you evaluate your own company's collective IQ. The second half presents a case study and some tools from companies that have worked to expand their collective intelligences.

HOW DO YOU KNOW IF YOUR COMPANY HAS A HIGH IQ?

Thomas M. Koulopoulis, President of the Delphi Group, recommends that you "Take a corporate IQ test. How smart is your company? Like an intelligent person, an intelligent company understands itself and its environment."[5] The Delphi Group assesses knowledge management for organizations and helps them understand their corporate IQ. Delphi uses 100 attributes to study corporate IQ, including how teams are structured, what specific technologies are used to manage knowledge, and the percentage of profits attributable to recent products. The group focuses on four areas of organizational behavior:

1. *Internal awareness:* The organization's ability to understand itself—its core competencies.

2. *Internal responsiveness:* How an organization rallies and coordinates resources to prepare for a response when challenged.

3. *External awareness:* Understanding how the market sees the value of your product and services.

4. *External responsiveness:* The ability to respond to turbulence.

The Delphi Group studied corporate IQ in a survey that included 350 companies responding via the Web. The most important results of the study were the following:

- Companies in mature industries are 40 percent less likely to have above-average corporate IQs.

- High-IQ companies are almost twice as likely to be made up of cross-functional teams from across the organization.

- Companies in which employees are involved in shaping their work have much greater flexibility to adapt to changing conditions.

---

[5] Thomas M. Koulopoulos, "Take a corporate IQ test: How smart is your company? Like an intelligent person, an intelligent company understands itself and its environment," excerpted from PLUG-IN-DATAMATION (June 1998) by Cahners Business Information, unpaged reprint.

- Companies in which teams of employees had a say in how they did their work are 500 percent more likely to rank high on both internal and external responsiveness.
- Learning trumps experience. High-IQ organizations are three times more likely than average organizations to prefer employees who have a well-honed learning ability over ones with experience of how things are usually done.
- Most organizations in the survey believe that corporate culture plays a disproportionately large role in shaping their corporate IQ.

SYMPTOMS OF A HIGH IQ CULTURE

If, as Delphi found, corporate culture plays a disproportionately important role in shaping corporate IQ, then it is essential to learn to recognize the characteristics of a high IQ organization. The corporate IQ cannot be measured by taking the sum of individual intelligence and then dividing by the number of people in the organization. The corporate IQ is a whole that is greater than the sum of all its parts. Corporate IQ is not just about the managers and formal leaders—it includes everybody contributing to the goals, strategies, and mission as they drive the organization to the future. Everyone in an organization needs to contribute.

Corporate IQ can be thought of as the aggregation and internalization of the important data, information, knowledge, and mastery of tools needed to effectively run the organization and compete. In the high IQ organization, employees at all levels, not just the managers, know a very great deal. Their knowledge and mastery include the following:

- Knowing what you know and where the knowledge is.
- Knowing how you use the data, information, and knowledge to make decisions.
- Knowing what the current decision-making processes are in the company.
- Knowing what important decisions must be made.
- Identifying the direction and focus of the organization and how that relates to its mission, goals, and strategies.

• Recognizing the networks the business operates in and how to use them effectively.

In the academic and popular cultures, educators and psychologists often identify IQ not only as a measure of raw or native intelligence but also as the ability of an individual to adjust and adapt. In other words, higher IQ people can better meet changing conditions. So it is with organizations. High levels of corporate IQ increase the odds that the organization can effectively shift its ground when market and environmental conditions indicate the company must adjust and adapt. Adapting and adjusting are particularly related to decision-making. Incremental decisions that depend on the past are a hallmark of a low corporate IQ. In the .com world, incremental decisions trap an organization into remaining stuck where they are right now. Boldness and quickness in decision-making are the hallmark of the smart company. In the e-business environment, this is even truer than it was in the past.

TIP IT is especially important in the .com world that high corporate IQ emphasizes focus and direction. Encourage people to think about the future and adjust continuously in moving toward the future. If your organization concentrates only on current job IQ and knowledge, it really isn't very smart. The future for most companies in a .com world will not look like the past or even the present.

SYMPTOMS OF A LOW IQ CULTURE

Authors Haim Mendelson and Johannes Ziegler express strong, terse opinions about companies with low corporate IQs. Their basic message: it takes a high organizational IQ to compete against world-class competitors and to survive in both the short and long term.[6] In the evolving .com world, companies operate rapidly in multiple complex

---

[6] Mendelson and Ziegler, 4-8.

environments, bombarded by massive amounts of data and information. The authors note that companies must quickly process the information, make effective rapid decisions, and implement them. If they don't, a competitor takes market share away in the blink of an eye. High corporate IQ companies do this better than their low corporate IQ counterparts.

Mendelson and Ziegler developed a complex model[7] designed to describe and measure corporate IQ that differs somewhat from the Delphi Group model described earlier. What is most significant about the Mendelson and Ziegler model is their description of low corporate IQ companies.[8] Much of what they describe relates to corporate culture.

Below is an adaptation of some of Mendelson and Ziegler's descriptors along with several others based on research and observations. Taken as a whole, the following traits provide a pattern of behavior common in organizations with low corporate IQs.

- It is business as usual, even when conditions change.
- Top-level management makes tactical decisions, even when they do not have the best knowledge to make decisions.
- Communications are rigid, going only through the lines and boxes on the organization chart.
- People are told to do things, and they follow instructions, even though poor productivity is the result.
- Access to both internal and external information is restricted.
- Deadlines are frequently missed.
- Work is repeated, and the wheel is constantly reinvented.
- The bottom line is not good, but managers deny that problems exist.
- Tight controls are coupled with power concentrated at the top.
- Management suggests the same old solutions to whatever problems surface.

---

[7] The Mendelson and Ziegler model dimensions are (1) external information awareness, (2) effective decision architecture, (3) internal knowledge dissemination, (4) organizational focus, and (5) Information Age Business Network. Readers are referred to the details of the model and pp. 221-229, for how to apply the model in Mendelson and Ziegler cited above.

[8] Mendelson and Ziegler, 4-7.

- Individuals and organizational units criticize (rather than constructively evaluate) and blame each other, have turf wars, and engage in infighting
- The organization lacks focus.
- Top managers view their status and success in terms of the number of people they supervise and the size of their budgets. They therefore accumulate power at others' expense by creating, holding on to, and increasing turf. Often they refer to the size of their staff by noting how many people they "control."
- Resources are allocated on an incremental basis, making it difficult to fund new ideas and initiatives that would respond to market conditions and the external environment.
- Mistakes are hidden and discussion of them becomes taboo.

Only a few tools are available to evaluate corporate IQ as the concept has only been developed in the last few years. Your company may profit from the instrument developed by the Delphi Group, the Mendelson and Zeigler model noted earlier, or from work done by other consulting companies. The formal processes of determining an organization's IQ, as noted elsewhere in this chapter, are detailed, sophisticated and comprehensive. In a .com world you may not have time or resources to conduct a comprehensive assessment of your organization's IQ. However, the conceptual framework, the principles of organizational IQ evaluation, and the tips and cues provided in this chapter can be used informally to gain an understanding of the strengths and weaknesses of your company's IQ. The numbered and bulleted lists shown above can serve as guideposts or baseline criteria for getting your bearings, setting you off, and keeping you on the right track. You'll be most effective with an informal assessment of your company's IQ if you educate a few managers about the IQ concept and how the models and instruments work. Then, involve them with you in creating your own informal method and instrument, conducting the evaluation, and understanding your company's IQ.

This chapter is designed to alert managers and employees to the conceptual framework for an organizational IQ evaluation and to provide tips and cues that can serve as a threshold or beginning point for getting your bearings. In the absence of comprehensive assessment, the principles of organizational IQ evaluation noted above in the bullets can serve as guideposts or baseline criteria to set you off and keep you on the right track.

If your company culture matches several of these behaviors, your challenge is to get smarter—increase your corporate IQ. If you do not smarten up, the odds increase against your company's competitiveness and survival. Undoubtedly tens of thousands of companies, non profits and governmental agencies match many or all of these negative characteristics. These organizations survive, but relatively few prosper or reach their potential. Worse yet, they will become irrelevant as the .com world inevitably overtakes them. The limitation of the low IQ organization is the relentless syndrome of inability to change.

LEARNING TO IDENTIFY WHAT YOU DON'T KNOW IS A KEY TO GETTING SMART

A young employee, who had previously worked for several start-ups and now works for a more established high-tech Silicon Valley company describes her view of her current company's corporate IQ. She believes that the company was at risk of becoming a low-IQ corporation because the skills needed to take a start-up to 75 employees are distinctly different skills from those needed to grow from 75 to the 400 or 500 people level. While the company, had, indeed grown to the 500 employee level, she believed the company could nonetheless fail because of managers who did not recognize, "OK, I've done everything I can. I'm limited now, and I need another skill set." She went on to describe managers who were directive, and who held on to decision processes by undercutting team decisions.

Part of the learning process for an organization is learning to identify what it does not know. In this example, the employee believed that the managers were failing because they could not identify the needs for different skill sets and because they were not willing to let skilled employees make decisions about programs when the employees had greater expertise.

The future belongs to those who learn how to unlearn—
letting information go as soon as it becomes irrelevant—
and how to confront the unknown without fear, the
biggest obstacle to learning.[9]

These symptoms of a low-IQ company are not the profile of success in the .com world. The culture of organizations making the move to e-business can claim adaptability and innovation as two of their dominant characteristics. E-business environments favor informal, non bureaucratic methods for making decisions and organizing to accomplish things quickly. In the tightly controlled, risk-averse culture of the low-IQ organization, a company finds it difficult to tap into and use and rely on the talents, knowledge, and skills of its individual employees. It is impossible for companies with rigid cultures to pull all these talents together into a collective IQ in which employees work together effectively. Individuals with the most sophisticated collaboration skills and attitudes would be defeated by a corporate culture that created this many barriers to sharing and working together effectively. It is true that a company must have a large percentage of smart individuals working in the organization to have a high corporate IQ, but it is equally true that these individuals must have a supportive corporate culture to succeed in collectively using their abilities.

Unfortunately it is not easy to discover what your company and its employees do not know. As noted above, you are dealing mostly with symptoms, indicators, and comparisons. You can increase the odds of gaining insight into what you do not know by engaging consultants who perform extensive performance and cultural audits and who are skilled in analysis and diagnosis. If you wish your assessment to be less costly and more internally oriented yet still formal, you can conduct benchmarking projects or do research to find best practices in your industry. An immediate, informal approach would be to attend conferences where speakers from other companies brag about

---

[9] Tim Gallaway, "Observe Performance," *Knowledge Management* (April, 2000), 33.

their best and to network with other professionals in your industry and specialty. Information gathered from these informal sources will enable you to compare and contrast your own organization with what's working elsewhere.

INDIVIDUALS IN HIGH IQ CULTURES HAVE THREE KINDS OF SMARTS

When describing the types of individual smartness that a company needs among its employees at all levels, we are not talking about the academic intelligence people used to pass college courses. We all know lots of people who scored high on their SATs, Stanford-Binet IQ tests and earned great grades in college because they mastered the art of studying, taking tests, and psyching out their professors. We are talking about three other kinds of smartness that are needed. The three types are:

1. job smarts
2. thinking smarts
3. emotional smarts (sometimes referred to as emotional quotient or EQ)

These are very different kinds of intelligence than academic and intelligence quotients. Without a critical mass of all three types of intelligence represented in your organization, creating a high collective organizational IQ will be difficult.

JOB SMARTS FOCUS ON THE CAPACITIES TO DO THE JOB WELL

Job IQ is what people use in doing their jobs. These people have brain power, access to the data, information, knowledge, and wisdom needed to do their jobs well. People with high job IQ, as we discussed in Chapter 7, constantly and effectively use the creed of know how, know why, know who, know what, know where, and know when. Smart people in the workplace apply their knowledge and brain power to make better decisions, be creative and innovative, and improve their business processes so the organization runs more efficiently and effectively. These people almost always have a reputation within a company for being incredibly good at what they do.

HOW to expand employees' job IQ beyond just their own individual jobs.

- Employees usually know the language of their own specialty or discipline and of their own work unit. It's critical that they learn the business language of your company. Your business language might include the business and financial models you use, supply chain management, strategy, and issues the company faces.
- Cross-train your employees so that they know more about each other's work. This will allow them to do their own work better. For example, in the transition to e-business processes, many companies are cross-training their IT and business unit staffs. "The more our technology people are trained on sales and credit, the faster they can translate and integrate what we do into e-business."[10]

THINKING SMARTS IS NOT NECESSARILY LEARNED IN SCHOOL

Thinking IQ involves a combination of five different types of cognitive skills.

1. *Systems thinking:*   Everything in life now is complex so you must think about whole systems, complexity, interconnections, interrelationships, patterns, and interactions because everything interacts with everything.

---

[10] Diane Rezendes Khirallah, "The ABCs of E-Business," *Information Week* (March 20, 2000), 158.

2. *Logical thinking:* Many of the visual symbols that dominate our popular culture (e.g., advertising and MTV) are no longer linear or chronological. This places a premium on logical and sequential thinking. This is the ability to understand the logical sequence of words and phrases, the premises on which they are based, the pattern or way the premises are put together in the form of an argument, and the conclusion(s) arrived at by applying the argument to the premises.

3. *Critical thinking:* Bad information is everywhere. Bad Web sites, sloppy research, and urban myths are just a few sources. Workers need to be able to step back and say, "Does this make sense?" Critical thinking requires adequate and multiple investigation and interpretation of facts, data, and information; separating opinion from the facts; challenging assumptions and norms; understanding bias, prejudice, and hidden persuaders from the world of advertising and separating personality from argument.

4. *Creative/innovative thinking:* Breakthroughs occur when someone says, "Wow!" Creative thinking builds on what already exists and breaks the bounds of present reality to see multiple solutions and possibilities.

5. *Synergent thinking:* Combining analytical, detailed, and focused convergent thinking with diffuse, creative, and multidirectional divergent thinking.

We can no longer approach information-age problems with industrial-age thinking.[11]

Unfortunately, these five kinds of thinking are not what most people learn in colleges and universities. Mostly students learn a lot of facts. They learn how to find facts and sometimes how to keep an open mind about them so they can move beyond taking the facts for granted. If they expand their skills, they also learn how to interpret the facts and knowledge. A few even become curious about some subjects. But few students move beyond that basic kind of thinking and learn to reflect on facts and information long enough to relate them to a context or find out how what they have learned may relate to something else. Even (or sometimes *especially*) in graduate school, some curriculums and subject matters do not move students much beyond doing rudimentary analysis and number crunching thinking tools that "ill equip them (graduates of business school, engineering, and law) for the complex real-world problems they encounter in their professional lives."[12]

The by-product of this "find-a-fact-and-learn-it" education for most people is that they are not very skilled at thinking when entering the workplace. They are mechanical thinkers, expressing little curiosity, and seldom looking for new information or questioning things and challenging assumptions. If you have a majority of this type of person on your staff, you will likely end up with a culture in which good thinking is not very highly valued. Using the definition of the five types of thinking previously described, people only "think" when it is absolutely necessary. There is also a tendency toward uniformity of thinking in which "the chances are that everyone will see

---

[11] Michael J. Gelb, *Thinking For A Change: Discovering the Power to Create, Communicate, and Lead* (New York: Harmony Books, 1995), xiii.

[12] Ian Mitroff and Harold A. Linstone, *The Unbounded Mind: Breaking the Chains of Traditional Business Thinking* (New York: Oxford University Press, 1993), vii.

the problem much the same way (if only because anyone who does not, soon finds himself on the outside of those organizations)."[13]

> People in this kind of uniform-thinking culture tend to have limited conceptions of their world, use lots of "slogans, stock phrases, categorical statements... love to pass judgment on people, ideas and things," and you'll hear "a large proportion of declarative statements, many phrased in dogmatic terms."[14]

EMOTIONAL SMARTS BRING IT ALL TOGETHER

It is not enough to be smart about how you do your job and thinking. You must also be smart in the area of emotional intelligence.[15] EQ is a high level of self-awareness in which individuals can monitor their emotions, assess the actions and behaviors that follow, and influence those actions and behaviors in a beneficial way. EQ is the type of smartness that plays a critical part in the formation and maintenance of a corporate culture, primarily because EQ is about how people behave, especially in their relationships with others. If your company has employees with high EQ, you will have a positive organizational culture manifested by people managing their emotions; constructively interrelating with others, especially on teams; and solving problems that otherwise would hold the company back.[16]

---

[13] Mitroff and Linstone, 19, quoting Michael Thompson and Michael Warburton, "Decision Making Under Contradictory Certainties: How to Save the Himalayas When You Can't Find Out What's Wrong with Them, " *Journal of Applied Systems Analysis* (Vol. 12, 1985), 3-4,11.

[14] Karl Albrecht, *Brain Power: Learn to Improve Your Thinking Skills* (New York: Fireside/Simon & Schuster, 1992), 39-41.

[15] The theory of EQ was developed and expanded over the past 25 years by scores of psychologists at universities and consulting firms. Most of their work stems from Harvard psychologist John Gardner's research on seven varieties of intelligence. Expansion of Gardner's work came from questions about why people with high scores on traditional intelligence tests and high grades in school fail in their work and private lives. Research designed to deal with these questions pointed to human emotions and how people manifest and manage them. John Mayer at the University of New Hampshire and Peter Salovey at Yale developed an EQ model that answered these questions and guided further development in this field.

[16] Robert K. Cooper and Ayman Sawaf, *Executive EQ: Emotional Intelligence in Leadership and Organization* (New York: Grosset/Putnam, 1997), 198.

Emotional intelligence specifically includes the following:

- Positively relating to people and getting along with them.
- Constructively confronting people problems, including conflicts.
- Influencing people through informal power and leadership.
- Minimizing distress so it is possible to think effectively.
- Having hope and being resilient to spring back after setbacks.
- Confronting and working through problems so that solutions lead to organizational opportunities.
- Applying the power of personality and emotions.
- Being aware of other people's overt and innermost emotions and feelings to empathize with them and effectively work with them.
- Managing your own negative emotions such as putting the brakes on inappropriate anger (controlling but not stifling impulsive behaviors).
- Delaying gratification.
- Constructively regulating moods.
- Communicating to others through self-disclosure your thinking, desires and feelings.[17]

INCREASING YOUR EQ: PARK YOUR ROAD RAGE AT THE DOOR

Note how many of these characteristics of EQ are mirrored in the "Citizenship and Study Skills" evaluation section of the Fairfax County, Virginia elementary school report card. Children in grades one through three in the school system are evaluated on these characteristics with standards that range from a high of "Outstanding" down to "Needs Improvement." At this early education stage, part of each day's instruction includes lessons in these qualities.

---

[17] A number of instruments for measuring these EQ components have been developed. Some have and some have not been scientifically tested for reliability and validity. See examples in Robert K. Cooper and Ayman Sawaf, *Executive EQ: Emotional Intelligence in Leadership and Organizations* (New York: Grosset / Putnam: 1997), 13-14, 85-88, 172-174, 245-249, 273, 288; Paul G. Stoltz, *Adversity Quotient: Turning Obstacles Into Opportunities* (New York: John Wiley & Sons, 1997), 289-298; and Hendrie Weisinger, *Emotional Intelligence at Work: The Untapped Edge for Success* (San Francisco: Jossey-Bass Publishers, 1998), 213-218.

Elementary School Progress Report
Fairfax County Public Schools

Citizenship and Study Skills

Accepts responsibility
Complies with established rules
Exhibits courteous behavior
Exhibits self-control
Follows through on assignments
Listens to and follows directions
Organizes materials
Respects personal and school property
Uses time constructively
Works and plays cooperatively

Form No. SS/SE - 53B 7/93

Just as the elementary school emphasizes the early formation of these EQ qualities, the successful .com corporate culture is trying to unleash the mature versions of these personal attributes that are closely linked to citizenship and character. Only when a company achieves a high level of performance in these areas can its EQ—and thereby its Corporate IQ—increase. In some respects, a high Corporate IQ requires workers who are well-formed in personal and interpersonal skills. If employees didn't perform well as children on the skills listed on this elementary school report card, there are few external sources they can turn to as adults to develop them, even though they are the basis of success in the workplace. For example, some people have very few skills for confronting mistakes or anger. Others may be very competent at interaction with others but lack resilience. The central challenge for companies and their managers is to find ways to finish the work begun by everyone's mom, dad, great aunt, or third grade teacher.

You can begin by seeking out training courses that teach EQ skills to employees and hope they will retain what is presented to them. When employees have taken the EQ training, the critical challenge for managers is to follow up and reinforce the principles and skills employees learned in the courses. Managers are not always effective in this role. Inevitably, the question "How did you handle your frustrations today?" is a more disturbing question for both the manager and the worker than "How many widgets did you make today?" Despite any limitations of the manager of the employee in tackling EQ problems, however, these EQ qualities are the foundation of a strong organization.[18]

An Example of Emotional Intelligence in Action

A manager had little success at two performance appraisals in getting an employee to open up. In preparation for a third session, she thought through possible explanations of the employee's reticence to talk. The employee might have had other things on his mind, thought that the supervisor would ignore things he had to say, or perhaps he felt threatened. The manager then developed tactics she thought might improve the dialogue between them. When the employee gave terse answers during the review, she asked follow-up questions such as, "Can you tell me more?" or "Can you give me an example?" When the employee elaborated, the manager provided positive reinforcement and summarized what the employee said—"I appreciate your input," or "That's helpful."Managing her own emotions, the manager took charge of her own behavior by following the same process when she spoke. "I asked for his thoughts of what I was saying, and when he disagreed, instead of getting defensive, I asked him to elaborate to clarify his own thinking. Whatever disagreements there were, I found that

---

[18] For a good exposition of emotional intelligence see Daniel Goleman, *Emotional Intelligence: Why It Can Matter More than IQ* (New York: Bantam Books, 1995).

by getting him to express his own thoughts and feelings
we were able to create an accurate appraisal of his performance." The result was continuous improved communications: "Ever since, he has been much more expressive
with his thoughts and feelings in dealing with me, and we
have a much more productive relationship."[19]

The primary responsibility for increasing EQ lies with each employee in the organization. Fortunately, everyone has some level of EQ and can increase their EQ competencies. According to leading experts in this field, it is possible to nurture the EQ you have, fine tune and further develop your EQ strengths, and even add to your strengths.

THE BASIC BUILDING BLOCKS OF EQ

The basic building blocks of EQ development revolve around:

- Becoming more aware of yourself, your emotions, and behaviors.
- Managing your emotions.
- Motivating yourself.

A number of specific tools, suggestions, and practical advice on how to apply EQ principles in the workplace can be found in two groundbreaking books by Hendrie Weisinger and by Robert Cooper and Ayman Sawaf.[20]

One tool recommended by both authors is keeping a work-related journal in which you jot down the feelings you experience and what caused them, such as frustration when your computer crashed, anger when your supervisor told you he needed you to work the next weekend, or joy when you closed a difficult sales deal. The journal entries should be periodically read and analyzed to look for patterns

---

[19] Hendrie Weisinger, *Emotional Intelligence at Work: The Untapped Edge for Success* (San Francisco: Jossey-Bass Publishers, 1998), 179-180.

[20] Robert K. Cooper and Ayman Sawaf, *Executive EQ: Emotional Intelligence in Leadership and Organizations* (New York: Grosset/Putnam, 1997); and Hendrie Weisinger, *Emotional Intelligence at Work: The Untapped Edge for Success* (San Francisco: Jossey-Bass Publishers, 1998).

of recurring emotions. Do the same people or situations always make you angry? Are you often happier when you are assigned to tasks outside of your normal routine or responsibilities? These recurring patterns provide a basis for making improvements. Journals can also help you look for emotions that you do not experience that are nonetheless appropriate to the circumstances. Do you fail to find pleasure in the success of others? Do you shrink away from the limelight when you've succeeded? There is not a list of "correct" responses to every situation, but the individual with a strong EQ will recognize the unrealized possibilities in a variety of circumstances. The next step after analysis is to explore how the conditions under which negative feelings and behaviors arise can be avoided or altered.

Another helpful tool noted by Cooper and Sawaf is an " Integrity Time Agreement,"[21] a contract with yourself that you write in your own words. The commitment you make is to schedule the necessary time each day for reflection and exploration of your emotional intelligence in the workplace. Cooper and Sawaf say that the purpose of the contract-agreement is to get you to look carefully at your inner life as it propels you forward into the future. The examination centers on "the full range and depth"[22] of your feelings and the images that accompany the feelings. The environment that most requires this reflection is the high pressure, on-the-fly .com business setting. The speed of the environment requires frequent deep breaths and pauses to tune in to your EQ so that it's in balance. The ping-pong tables, volleyball courts, and foosball rigs in many offices are part of the deep breath, but the pause and essential reflection requires some moments and spaces for quiet, as well.

HOW TO SMARTEN UP: CREATING A LEARNING CULTURE THAT PRODUCES A HIGH CORPORATE IQ

At the beginning of this chapter we emphasized the importance of learning fast. The ability to learn fast involves three different learning

---

[21] Cooper and Sawaf, 179.
[22] Ibid.

challenges for organizations trying to move to e-business operations. This first challenge is learning faster than your competitors to keep them from passing you. The second is the geographic dispersion of employees and the need to conduct virtual learning. The third is learning faster than the pace of market changes that threaten to engulf your organization. These market changes are a multifaceted challenge, given the volume and complexity of the changes and the mass of new products, technologies, and knowledge that you have to learn and master.

WHO IS RESPONSIBLE FOR THIS RAPID, COMPLEX LEARNING?

In a word, "everyone." Everything about life has gotten more complex. More rapid changes are taking place in the business environment, and everyone in the company must learn.

> Since at the present rate of technological change the problems to be solved differ from one day to the next, it follows that everybody in the organization, from those who frame the policies to those who manipulate the ultimate details of technique, must be endowed to the greatest extent possible with the means of learning.[23]

While everyone is responsible for their own learning, senior and other management in the company needs to lead, foster, and encourage learning. There are several things management can do, including:

- Make learning part of the employee's job description.
- Make learning part of the employee's performance appraisal.
- Provide resources and time for employees to learn.
- Provide frequent information about what learning opportunities are available.
- Encourage employees to tell you about their learning experiences, what they learned, and how they intend to use what they learned.

---

[23] Reg Revens, "Linking artisan and scribe," *New Society* (June 1964), quoted by Jerry Rhodes, *Conceptual Toolmaking: Expert Systems of the Mind* (Oxford UK: Basil Blackwell, 1991), 2.

- Use both formal company in-house publications and informal conversations to highlight stories about employees who successfully did something in their work that came as a result of what they learned.

If learning does not take place at the individual and corporate levels, everyone quickly becomes obsolete. No one can afford to risk failing to keep up during times of rapid technological change in which skills and knowledge quickly become obsolete. You risk getting downsized and will find it increasingly difficult to land a job or even temporary work. And if your company does not smarten up its collective corporate IQ, the company will become less relevant day by day and more likely to go out of business.

HELPING EMPLOYEES IMPROVE THEIR EQ

The preceding section illustrated the importance for individuals to increase their EQ skills. Since your employees constantly interact with each other, work in informal groups, and on teams, your company must also enhance its collective EQ. As basic as it sounds, the experts in organizational learning[24] emphasize one basic building block: workers must talk together using dialogue or conversation. As employees acquire mastery of this tool, they can then move forward to the enhanced skills of virtual learning, learning by doing, and mistake learning described in the sections that follow.

One tool is dialogue or conversation. Conversations centering on the work of a team, for example, can effectively aid learning by team members. Conversations have several advantages, particularly when EQ learning is one of your goals. Conversations tend to equalize people and take them out of their formal positions and power. Therefore they do the following:

- Build relationships and trust among people.
- Help people move from advocacy to inquiry and from judgment to acceptance.

---

[24] Organizational learning leverages reflective insights about how an organization does things so that people can improve themselves. The organizational learning theorists believe that this individual and collective learning experience takes on a life of its own, thus raising the corporate IQ and improving the organization's outcomes.

- Help people explore their feelings, beliefs, and especially their opinions.
- Are not threatening to people since they are informal.
- Lead to new insights since the thinking of several people is usually superior to the thinking of just one person.
- Help bring to the surface assumptions and people's beliefs.

Following are some suggestions about holding conversations to maximize the benefits:

- *It may be necessary to informally coach a team on how to hold conversations.* One effective way of doing this kind of coaching is to ask people to remember a good conversation. Then, ask them to think about and write down on what was memorable. Ask participants to read aloud what they have written. Record the words and phrases on a whiteboard or blackboard. Then ask the participants to come up with a set of guidelines about holding conversations based on what they have developed.

- *Establish comfortable places in your facility where people can talk and reflect.* The current jargon for these is "collaboration zones" and "neighborhoods." Provide collaboration tools such as whiteboards in these zones and neighborhoods.

- *Encourage people to converse by allowing them time to do so.* In many companies conversations are viewed as wasting time, but as we discussed in Chapter 2, even in an e-business environment there are times when you need to slow down so you can move fast and effectively.

- *Reward conversations.* Rewards send an important signal that action preceded by reflection can be more powerful than action alone. The criteria for rewarding productive conversations are likely to be subjective in nature and based on the manager's judgment. Look for some of the following characteristics when evaluating the merits of conversations in the workplace. If the conversations focus on expanding both parties' knowledge of the subject, building on each other's ideas, and generating new ideas, these are corporate IQ enhancing conversations. If, on the other hand, the conversations take the form of arguments and debates that focus on tearing down the other person's ideas, defending an old way of doing a work process, or explaining why a new idea cannot be done, then these are not productive conversations and should not be rewarded.

* *Reward good thinking and unique contributions that result from the conversations.* As we have said repeatedly throughout this book, if you want a characteristic to become a part of your culture, you must recognize and reward it regularly. Rewards can be as simple as public praise, a free day off or a gift certificate.

THE COMPANY THAT CHANGED BY USING CONVERSATION AS ITS LEARNING TOOL

One organization (we will call it Realco) had a "silo" culture for many years. Hoarding information was the norm, and there were many layers of bureaucracy. Individuals within units did not speak with each other, and divisions did not share information. Often more than one division was working on projects that related to the same subject matter, but the divisions were seeking opposing outcomes on the same issue. Then, a new CEO was hired. On his arrival, he announced that the silos were coming down and everyone would work on teams. The managers were not given any training on teamwork, so everyone had differing ideas about what that meant. The company had two locations. At one, the managers simply announced, "Now we're going to work on teams. Here are the issues we'll be working on. Anyone from any division here who is interested in participating on a team related to issue X should arrive at conference room A at 10 a.m. Monday."

What ensued was chaos and a highly frustrating year for everyone involved. Members of the teams never stepped back to develop some common definitions of teamwork or the methods the teams would use. The desired outcome was well known to the employees, but since they had never worked together they did not share a common language about the goals or processes. Further, because they really had never interacted, there was little trust. Because the employees had few interactive skills, the teams never developed cohesion and conflicts were never resolved in a constructive manner. Also, because the group chose team leaders, the division with the greatest representation on the team could manipulate the results. Few of the team leaders were effective. Some individual alliances were formed among the workers, but successes were mostly the result of serendipity.

The work in that location of the company was cyclical, so the managers went back at the beginning of the second year to try again. Fortunately, they had apparently learned from their mistakes and had also had some training, although the staff still remained untrained in any team or interpersonal skills. The managers built on some of the alliances that had formed and took care to appoint team leaders who had shown some skills in leadership and working with others. The managers provided the teams with opportunities for learning conversation by devoting some budget funds to lunches and informal gatherings for the teams. Larger groups of two or three teams from the first year were brought together to discuss what had worked—not much—and what needed to work better—almost everything. These formal and informal conversations helped the workers learn from past mistakes to gain insights into each other's assumptions and behaviors. During the conversations the managers coached the employees and helped them identify counterproductive behavior, thereby enhancing the individual and collective EQ of the teams. By the third year, the team concept was entrenched among the employees and few could imagine any other way to work. The organization was able to meet its goals more frequently and in a less stressful manner.

It is notable that during this period, one senior manager took it upon himself to learn more about effective team management. He took a series of courses, making sure that the employees knew he was working on his own skills. He took this effort very seriously and successfully shed a few of his bad habits. As the employees saw him grow and become a better coach, the tone among the workers improved. The boss seemed more approachable, so the trust level between him and the workers improved. This encouraged the employees to reach out more to each other. Some workers believed that the best barometer of the improved culture at the location was the increase in laughter and banter at staff meetings.

These changes in Realco's culture and its enhanced learning environment illustrate why it is important, even when there is no bottom line impact, to pay attention to building individual and collective EQ and to organizational learning. The workers at Realco came to admire the manager's efforts to lead them, create a learning environment, and coach them for improved performance through EQ skill development. They simply became more effective. The work at the location remained cyclical, and the nature and timing of the cycles did not change. However, worker satisfaction changed and the workers all felt they worked smarter.

TIP

FOR the company to succeed, each individual is responsible for developing their personal EQ. The collective EQ only rises as individuals enhance their own EQ.

You can enhance your company's conversation culture by doing some of the things Realco did:

- Break down some organizational boundaries.
- Provide training on teamwork and interactions to managers and team members.
- Communicate desired outcomes.
- Structure learning conversations around successes, mistakes and behaviors.
- Managers and team leaders coach more than manage.

SHEEP DIP TRAINING IS NOT ADEQUATE ANYMORE

The learning burden increasingly is on the individual. While many companies continue to provide access to training, there is less emphasis on so-called "sheep dip training" in which people all take the same course at the same time in classroom training sessions. Today, corporate America generally understands that frequently the most it can do is encourage workers to prepare for the real learning that takes place on the job. So, there is more self-learning tailored to the individual's current job demands. The next two sections provide examples of self-learning. Management can enhance the company's learning culture by following these examples and by assigning tutors and mentors and by providing learning hardware such as mobile learning stations using computer-based training.

ALTERNATIVES TO SHEEP DIP TRAINING— VIRTUAL LEARNING AND E-LEARNING

Virtual learning and e-learning are the latest trends in corporate learning because of employment dispersion and telecommuting, but they are hardly new concepts. They are essential components of a rapid learning culture. Companies have been using distance learning (e.g., teleconference training for employees in several locations) for years. Now, however, the Web brings new promise, so more and more distance learning, often called virtual or e-learning, is becoming available.

A company can customize its training requirements by creating its own Web site portal with links to customized training packages developed by e-universities and e-vendors.[25]

KPMG Consulting uses a Web portal developed by DigitalThink for increasing their consultants' knowledge and skills. The e-learning portal "contained a pre-test to determine their current knowledge, provided access to white papers and articles, facilitated the shipping of books and CD-ROMs," and a post test which all 8,000 KPMG consultants were required to complete. The portal also providing "tracking and reporting tools for managers and partners to follow their consultants' progress and success.[26]

Net-based programs are now run by 58 percent of American universities. The next major educational start-up appears to be UNext, which is developing an Internet-based interactive higher education institution using a consortium of business schools at Columbia University, University of Chicago, Stanford University, Carnegie Mellon University, and the London School of Economics and Political Science to develop on-line business courses. UNext also has hired Dr. Donald Norman, Professor Emeritus at the University of California, San Diego, and a specialist in psychology and cognitive sciences, to gather the best academic resources in the country. Norman predicted that UNext's student body will be primarily made up of professionals from all over the world seeking to improve their job performance and their "human capital."[27]

Corporations also are heavily involved in running their own universities. The big names in this field are General Electric, Unisys, and FedEx. Corporate Xchange, a New York research and consulting firm, reports that the number of these company-run universities jumped from 400 in 1988 to more than 1,600 in 1999.[28] CSC, a global IT consulting firm, is an example of a company that has devoted

---

[25] Alan S. Kay, "The Truth about Training: pay for IT now or you'll pay for IT later." *Small Business Computing* (April, 2000), 51.

[26] e-Learning Success Stories, "KPMG: Staying in the know at Internet speed," http/www.digitalthink.com/els/client/kpmg2.html.

[27] "School's Out," *Business 2.0* (October, 1999), 30.

[28] Joseph Webber, "School is Never Out," *BusinessWeek* (October 4, 1999), 164-168.

great effort to virtual learning. Chris Malcolm of CSC said, "During the first quarter of this fiscal year alone, a record 41,458 courses were accessed by various CSC employees." Malcolm says CSC uses a "Learning Database" that employees access through Lotus Notes, CD-ROMs, and its CSC Web site. Initially, CSC had 200 computer-based programs to help employees maintain technical currency. CSC in partnership with CBT Systems, a computer-based training firm, developed these programs. By October 1999, the resources had increased to 1,500 courses, some in Spanish, German, Portuguese, and French.[29]

In some companies, a significant driving force for e-learning has been cost. IBM estimated that it saves $400,000 for every 1,000-classroom days that are converted into electronic Web-based training. IBM expects to deliver 30 percent of internal training courses on-line at a cost saving of more than $120 million a year.[30]

The University of Phoenix has 50,000 students at 65 campuses and learning centers in 12 states. It conducts much of its education using distance learning that centers on a culture of collaboration in which students are required (it is not an option) to participate in open-ended question discussions. Terri Hedegaard-Bishop, vice president of distance learning says, "the real learning comes from adults sharing their ideas and perspectives about the subject matter."[31]

WHAT IS HIGH-QUALITY E-TRAINING?

We want to provide a few cautions about the quality of electronic training. Just like bad Web sites (and we have all seen them), e-training can be poorly thought out and constructed. It is essential to provide rapid on-line responses in the form of feedback to the students. For example, when a student completes an assignment or a test they should quickly be notified about how well they did, what they didn't do very

---

[29] Provided by Christine Malcom of CSC in conjuction with an interview with the authors, taken from CSC's Healthcare Group Bulletin.

[30] Ira Sanger, "Inside IBM: Internet Business Machines," *BusinessWeek E-Biz* (December 13, 1999), 20-38.

[31] Ibid., 23.

well, and what else they could do. The Net and e-mail can be used to explain things to students. Using expert on-line tutors and mentors to complement the instructor's work is also helpful to provide on-line references so the student can do just-in-time learning anytime and anywhere. Immediacy and personalization of the feedback and assistance are the critical elements.

University and corporate experience also highlight the importance of learning by doing. Despite the recognition that training is almost always a good thing for workers, managers sometimes are resistant to letting their workers attend training sessions or take time from their formal tasks. To overcome this resistance from management, chemists at Eli Lilly submit "learning proposals" to their managers showing how the training or e-learning opportunities will relate to and facilitate the work on their "current real-world research."[32]

The net cannot do it all. Learning must be supplemented by one-on-one meetings and coaching. On-line courses conducted by the Fordham University Transnational MBA program found that while e-learning may foster community among dispersed participants as they communicate on-line about the course work, the learning actually becomes richer as the on-line students discuss their new discoveries with their colleagues. This is where knowledge management and high IQ intersect. The on-line classroom work and discussion are inevitably enhanced by the one-on-one meetings that happen when discussions spill into hallways and pubs.[33]

Virtual learning also requires a great deal of self-motivation. Some authorities estimated that there is a 70 percent dropout rate from e-learning. Chuck Martin, cyberfuturist and author said, "The flip side of 'learn what you want, where you want' is that the student must be motivated to learn.... When the virtual classroom is open 24 hours, 7 days a week, self-motivation will be needed to get the student in front of the computer and into class."[34]

---

[32] Chuck Martin, *Net Future* (New York: McGraw-Hill, 1999), 55.

[33] Joseph Webber, "School Is Never Out," *BusinessWeek* (October 4, 1999), 164-168.

[34] Chuck Martin, *Net Future* (New York: McGraw-Hill, 1999), 231.

LEARNING BY DOING

Some of the best learning takes place on the job—not in the class-room. Keri Perlson and Ray Yeh, professors at the University of Texas at Austin business school, use the term "stealth learning" to describe learning that is built into the work process.[35] At Dell Computers, on-the-job training for new hires centers on mentors and buddies. Managers also are mentored. Once hired, you do not just settle in at Dell. To ensure quick assimilation, every new employee is given specific performance goals to reach in 30 days. Informal and formal buddy systems pair newbies to vets. Executives host informal monthly chat sessions with small groups of managers to mentor them along.[36]

Dave Barram and Martha Johnson, respectively Administrator and Chief of Staff at the General Services Administration (GSA), the federal government's infrastructure agency, discussed incorporating learning-by-doing training at the agency. Dave Barram described it this way: "What I've been wishing for about eight years now is for hundreds of people to become five-minute seminar givers. Most of us learn by overcoming something, by looking at the guy next to us and saying, 'Hey Charlie, I can't change the colors on this graph. How do you do it?' I can go look at the manual. I could click on Help. But I don't want to do that... So Charlie comes over and says, 'All you do is this, dummy.' And there it is. He's given me a one-minute seminar or a 30-second seminar." Martha Johnson added, "You don't learn the important lessons by passively sitting through traditional training. It's out of date by the time you get back to the workplace, and it's sterile and antiseptic."

MISTAKE LEARNING BECOMES
ACCEPTABLE IN THE CORPORATE CULTURE

A mistake is not the end of the world. Historically, tolerating mistakes has run counter to American management style and practices. Usually workers at any level hesitate to own up to a mistake because they will

---

[35] Gina Imperato, "Time for Zero Time," *net company* (Fall, 1999), 6.
[36] John Byrne, "The Search for the Young and Gifted: Why Talent Counts," *BusinessWeek* (October 4, 1999), 108-116.

likely be punished when their boss hears about it. But mistakes are the basis of learning, and this cover-up mentality does not reinforce a learning culture. It does not have to be this way.

YOU will make mistakes. Count on it. A key quality of a learning company is the ability to discover how you can benefit from the mistakes that occur in the workplace. By sharing mistakes, you will enhance the company's knowledge base. Employees will feel less threatened about taking risks and they will learn from each other.

The US Army has a process in place to learn from its mistakes with its After Action Reviews (AAR) process. It consists of one primary and two subsidiary learning principles:

1. lessons can be learned from mistakes,
2. shared learning is often superior to individual learning, and
3. action learning comes from dynamic on-the-job insights.

The AAR process is used after each Army action.

In the AAR process, officers and enlisted personnel use a specific form to record a description of what happened during a particular action or activity. This illustrates the first value (lessons can be learned from mistakes) of the AAR system. The participants can identify what decisions were made and how the participants used available knowledge to make those decisions. The second value (shared learning is superior to individual learning) arises from discussions by participants about the action and decisions. The process builds collective, shared, and action learning. The third value (dynamic, on-the-job insight) is the immediacy and practicality of the learning opportunity. Authors Thomas H. Davenport and Laurence Prusak described the Army AAR process as a good example of mistake learning. The authors believe that the Army has "an admirable culture that allows for this type of discussion without blame or recrimination."[37]

---

[37] Thomas K. Davenport and Laurence Prusak, *Working Knowledge: How Organizations Manage What They Know* (Boston: Harvard Business School Press, 1998), 171. See also "Learning in the Army," *Knowledge Management* (March, 2000), 47.

The form is simply a record. The important parts of the AAR process are the shared opportunity to identify what caused the mistake, the judgment-free context for the discussion, and the opportunity to plan what needs to take place to keep from repeating the mistake.

WHEN you are conducting or participating in action learning or learning by mistakes, be sure to emphasize both what went well and what went wrong.

A CONVERSATION TOOL FOR DEVELOPING JOB, THINKING, AND EMOTIONAL IQ

Believing that experience can be an excellent teacher, MIT's Center for Organizational Learning developed a tool that is useful in collective learning situations. Analogous to a journal, the tool helps people document a written history of critical events. The journal is structured with two columns. One is for people who participated in an event or were affected by it. In this column, the individuals described the events as they unfolded. The second column is for a team of trained people outside the event to analyze and comment on the events. MIT recommends that this team be composed of a few people who know something about organizational learning and are knowledgeable about the organization. Frequently, the team is drawn from human resources personnel or organizational development and effectiveness coaches.

After both columns are completed, the learning begins. Follow-up is designed to encourage reflection and insights about such things as incidents that went well, those that didn't work out, inefficiencies, scheduling problems, coordinating problems, bureaucracy glitches, and human interaction problems. Small groups discuss the journal. Those discussion participants are not limited to those who worked on the project or event. Others are encouraged to learn from the journals and discussions as well. One company used a journal as a general teaching tool by removing some of the identifying information and then duplicating the edited document and sharing it with other divisions as part of the effort to boost employee skills.[38] By augmenting this organizational learning journal with discussions about EQ behaviors, a company can improve the collective EQ of the company.

YOU MUST BE WILLING TO CHANGE YOURSELF

> You cannot change the system of which you are in command, fundamentally, unless you are changed in the process.[39]

There is hardly a company that is not trying one change initiative after another. Most fail and the company never knows why. One of the reasons is the focus on organizational change and transformation totally ignores the fact that the *people* in the company also have to change.

Unfortunately, almost every change consultant and writer has ignored this obvious fact for the last decade. If you're an informal leader, team leader, manager, or executive working on a change in the company, you must change the way *you* think, the way *you* do your job, and how *you* handle your emotional quotient. *You* have to know how change processes work and how to work them. This requires *you* to be in a state of continual learning, then *you* apply what you have learned *every day* to think more, do your job, and manage your emotional IQ better.

---

[38] Art Kleiner and George Roth, "How to Make Experience Your Company's Best Teacher," In *Harvard Business Review on Knowledge Management* (Boston: Harvard Business School Press, 1998), 137-151. Originally published in September-October 1997, Reprint 97506.

[39] Jerry Rhodes, *Conceptual Toolmaking: Expert Systems of the Mind* (Oxford UK: Basil Blackwell, 1991), 5.

WHEN you encounter resistance to learning and to changes in your company:

- Move or remove people who resist or cannot adapt.
- Provide time and facilities for dialogue and reflection.
- Move from control to leading and pulling people.
- Start small and accumulate small wins.

APPLYING THIS INFORMATION IN YOUR ORGANIZATION

1. How smart is your organization? Do you have a profile of your organization's current level of smarts—job starts, thinking smarts, and emotional smarts? What dollar and people resources are you allocating and spending for individual and collective learning in these three areas?

2. Does your organizational culture inadvertently foster or encourage employees to resist learning, resist changing their behaviors, or resist the changes your company is trying to make?

3. How often do you reward your employees who make mistakes and learn from them?

4. How often is talent and knowledge ignored when talented and knowledgeable employees are not liked? How does your culture respond?

5. Do you have people in your organization who could be more effective and productive if they would manage their emotions and constructively relate to others.

CHAPTER NINE

Linkages and Relationships Outside the Organization: A Cultural Challenge

A uthor Chuck Martin identifies key business practices required for doing business in the net environment. One of the most important of these is creating linkages with other companies. "Buddies everywhere. Partnering with others is a way of life in this arena. Collaboration often replaces make-or-buy decisions."[1] Even without the arrival of the Internet and the wired economy, the volume and speed of change in today's business world would possibly have forced companies to look at their organizational models. Add the Internet, and the pace of business activity increases by a factor of ten. There is no doubt that organizations need to immediately jump to warp speed to survive in the e-business environment. One of the ways companies can do this is by linking with each other and using a wide variety of business models for forging alliances. In this chapter, we describe the different types of alliances that are being tried, give examples of each, and provide you with a road map for the culture implications of the different choices.

---

[1] Chuck Martin, *The Digital Estate: Strategies for Competing, Surviving, and Thriving in a Internet-worked World* (New York: McGraw-Hill, 1997), 21; *Net Future* (New York: McGraw-Hill, 1999), 5.

Nowhere is this jump to warp speed more necessary than in the traditional organizations moving from bricks-and-mortar to clicks-and-mortar. Globalization, mass customization, and the customer-driven net present more opportunities than most organizations can respond to on their own. To take advantage of these opportunities, they are searching for ways to increase their capabilities, markets, and resources. The traditional method for rapidly adding this capacity was mergers and acquisitions, and many companies still use this method to move into or expand their e-business presence. Alliances are a newer model now used more frequently to link with other companies, sometimes even with companies once seen as competitors. Alliances describe several types of relationships that are less permanent than mergers and acquisitions. The alliances discussed in this chapter are:

1. transactions
2. performance contract
3. specialized relationships
4. partnerships

As companies move from a simple transaction model to complex partnership model, they give up more independence and expect the duration of the relationship to be longer.

Alliances of all four types can usually be established in shorter periods of time than it takes to complete a merger/acquisition because there are fewer legal and financial issues to negotiate. Another benefit of creating an alliance is that there is usually more flexibility for ending the relationship if it is no longer required. From the perspective of corporate culture, there is less impact on the culture in the creation of most alliances. There is no intention of combining the two companies completely, so it is usually possible for the two cultures to continue to function separately and simply tolerate the differences when they come in contact with each other.

> Companies have formed partnerships in the Digital Estate for many reasons. One reason is that with such a fast-growth market, the make-or-buy decision is replaced by the benefits of simple teaming. There are simply too many good ideas to buy them all up. [2]

These alliance relationships between companies are not mergers. They fall on a continuum from the least permanent, the transaction, to the most long-term and durable relationship, the partnership. Mergers and alliances are described in this chapter with the cultural challenges that accompany each model.

MERGERS AND ACQUISITIONS: THE TRADITIONAL OPTION IS STILL USED IN A .COM WORLD

Mergers and acquisitions are not new, and business publications and television news programs seem to detail mega-size deals in the banking, telecommunications, utility, and pharmaceuticals industries every month. Mergers and acquisitions are one way organizations answer the question of build or buy to expand capacity or meet the new e-business market opportunities. The total number of mergers and acquisitions taking place cannot be accurately stated because some small or privately held organizations have no reporting requirements but the announced worldwide merger activity for the initial three quarters of 1999 was $2 trillion.[3]

WHY MERGE AND WHAT ARE THE RISKS?

> One of the most important causes for failure or success is really knowing why you want to acquire a company. If you want existing product in a market and the customers it brings, then you don't care about the sales force and all

---

[2] Ibid., 155.
[3] Michael J. Mandel, "All These Mergers Are Great, but…" *BusinessWeek* (October 18, 1999), 48.

these other things. So focus on that and implement well. Don't try to play footsie and con people. It gets down to make, sell, and cash. What am I buying? I think that is where most mistakes are made. People deceive themselves as well as the organization that they are acquiring. They tell the organization that they are acquiring, "We love you. We're going to let you be autonomous." And in some cases, it is just bull.

—*Jim Hammock, Chairman and CEO of Hire.com*

The reasons organizations merge are almost as numerous as the number of organizations that are merging. For example, World-Com, led by CEO Bernard J. Ebbers, acquired the long-distance phone company MCI in 1998. One year later WorldCom acquired Sprint Corporation for $129 billion.[4] These acquisitions were triggered by a technology strategy for becoming the leading supplier of wireless, data, and long-distance services to corporate customers. This was a direct challenge to AT&T, which, led by CEO Michael Armstrong, acquired a local telephone company (Teleport) and two cable television companies (Tele-Communications, Inc., and Media One Group) between January 1998 and May 1999. These acquisitions totaled $121 billion.[5] AT&T is using them to define its position in the global telecommunications market. Through acquisitions MCI WorldCom and AT&T are adding the technologies, skills, and markets needed to move from the highly competitive, cost-sensitive world of long-distance service to a position of offering business and residential customers a total array of services for local, long-distance, data, and wireless telecommunications. Both companies have a history of acquisitions and have had success in blending different technologies to support their business strategies.

So what is the risk? One of the biggest risks companies face when orchestrating a successful merger is combining the organizational

---

[4] Andy Reinhardt, Catherine Yang, and Roger O. Crockett, "The Main Event: Bernie vs. Mike," *BusinessWeek* (October 18, 1999), 32.

[5] Peter Elstrom, "AT&T: The Problems Keep on Coming," *BusinessWeek* (October 18, 1999), 41.

cultures. This task is much more difficult than merging dissimilar technologies, but it is often minimized or ignored when planning an acquisition. Most planning and due diligence focus on financial and legal issues but the culture clashes are often a source of huge problems for the combined companies after the merger.

One of the greatest challenges for AT&T and MCI WorldCom is blending the various cultures of their acquired companies. If these differences are not addressed, they could lead to the unintended loss of key executives and other valuable employees from the acquired organizations. AT&T has more than a 100-year tradition of operating in a highly regulated business that only started to become a competitive marketplace in the late 1960s with the court decision in a case about allowing devices not manufactured by the phone company to be added to their networks. Since that time AT&T's acquisitions have focused on smaller, more nimble organizations with a more entrepreneurial culture. MCI WorldCom will likely experience similar problems. It has a proven record of making acquisitions work, but trying to integrate Sprint, the more traditional organization into the high-flying parent may put their merger skills to the test. In addition to the basic cultural differences, WorldCom has the additional challenge of getting MCI and Sprint to work together after years of in-your-face competition. This rivalry is embedded in the culture of both organizations and will not be easy to leave behind.

THE ODDS ARE AGAINST PULLING OFF A SUCCESSFUL MERGER

Mergers and acquisitions usually are announced with great fanfare, media attention, and high expectations. When the smoke clears and the plans degenerate into work, what is the success rate of mergers/acquisitions? The literature indicates that the results companies hoped to achieve, either financial or operational often are not realized. Harvard Professor Michael Porter studied acquisitions of major companies over a 36-year period and found that more than half of the acquisitions were subsequently divested.[6] A study by McKinsey &

---

[6] Terrace E. Deal and Allan A. Kennedy, *The New Corporate Culture* (Reading, MA: Perseus Books, 1998), 115.

Company found that 61 percent of 116 acquisition programs failed to earn returns larger than the cost of capital involved in the deal.[7] Acquisition Horizons found that of 537 companies studied, more than 40 percent of the companies reported that their acquisitions were unsuccessful or only somewhat successful.[8]

What qualifies as a successful acquisition may be in the eyes of the beholder, but it is safe to say that getting successful long-term results from a merger/acquisition may be no better than fifty-fifty. The story of Thomas T. Stallkamp of Daimler/Chrysler provides some insight into what can go wrong. He was responsible for merging the German-based Daimler-Benz and the United States-based Chrysler Corporation. After a year of trying to blend the two organizations, he was forced to resign. His parting words were, "you can't ignore culture."[9]

Stallkamp ran into many culture clashes between the two companies—travel policies (e.g., who gets to fly first class), establishment of emission-control policy, and labor relations. These issues go to the heart of each organization's corporate culture. This type of cultural conflict has been a key component in the poor track record of many mergers and acquisitions.

THE CULTURE CAN BE A STUMBLING BLOCK

Corporate culture has been present since the first groups banded together to accomplish a common task (e.g., hunting, farming, or defense). Corporate culture is the beliefs of an organization—its values and actions. It makes up the corporate personality and is an accumulation of the organization's shared experiences. The most visible level of the culture is symbols—how the people dress, how they treat each other, how their offices look, and how they use time. During a merger, there can be clashes at all levels of culture.

---

[7] Ibid.

[8] Price Pritchett, *After the Merger: Managing the Shockwaves* (Dallas: Richard D. Irwin, Inc. 1985), 8.

[9] Joanne Muller, "Lessons From a Casualty of the Culture Wars," *BusinessWeek* (November 29, 1999), 198.

The cultural differences of two organizations can lead to conflict even if both groups favored the merger. *BusinessWeek* reported a view of the cultural differences between America Online (AOL) and Time Warner as merger partners shortly after the merger announcement. "The deal-a-minute, scream-until-win culture of AOL is not likely to tolerate the stately pace of a company (Time Warner) whose decision-making arteries are often clogged with consultants and task forces."[10]

A number of these merger culture clashes have occurred in recent years in health care. A typical situation involved the attempt to merge a hospital run by a religious group with a secular, profit-oriented hospital. While both had been successful on their own and provided very high quality patient care, their merger brought many conflicts to the surface. Many of these conflicts were based on the differences in corporate culture. The way the two institutions "do business" differed in areas such as negotiating with vendors, handling of finances, speed of decision-making, and tolerance for risk. The religious hospital was more hierarchical, including strong ties back to the sponsoring religious organization. The people from the two organizations often did not even laugh at the same jokes. In many cases, mergers of organizations with such different cultures do not work. In this case, the merger fell apart in the negotiation phase. But even after the deal is signed, the merger often does not work, and the organizations eventually end up going their separate ways.

MDS, an international health and life science company headquartered in Toronto, has acquired 11 companies in the past five years and has been unusually successful in integrating these companies into the MDS business strategy and culture. The company has also participated in eight joint ventures during the same time frame. Jim Reid, Executive VP of Organizational Dynamics, described their approach:

"When we are considering acquiring a company, our first and most critical test is fit. We look at two kinds of fit. One is fit with our strategy. In other words, it has to make sense from a business perspective. But then even more important is the core

---

[10] Daniel Okrent, "Happy Ever After," *BusinessWeek* (January 24, 2000), 41.

values and management fit. If the values and management fit is not there, we generally do not make the acquisition unless the company has a technology or critical strength that we need. In that case, we recognize the requirement to make a quick leadership change. At MDS, we like to say that our biggest challenge is not people, it is the *right* people. That means that sometimes you have to make tough people decisions that are right for long term business success."

WHAT HAPPENS WHEN A MERGER IS ANNOUNCED?

Mergers increase tension and unrest for everyone involved. From a cultural perspective, this means that the atmosphere in each organization is under great strain. Because of this, the cultures do not necessarily function at their best when they come into contact with each other.

Psychological Dynamics of a Merger

- Ambiguity
- Weakening of the Trust Level
- Focus on Self Preservation[11]

In an environment dominated by this atmosphere, employees typically have a whole series of reactions. Author Price Pritchett identified the following employee reactions that often occur in organizations after an impending merger is announced.[12]

- Communication deteriorates
- Productivity suffers
- Momentum suffers
- Parochialism increases
- Team play deteriorates
- Power struggles occur

---

[11] Price Pritchett, *After the Merger: Managing the Shockwaves* (Dallas: Richard D. Irwin, Inc. 1985), 42-44.

[12] Ibid., 46-52.

- Commitment is lost
- Employees bail out

The negative effects on employee behavior can cause serious problems. If the acquiring company fails to respond to employee concerns in a way that gives them hope that the new company will be a good place to work, there can be serious fallout. The reasons for purchasing the company may be lost if there is an exodus of skilled people, a disruption in production or service, or a decrease in customer satisfaction.

DO MERGERS REALLY EXIST OR ARE THEY ALL REALLY ACQUISITIONS?

> I don't believe mergers of equals work.
> —*John Chambers, CEO of Cisco Systems*[13]

No matter how the press releases define the merger/acquisition or how executives from both organizations explain it, in almost all cases one organization purchases another. It may not be politically wise to word it that way when talking with board members or the press, but in reality that is what happens. There are very few examples of successful mergers of equals. The usual model is for the acquiring company to place its people in key positions and install its procedures and systems. This means that in most cases one culture prevails over the other after the acquisition.

THE DIFFERENT WAYS TO DEAL WITH CULTURE AFTER THE MERGER

From a culture perspective, there are three possible patterns in an acquisition. Edgar H. Schein, author of *The Corporate Culture Survival Guide*, described the three options a company can implement as:

---

[13] Henry Goldblatt, "Cisco's Secrets," *Fortune* (November 8, 1999), 17.

1. keeping separate cultures after the merger
2. the acquiring company dominates and absorbs the other culture
3. blending cultures as an attempt to retain the best of both cultures. [14]

The first two options usually happen after an acquisition, but the third option is usually what the company announces it is going to do.

I. KEEPING SEPARATE CULTURES AFTER THE MERGER

In this case, the two cultures remain separate, (i.e., a subsidiary that retains its separate identity). IBM's acquisition of Lotus is a example of an acquiring company recognizing the value of allowing a purchased company to remain separate rather than absorb it and risk losing the creative Lotus culture. In 1995, IBM purchased Lotus Development for $3.5 billion. IBM senior management made a concerted effort to reassure the people at Lotus Development that they would be supported but left to work on their own.

An amusing incident about the first meeting between IBM and Lotus leadership demonstrated the difference in cultures and the efforts both companies made to be respectful of the other's culture. IBM Senior Vice President, John Thompson, came to the meeting dressed in a T-shirt and jeans, not the usual IBM garb. The normally casual Lotus contingent showed up wearing what they assumed was expected at an IBM meeting: the traditional blue suits and ties. During the merger process, there certainly was skepticism on the part of Lotus employees, and some people did leave. But five years later Lotus still maintained the dual benefit of operating separately and at the same time having IBM's support with marketing, sales, and resources. As Marjorie Tenzer of Lotus put it: "they allow us to play in our space."[15]

---

[14] Edgar H. Schein, *The Corporate Culture Survival Guide: Sense and Nonsense about Cultural Change* (San Francisco: Jossey-Bass, 1999), 176.

[15] Stephanie Armour, "IBM, Lotus Transcend Often-Fatal Culture Clash," *USA Today* (March 26, 1998), 2.

2. THE ACQUIRING COMPANY DOMINATES
AND ABSORBS THE OTHER CULTURE

In this case, the acquiring company intentionally dominates and absorbs the other company's culture as quickly as possible. The goal is to create one seamless culture that looks very much like the acquiring company's culture.

IBM's success with the Lotus acquisition shows that companies can learn from experience. When IBM purchased the ROLM phone company in 1985, the blending of cultures did not go smoothly. In this case, IBM's intention was to absorb the other company's culture, but it never was able to make that happen. If there was any discussion at any stage about the cultural differences between the 70-year-old Armonk, New York-based IBM and the 15-year-old Santa Clara, California-based ROLM, it was lost in the execution when the two started working together. In 1985, as ROLM prepared to launch a new phone system, IBM sent large numbers of its staff to Santa Clara to run the product launch. The IBM employees were dedicated, skilled, and extremely professional, but their skills and experience were in selling large mainframe computers in a nearly monopolistic environment. This experience was in sharp contrast to the Rolmans, as they called themselves. They saw themselves as street fighters succeeding against giants such as AT&T and Northern Telecom (Nortel Networks).

The clash of cultures showed in a number of ways. The new system had a faster central processing unit (CPU) than the older models and a much larger memory. These improvements did not have the same selling power in the phone business as they did in the mainframe market. The IBM staff on the task force had a hard time understanding that some customers were happy with their existing phone systems and would not trade them for one with a faster CPU and more memory.

On the local level, these differences showed up in symbolic ways. ROLM repair technicians were assigned company vehicles, while IBM technicians at the same location were not given cars. At one location the IBM personnel manager assigned to ROLM did not invite the ROLM employees to the IBM company picnic because they were not IBM "heritaged." Many similar conflicts occurred at all levels between the two organizations until IBM finally sold ROLM to Siemens. The acquisition did not live up to expectations, and cultural differences clearly played a role in the disappointing outcome.

Successful Examples of an Acquiring Company Absorbing the Other Culture

On a more positive note, some of the most successful acquisitions were ones where the acquiring culture dominated and absorbed the culture of the purchased company. Cisco Systems is famous for its skill in acquiring large numbers of companies and succeeding with most of these transitions. Cisco's approach is detailed later in this chapter.

Acxiom Corporation also has a successful track record of acquiring and absorbing the other company's culture. It acquired nine companies within four years, and like Cisco Systems, Acxiom has learned to move fast. In the past, Acxiom set a two-year time line for integrating the new company into the fold but found that two years was too long and important issues would drag on instead of being resolved. The company shortened the process to ten months or less, and it seems to work better. Clear objectives and time lines for implementation were set to convert the newly acquired company to the Acxiom way. Charles Morgan, Acxiom's leader (he does not use the term CEO), personally delivers the training for the new leaders joining the company; they hear directly from him about the way Acxiom operates and what is expected in this culture.

One story the Acxiom people tell illustrates how they balance a determination to create one seamless culture and at the same time make an effort to be sensitive in how they implement this strategy. Pete Hoelscher and Cindy Childers explained that they usually move fast on items such as replacing old signage with the new Acxiom signs. But in one case they did not do this. The company Acxiom had purchased had been in existence for several decades, and many employees were long tenured and very loyal. In addition the company founder was on his deathbed at the time of the acquisition. Hoelscher and Childers pointed out, "We waited for months before we changed things like the signs on their buildings. We wouldn't have gained anything by changing these things, and it would have caused a lot of harm." As this story points out, the route of absorbing the culture of the purchased company can be chosen without being callous or disrespectful about it.

HOW to absorb the culture of an acquired organization in a way that creates the minimum amount of resistance.

- The leadership of the acquiring organization needs to clearly state their philosophy, vision, missions, and goals—tell everyone directly that this will be the culture of the newly combined company.

- Think carefully about the timing for changing the symbols, the dress code, the signs, the letterhead, the business cards, and employee ID badges. In most cases you will want to do it immediately.

- Assign mentors, coaches, and assistance teams to help the employees of the acquired organization understand the new business systems and processes.

- From the first day, have welcome packets explaining the new benefits, vacations, rules, and expectations.

- Take care not to minimize the contributions of employees from the acquired company.

- Encourage your employees to make an effort to get to know the people from the acquired company and make them feel welcome.

- Get employees from the acquired company involved in figuring out how to handle the changes such as different technologies, customers, and products.

3. BLENDING CULTURES IS AN ATTEMPT
TO RETAIN THE BEST OF BOTH CULTURES

Blending cultures is an admirable goal but rarely works. It is very difficult to do and may take a longer time than the senior managers or Wall Street are willing to spend. In some cases, the senior management teams blend by having the CEO come from one company and the president from the other. But this practice is as likely to produce infighting as it is to produce a blended culture. To create a truly blended culture, it is necessary to create a new common mission and start developing common values about everything from customer service to employee benefits. It is possible to do so, but again it is important to stress that this is a very slow and time-consuming process unless the two companies had similar cultures before the acquisition.

There is a case of two technology organizations merging to use their strength to compete with IBM in the large computer market. Their aim was to create a new blended culture so they began by creating a new name and a new logo to help with this blending process. But five years later, the employees still identified themselves with their previous company. In fact, they even continued to use the old forms and letterhead of the old organizations internally, because "they had left over paper."

The creation of a blended culture is easy to talk about, but in reality it is difficult to achieve. In almost all cases, over time, one culture will become dominant. Many times companies claim that they intend to blend the best of both cultures, but when you investigate the reality of what actually happened, one culture dominated.

CHOOSING AN OPTION: SEPARATE, DOMINATE, OR BLEND

The cultural challenges make mergers/acquisitions a high-risk proposition. The risks must be reduced as much as possible by clearly thinking through your plan for handling the purchased company's culture. You can choose to separate, absorb, or blend. There are different benefits and problems with each. If it is possible in the political climate you are facing at the time of the merger, tell people which approach you are taking. Do not confuse employees by saying your goal is a blended culture when you really are planning to absorb their culture in due time. This mixed message leads to unnecessary conflict among employees at all levels during the transition and damages trust in the long run.

Your business strategy is the determining factor for which approach to take in dealing with the culture of an acquired company. Why did you buy the company? Did you want its customer base, its products or technology, or its talented employees? If you purchased this company for valuable customers who are loyal to the acquired company, you may want to keep the cultures separate so the customers see no change at all. Any disruption from the customers' perspective could cause them to discontinue their business relationship with the newly merged company and destroy the value of the acquisition. If, on the other hand, you purchased the company for its product or technology, it may make much more sense to absorb their culture as rapidly as possible. The more integrated all the production and distribution processes are, the more likely you are to profit from your new combined products and technology. If you purchased the company for their talent pool, do not do anything that will anger those employees and cause them to leave. If they loved the old company, leave it alone. If they were disgruntled and disillusioned with their old employer, absorb them quickly into your company culture and promise them a new and better era. If those talented employees see pros and cons of both companies, then get them involved in helping you figure out how to blend cultures to retain the best of both. The most important advice on this issue is start with your business strategy. Choose what you do with the culture of the acquired company—separate, absorb, or blend—based on which approach is most likely to produce the results you were looking for when you bought the company.

MERGING AT .COM SPEED

The need for speed exists in all aspects of e-business, including the way companies acquire other companies. Interactive marketing company CMGI made a bid to buy FLYCAST, an on-line advertising network, but one condition was the deal must be completed in four days. After an all-night negotiation session, the $900 million deal was done.[16] In the .com world the battle is for capacity and mind share. If CMGI were to allow FLYCAST to delay the acquisition, other companies might enter the bidding resulting in a feeding frenzy with the companies rushing to stake out their market position and product content.

Mergers and acquisitions among .com companies happen at the speed of light compared to those in the traditional world in which the negotiations, due diligence, and other activities can take a year or longer. The fact that the companies often are buying concepts or "mind share" makes .com mergers unique. Many companies involved are in the early stages of their start-up, and this lack of history makes the speed easier.

HOW to determine the speed with which you are likely to be able to negotiate mergers. The more established a company is in these characteristics, the longer it is likely to take to negotiate the merger and to create a common culture after the deal is completed.

- Does the company you are merging/acquiring have an existing product line?

- Have they already delivered products and have a customer base?

- Have they been in existence long enough to have developed a strong culture?

---

[16] Bethany McLean, "Merging at Internet Speed," *Fortune* (November 8, 1999), 164.

CISCO SYSTEMS: AN ACQUISITIONS SUCCESS STORY

Cisco Systems, provides an excellent example for how to do a merger/acquisition in .com time. During a six-year period, Cisco acquired 42 companies for $18.8 Billion. Cisco is the epitome of an organization operating at net speed. Cisco's model for choosing its acquisition targets is one that can be copied by traditional companies. One objective for Cisco's acquisitions is to fill holes in its product line or support entry into new markets. The company also uses the process to find technical talent in an environment where recruitment is very competitive. One of the things that distinguishes Cisco when it considers an acquisition is the importance the company places on the cultural fit between Cisco and the acquisition target.

> Cisco's strategy can be boiled down to five things. We look at a company's vision, its short-term success with customers, its long-term strategy, the chemistry of the people with ours, and its geographic proximity.[17]

Even at the speed Cisco moves in making acquisitions, the company thoroughly evaluates the organizations it is interested in acquiring. If only four of the five elements on its checklist are present, Cisco approaches the acquisition with caution. If only three elements are present, it walks away from the deal.

During the evaluation phase, Cisco uses a team approach for the review. Engineers evaluate technology, while the finance group reviews the books. Cisco's evaluation model is based on the present technology, projections of future technology, and the strength and depth of the acquired company's talent. Cisco looks for companies that are new in their life cycle and privately held. It searches for a company with a finished and tested product but no customer base.

---

[17] Henry Goldblatt, "Cisco's Secrets," *Fortune* (November 8, 1999), 178 (quoting Mike Volpe of Cisco Systems).

In its experience, more mature companies require a longer period of time to integrate into Cisco after the deal is closed.

Since Cisco is buying talent as well as technology, it leaves nothing to chance when integrating the acquired organization into the Cisco way. Cisco's dedicated integration team is on site with the company being acquired from the start of the negotiations until the integration is in place (usually 30 days). On the first day after the acquisition, the employees arrive at their office to find the Cisco name on the building and other Cisco touches down to the bottled water in the break rooms.[18]

By just about any measure you could apply, the majority of Cisco's acquisitions have been successful, even from the view of personnel in the acquired companies. Cisco's strategy is to build a corporate culture to which people want to belong. Its strength is that it welcomes the people from the acquired companies and values their contributions. The employees of the acquired company know they must leave their old culture behind, but they also know they are joining a great company that welcomes them.

If traditional bricks-and-mortar companies pay as much attention to the issue of culture as Cisco, Acxiom, or IBM/Lotus have done, they will likely have a success rate for mergers that is higher than the average 50 percent. One challenge for a traditional organization is reducing the time required to complete a merger/acquisition that is needed to increase resources, add products, or meet competitive threats. This time lag is even harder to overcome when the merger occurs between two established organizations with products and customers.

CREATING ALLIANCES: ANOTHER OPTION

Alliances of all types are not new to business organizations, but they have become more important in the past few years. To meet the speed requirements for the .com economy and avoid some of the risks of acquisitions, alliances are an alternative worth serious consideration.

---

[18] Ibid., 180.

The key is to be aware that the options exist, choose carefully what best meets your needs, and communicate your objectives clearly to the company with whom you are trying to link.

Many people informally call any business relationship a partnership and do not distinguish between different types of relationships they may be establishing. This lack of precision can lead to misunderstandings and conflicts. In this section we describe four different categories of alliances and consider the culture implications of each option. Examples of each are:

1. Transactions: Buying a product at a Web site.
2. Performance Contract: Contracting with a company to develop a Web site for your company.
3. Specialized Relationship: Working with a retail Web company to advertise your products on its site.
4. Partnership: Owning a 50 percent share in an Internet company.

If you decide which version you are trying to establish with another company, it will help you to avoid the misunderstandings that can occur when two parties use the same words but mean very different things. For example, you might think you are in a partnership with another company and ask for some special help because of unforeseen circumstances. If your partner checks the contract and then turns down your request while referring to a specific contract clause that justifies their refusal, you do not have a partnership. You only have a performance contract with that company. If you think you have a partnership and the other company thinks it has a performance contract, you have a set-up for trouble.

ALLIANCES ARE NOT NEW TO THE .COM WORLD

In many industries, companies have been forming alliances for years before e-business entered the scene. The newspaper industry is an example of this. Newspapers have formed consortiums with wire services to expand news coverage. Because alliances are a part of the newspaper culture, expanding this model is not the leap it might be for other organizations.

> We feel it is critical to create partnerships and market-places that are compelling for customers. Partnerships extend our reach into niche and diverse marketplaces.
> —*Judy Kallet, Chief Information Officer of Los Angeles Times*

FOUR TYPES OF ALLIANCES

This section draws heavily on the work of John C. Henderson of the Systems Research Center at Boston University.[19] He looks at alliances as a series of relationships that reside on a continuum (Figure 9.1) rather than existing in only one form. The type of alliances is determined by two primary factors: the amount of independence each organization retains and the length or duration of the relationship. In all of the alliances, there is a trust requirement. The farther out on the continuum you go toward partnership, the more unconditional the trust becomes and the more merging of cultures will be required.

Figure 9.1: Relationship Portfolio

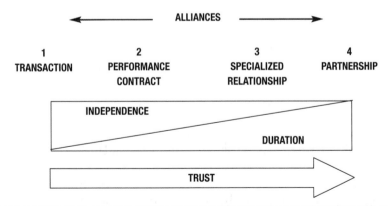

Based on a concept by John C. Henderson, "Plugging into Strategic Partnerships," *Sloan Management Review* (Spring 1990), 14.

---

[19] John C. Henderson, "Plugging into Strategic Partnerships," *Sloan Management Review* (Spring 1990), 14.

1. TRANSACTIONS

Transactions are the simplest form of relationship. The participants retain their independence, and the duration may be measured in minutes. The rules for participating in a transaction are well defined and fairly rigid. The type of transaction that we are most familiar with is the retail transaction. When you stop at a convenience store to pick up milk, you are participating in a transaction. You give up no independence and are out of there in a few minutes. This is a nonspecific process (i.e., it could take place at any number of locations, and the amount of expertise required is low). The trust is based on the belief that both parties will respond in a legal and ethical manner. The cultural component includes the greetings and any discussion you have with the sales clerk. It may seem almost scripted. You use a similar conversation every time you stop for milk.

This same type of exchange exists in the .com world. For example, when a company buys books from Amazon .com, both companies expect to maintain their independence and expect the contract duration to be brief. The company ordering the books trusts Amazon.com to deliver the order. And Amazon expects the other company to pay the bill. It is a simple transaction that may or may not be repeated in the future. The cultures of the two organizations are relatively unimportant in this type of alliance.

2. PERFORMANCE CONTRACT

As you move out on the relationship continuum, you become involved in a performance contract. In this case, you give up some independence, and the duration is longer. The relationship usually lasts for the length of the contract. If your organization contracts with another organization to create your Web site but not run it, you are establishing a specific performance contract with the Web design company. The group you contract with to develop your Web site has expertise in this area, but its expertise is not specific to your organization. The same design team could use their skill to design the Web site for many other companies. By contracting with this type of organization, you can add to your Web capabilities in a very short time period without permanently owning the capability. You trust your supplier to get the job done no matter what and the supplier's expectation is that you pay its bill in a timely manner. In this type of alliance, the two cultures of the companies begin to come into contact. They must have similar standards of fairness and business ethical practices, or they will run into conflicts.

An example of a performance contract is the work done by a Web design company called OnTargetInternet.com in Austin, TX that provides services in graphic design, printing, and creating Web sites. Organizations that want to increase the visibility on the Web but are not interested in adding the necessary skills to full-time staff will contract with this company to design and launch their Web site. The duration of the relationship will be the time defined in the contract, in this case a few weeks. Each party will retain their independence except where the terms of the contract are concerned. The performance contract is that the design company will perform the necessary design and technical functions to create the Web site. The client's responsibility in the contract is to provide the necessary content information and pay the amount required by the contract.

3. SPECIALIZED RELATIONSHIP

This type of relationship is used more frequently than in the past. An example is a .com retail company entering into a specialized relationship with a company such as FedEx to handle the shipping for the .com company. The .com company benefits from this arrangement by increased speed in product delivery and not having to buy trucks to do the shipping. The shipping company benefits from the alliance by becoming the sole provider of shipping for the .com company. Both companies can expand their business without moving away from their areas of competencies and resources. The customer also benefits from this relationship; receiving products is easier and more convenient.

Another example of a specialized relationship is the one between Wal-Mart and Brunswick Corporation. Brunswick is an old-line manufacturing company that produces sporting goods equipment ranging from bowling balls to top-line SeaRay boats. For Brunswick, the Web allows it to form alliances with retail partners to put its products on the retailer's Web site. "Content alliances and marketing alliances are very, very important," states Bob Sell, Brunswick CIO. Brunswick is positioning its products on a Web site controlled by Wal-Mart. Some companies would have difficulty with this sharing of control because it would be counter to their traditional corporate cultures, but Wal-Mart and Brunswick have made it work.

Wal-Mart and Brunswick have done a good job of avoiding channel conflicts by placing the Brunswick products on the Wal-Mart Web site. There have been cases where manufactures have started offering their products directly over the Web in direct competition with the retail outlets that have traditionally carried their products. If a company that makes athletic shoes starts offering their products directly to consumers over the Web and bypassing their traditional retail sales vendors, this can create conflicts. A business decision needs to be made to determine whether the manufacturer is willing to risk losing business to their retail customers by going direct to the consumer over the Web.

The trust involved in a specialized relationship requires both organizations to share information on internal processes. This strong linkage allows them to increase their capabilities and cover additional markets in much less time. Many elements of the two cultures come into play in a specialized relationship (e.g., behaviors, policies, and standards of performance). If the two cultures are dissimilar on many of these traits, the two companies will have difficulty working together and building trust.

4. PARTNERSHIPS

The term partnership became a business buzzword in the 1990s and many people use it to describe any business relationship or alliance that exists, but there are very few true partnerships because they are difficult to sustain over time. For a partnership to work, both parties have to give up much of their independence. Both groups must see themselves as being involved in something unique and expect the duration of the relationship to be very long or permanent. An example of a partnership is the alliance between Chase Manhattan's Chase.com and the on-line procurement vendor Intelisys Electronic Commerce LLC. Chase owns half of the company, and it plans to launch a business-to-business purchasing community. In this case, each organization gives up independence and expects the relationship's duration to extend past the date on any contract.[20]

In a partnership, the cultural issues are similar to those faced in a merger/acquisition. A partnership is intended to be long term or permanent and large segments of the two companies must work together seamlessly. The portions of the companies that must work together at the partnership level must either have similar cultures, or they must make the same decisions as companies that are merging (i.e., stay separate, one culture absorbs, or blend the two cultures). There are many legal, financial, and political reasons that impact a company's choice of whether to set up a partnership or negotiate a full merger. In the .com world, speed and flexibility are two of the overriding reasons that companies are opting for partnership arrangements more often than in the past.

FACTORS DETERMINING THE SUCCESS OF ALLIANCES

Six factors determine the likely success of an alliance. The first three factors affect the long-term chances of success and the last three factors how well day-to-day actions unfold.

FACTORS AFFECTING THE LONG-TERM SUCCESS OF ALLIANCES

1. Mutual Benefit

There is some level of mutual benefit in all four types of relationships—transactions, performance contract, specialized relationships, and partnerships—but it is most important in a partnership. Both

---

[20] "Chase Manhattan Forges E-Business Alliance," *Information Week* (October 18, 1999), 209.

organizations must clearly identify the mutual benefit, and it must be consistent with the business strategies and cultures of both parties.

2. Commitment

The contract in a transaction is a social contract rather that a formal one. As you enter into the other types of alliances, the negotiations become more important. Each organization discovers the capabilities and wants of the other group. When you are involved in a partnership, the contract becomes less important because of the lack of independence and the duration of the relationship. There is a mutual commitment that focuses on mutual benefits for both parties.

3. Predisposition

This is another word for core values and underlying beliefs, which is the most important cultural characteristic. Some people and organizations are predisposed to believe in doing everything on their own. The individual approach is deeply embedded in American culture, so this core value is quite common in US companies. If an organization is predisposed against relationships, creating an alliance still may be possible, but it makes the effort more difficult.

FACTORS AFFECTING DAY-TO-DAY ACTIONS IN ALLIANCES

4. Shared Knowledge

To be effective in an alliance, both groups must be willing to share knowledge about their processes, markets, customers, and plans. The farther out on the continuum toward partnership, the more knowledge you must share. In some specialized relationships and partnerships, it is difficult to tell where one organization ends and the other begins.

5. Distinctive Competencies and Resources

If your organization has a world-class manufacturing capability, you likely will not partner with an organization possessing the same skills. This is one of the primary reasons alliances and mergers take place. You align yourself with someone that has a *complementary* skill such as product design or marketing. Many of the new .com companies are creating alliances with traditional organizations to do their shipping and inventory control. Much of the work of making an alliance (or merger) work is developing the processes, systems, and joint cultural behaviors and habits to create a seamless operation. If you have conflicting cultures or do not make clear to employees whether you are using the separate, absorb, or blend strategy to the culture, you are likely to have a difficult time creating this seamless operation. People need to know whose culture dominates or which procedures, rules, and customs will be used in the future. If they are not told, they will defend their own histories and you will have endless turf battles rather than a smooth running operation that can capitalize on both sets of skills.

6. Organizational Linkage

These are the social linkages between the individuals involved in the alliance. Do they play sports together? Do they socialize with each other away from the work environment? Have they formed some type of social contact? In a virtual world, creating organizational linkages may be more difficult for the alliance. To work on a day-to-day basis, the groups must find some way to build relationships with each other.

THE E-BUSINESS WORLD REQUIRES THE FULL RANGE OF RELATIONSHIPS

Because the pace of business is increasing daily and there are more opportunities than any one organization can handle, it is essential that a faster, more flexible way to expand capacity be found. Mergers and acquisitions are certainly one option, but few companies can handle them with the success of Cisco Systems. Most companies need to hone their skills for developing all types of relationships described in this chapter. No organization will survive in isolation in the connected workplace. Learning to link up and make all these relationships work will help traditional organizations respond to the market opportunities in .com time.

APPLYING THIS INFORMATION IN YOUR ORGANIZATION

Below are questions to ask to determine how receptive your company's culture is to mergers/acquisitions or alliances.

1. Has your organization used mergers and acquisitions to expand its e-business capabilities? If so, was it successful?

2. Would you classify your organization as a "go it alone" type of organization?

3. Does senior management consider alliances as an asset or a necessary evil?

4. Does your organization have a corporate culture that supports openness and a willingness to share information with organizations when you enter alliances?

5. Does your organization understand that a clash of corporate cultures can derail a merger or partnerships? Does it look for culture fit as one of the important factors in making a merger or partnership work?

CHAPTER TEN

Leading the Journey to the Wired Enterprise

THE LEADER AS CULTURE CARRIER

Can today's leaders of traditional companies respond to the speed of the .com world? There are two primary roles that leaders must play in the transition from bricks-and-mortar to e-business. First, they must lead the organization in the creation of the new e-business strategy. Then they must lead the transition to a new corporate culture that supports this strategy. These are huge challenges. Are today's leaders up to the task? The probable answer is some leaders will succeed and others will fail. This chapter provides a road map of practical suggestions for succeeding in leading the transition to a new corporate culture that supports the e-business strategy.

Technology isn't always the hang-up. In some cases, it's a stodgy corporate culture. "For many older executives, converting to e-business is like changing their religion. —*John Thorp, Vice President of DMR Consulting Group, Inc.*[1]

---

[1] Steve Hamm and Marcra Stepanek, "From Reengineering to E-engineering Companies," *BusinessWeek* (March 22, 1999), 14.

Leaders are the most influential culture carriers in the organization. The leader's core beliefs and actions set the tone for the entire company. When a new CEO with a very different personality comes into a company, the culture almost always changes in response to the new person's leadership. If the new CEO does not convince the organization to change, his tenure usually is not long. Cultural fit between the CEO and the organization must develop. Without it, a strong culture that provides clear and consistent guidelines for employees cannot exist. Without those clear guidelines, it is unlikely that the company can accomplish its business strategy. Efforts are too fragmented with people pulling in too many different directions. The transition to e-business and Internet speed can only be accomplished with direct intervention by the formal leadership team.

Look at the current culture of companies to determine who is likely to succeed in leading this transition and who will fail. There are organizations which have been in existence for years with cultures that reward risk taking, teamwork, and autonomous decision-making (some examples mentioned in this book are Schwab, Acxiom, 3M, Southwest Airlines, Nike, Computer Sciences Corporation). These company leaders already get it. Their cultures are primed for the changes required to transition into a warp speed e-business culture. The journey to the wired enterprise will be much easier because they already have a .com-like culture. Their current leaders are responsible for having taken the company in this direction. Therefore, these leaders probably have the skills and mind-set needed to lead the company through the rest of the journey.

DEFINING LEADERSHIP IN THE E-BUSINESS ARENA

A cursory survey of bookstores reveals that the topic of leadership is one of the largest categories. There may be more words currently in print about leadership than about any other business topic. According to Warren Bennis and Burt Nanus, authors of *Leaders*, there were more than 350 definitions of leadership in 1985[2] and since their book

---

[2] Warren Bennis and Burt Nanus, *Leaders: Strategies for Taking Charge* (New York: Harper & Row, 1985), 4.

was written, the number of definitions has probably increased dramatically. A check of a library database identified 1,000 books or articles on leadership published in 1999 alone.

Whether all these books and articles actually inspire more frequent and skillful practice in the art of leadership is unknown. Consider the man who owns every book written on stretching. He loves to put on his jogging suit, lie on the couch, and read books about stretching, but that did not make him limber or flexible. Reading books on stretching or leadership may provide a good education on the topics, but the goal is to become a practitioner of the subject rather than a theoretician. Virtually any definition of leadership focuses on the practical activities of leading an organization and that is particularly true in the Internet-driven business world.

THE DIFFERENCE BETWEEN LEADERSHIP IN TRADITIONAL COMPANIES AND THE .COM WORLD

Leadership in traditional bricks-and-mortar organizations tends to be recognized only at the most senior levels of the organization in the form of official positions with clear titles and authority. The informal leadership that occurs at all levels in the e-business environment often was not recognized or encouraged in the past. This formal leadership was a keystone of the industrial revolution era of business and industry that existed for more than a century. The work of Fredrick Winslow Taylor and proponents of his scientific management views were a classic example of the thinking that dominated companies during that era.[3] In his view, work was based only on efficiency and increased production rates, and it was this concept that resulted in time and motion studies of work tasks. Traditional organizations historically have operated with a command and control, hierarchical structure where decision-making is consolidated as high up in the organization as possible. It was not considered desirable for workers to think or make independent decisions. They were strictly expected to do as they were told. Even though few companies today would

[3] Fredrick Winslow Taylor, *The Principles of Scientific Management* (New York: Dover Publishers, 1998) reprint from original publication in 1911.

claim to still follow these beliefs to this extreme, there is a cultural residue that remains in many traditional companies. Front-line employees are reluctant to take action because their actions will probably be second-guessed. Often there is the perception among employees that you will not be rewarded if you take a risk and are successful, but you are very likely to be reprimanded for a failure. Risk taking and independent thinking is discouraged. Historically, this type of organization was considered to be well suited to a stable environment. Leaders in well-run organizations of this era often functioned as benevolent dictators.

With the arrival of the Internet and the .com workplace, the industrial revolution's Taylorian model of leadership is rapidly being abandoned. The fluid nature and the speed of .com companies require leadership and responsibility to be shared and pushed to the lowest levels of the organization. Leadership is no longer a job title at the senior level of the organizational chart, it is a role, both formal and informal, that individuals play at all levels and in all parts of the organization. The speed of business activity in the .com world makes it impossible for all decisions to be controlled by a few people at the top of the hierarchy. The fact the e-business environment is driven by information and constant innovation means that all workers must be empowered to use their skills and knowledge to make decisions and take risks on a daily basis. In the case of remote workers or employees in direct contact with the customer, speed is particularly important. They no longer can afford to take the time to clear every customer decision with the managers above them in the organization, or the business opportunities are lost to competitors who are ready to act quickly. In the .com world leadership is everyone's responsibility.

TIP CHANGE your definition of leadership in your organization. If your company still carries the remnants of the old command and control leadership with a few formal leaders at the top, you need to change this mind-set as quickly as possible.

- Change your language about leaders in all written and spoken settings. Start using terminology that includes leaders at all levels—informal leaders, team leaders, and front-line leaders as well as formal leaders.

- Identify front-line or supervisory level people who take on leadership roles in teams or work units and turn them into corporate heroes by publicizing their actions, giving them high status assignments, and including them in decision-making groups that advise senior management on company-wide issues.

- Give project teams clear instructions on goals, provide them with the resources they need to get the job done, and get out of their way. Let them make their own implementation decisions without having to ask permission at every step along the way. Have periodic update sessions to keep senior management informed, but they should not have constant control over approval of all decisions.

Eight Key Activities of E-Business Leadership that Shape the Culture

Core Activities
Broadcasting the Guiding Principles
Creating a Vision

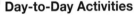

Day-to-Day Activities
Paying Attention to the Right Things
Reacting to Bad News
Allocating Resources
Being a Role Model
Rewarding the Right People
Using Influence More and Power Less

CORE ACTIVITIES OF A LEADER THAT SHAPE THE CULTURE

BROADCASTING THE GUIDING PRINCIPLES

 In many systems, scientists now understand that order and conformity and shape are created not by complex controls, but by the presence of a few guiding principles.[4]

Broadcasting the guiding principles of the organization constantly is one of the most important activities of all leaders in the organization. These guiding principles are the organization's internal compass. If the leaders successfully communicate these, everyone knows what to do without having to constantly ask for guidance or permission. An example of guiding principles exists at investment firm Charles Schwab, which identifies its values as "fairness, empathy, teamwork, and responsiveness, constantly striving to be worthy of our customers' trust."[5]

This emphasis on communicating the guiding principles is particularly important in an e-business culture because of the need for speed and independent decision-making. If the guiding principles are well defined and communicated so that they become the way the organization does business on a routine basis then employees will have a compass to guide them without detailed management directions. In the case of Charles Schwab the values have been developed and communicated throughout the organization so that all employees know what those values are and can explain what they mean in terms of daily actions.

This book provides many examples of leaders skilled at communicating the guiding principles. Amazon.com CEO, Jeff Bezos personally takes the message out to the employees, repeating the "customer-obsessed" theme everywhere he goes. Acxiom's Charles

---

[4] Margaret J. Wheatley, *Leadership and the New Science: Learning About Organization from an Orderly Universe* (San Francisco: Berrett-Koehler Publishers, 1992), 11.

[5] David S. Pottruck and Terry Pearce, *Clicks-and-Mortar: Passion Driven Growth in an Internet Driven World* (San Francisco: Jossey-Bass, 2000), 13.

Morgan set clear goals for the 100-Days Project and created a corporate culture in which people knew it was safe to make independent decisions once the project was underway. Lucent Technology's CEO Rich McGinn is successfully pulling disparate cultures together from the Silicon Valley and Murray Hill, New Jersey, by communicating that Lucent is now an Internet-age company that has left its Ma Bell culture behind. Relentless repetition and consistency is required to deliver the core message until that message takes hold. People do not necessarily believe the message the first few times they hear it. After hearing the message repeated many times and observing that the actions routinely match the words, employees start believing the message and understand that their actions must fit the guiding principles.

HOW to broadcast the guiding principles in your company.

- At least one (preferably several) of your senior management people needs to be the obsessed message carrier in the way Jeff Bezos of Amazon.com is. Talk about the guiding principles everywhere you go in every setting where you have an audience.

- Tell stories and give examples of the guiding principles in action. This helps translate fancy phrases into practical reality for employees.

- Make carrying out the guiding principles part of the goal for every team project. Make it explicit. If one of Schwab's principles is earning customer trust, then every project should be able to demonstrate that it was developed and implemented in a way that strengthens customer trust.

CREATING A VISION

While the guiding principles set the organization's internal compass, the vision helps establish the external direction. A vision is a picture of the future. It accomplishes three things: sets the general direction, motivates people, and coordinates the organization's actions. One of the greatest vision statements in US history was President John F. Kennedy's about lunar exploration. He said, "We will put a man on the moon and return him safely by the end of the decade," which was something people could see happening. It set a time limit so there was a target to meet but was not heavy on detail. A vision creates a picture of the organization's future and for it to be effective, it must be consistent with the corporate culture. The vision also must be something meaningful to the employees—becoming a billion-dollar company usually only inspires CEOs.

TIP

CHARACTERISTICS of an effective vision are listed below. Test your vision statement against these criteria. Come as close as you can to creating a vision statement that incorporates these characteristics, and it will make it easier to understand and more inspiring to employees at all levels.

Imaginable: Conveys a picture of what the future will look like.

Desirable: Appeals to the long-term interests of employees, customers, stockholders, and others who have a stake in the enterprise.

Feasible: Comprises realistic, attainable goals.

Focused: Is clear enough to provide guidance in decision-making.

Flexible: Is general enough to allow individual initiative and alternative responses in light of changing conditions.

Communicable: Is easy to communicate; can be explained within five minutes.[6]

---

[6] John P. Kotter, *Leading Change* (Boston: Harvard Business School Press, 1996), 72.

In the United States one of the oldest and most traditional industries is a railroad. In some cases, their resistance to change is only exceeded by government bureaucracies. How do you get a railroad company to move into e-business? It takes a leader with vision. Burlington Northern Santa Fe (BNSF) Railway has undergone many changes over the past few years. This includes a steady stream of mergers and acquisitions, technology projects, and competitive pressures in all segments of its market. The vision to move BNSF to the .com world comes from its CEO, Rob Krebs. Within a day of attending an industry seminar chaired by Jack Welch of General Electric, Krebs led a senior management planning session, developed a plan, and appointed an e-business czar.

Krebs did several concrete things to bring this vision to life in the company:

- Focused the attention of the leadership on e-business by calling an immediate and urgent planning session on the subject after the Welch meeting.
- Chaired the planning session himself to stress the urgency for moving to a .com strategy.
- Created a senior management position with the responsibility for the Web presence.
- Allocated resources, financial, people, and technology are all necessary for the transition to e-business.

Krebs not only identified the need to move into e-business, he sponsored the actions to make it happen. He knew this was the only way to fuel the growth needed to make the company successful in the future. If the company waits to prove a return on investment (ROI), it will be too late. Rob Krebs has the vision and is developing the plan to retool BNSF for the new economy.

DAY-TO-DAY ACTIVITIES
OF A LEADER THAT SHAPE THE CULTURE

PAYING ATTENTION TO THE RIGHT THINGS

Attention is the currency of leadership.[7]

Employees watch what the leader pays attention to and follow suit by paying attention to the same things. Effective leaders learn early in their careers that actions speak louder than words. If the senior management team spends its time listening to customers and asking employees about customers, the employees get the message that the customers are important. On the other hand, if leaders focus their attention internally on attending endless corporate meetings about budgets, corporate restructuring, and cost cutting, the employees get the message that the internal focus is more important than the customers. In some companies the leadership team pays more attention to the stock price than it does to employees, products, and customers—and everyone in the company notices. Paying attention is the most powerful tool available to leaders.

TIP

PAYING attention is the currency of the leader. Decide where to focus your attention. The right things to pay attention to are:

- Actions that will support the organization's business strategy.
- Actions that support the guiding principles.

---

[7] Ronald A. Heifetz, *Leadership Without Easy Answers* (Cambridge, MA: Belknap Press, 1994), 113

The industrial supply company W.W. Granger, Inc. launched a business-to-business Web site in 1996. This pilot led to the establishment of a separate on-line unit the following year. To emphasize the importance of e-commerce to the company, the leaders promoted the head of the new organization from vice president to president. Having a person with the title of president for e-commerce told the entire organization that e-commerce was important to the company.

> Many people hold the title VP of e-commerce, but they sit in either the marketing or IT group. Without direct access to top executives it's often too difficult for VPs of e-commerce to educate senior executives about the Internet.[8]

REACTING TO BAD NEWS

In large part, organizational cultures are formed by the organization's response to outside threats. One type of bad news is a company crisis. During a crisis, leaders must do two things:

1. respond in a way that is consistent with the culture's core value, and
2. create a sense of urgency to inspire an energetic response from employees.

For many companies, the arrival of the Internet is a crisis. If the leaders continue to conduct business in the same old way, the required sense of urgency is not transmitted to the organization. Creating a sense of urgency requires bold action from those in leadership positions. The urgency level can be raised by:

- Reporting poor financial results for the quarter and pointing out that that trend may lead to the demise of the company.
- Presenting low rankings for the organization in a recent customer satisfaction survey.
- Freeze pay or withhold bonuses. (Including your own pay and bonus).

---

[8] Gregory Dalton, "Web-organized: The Net is changing corporate structure and management," *Information Week* (January 25, 1999): 71, citing Lee Dingle, VP for Cambridge Technology Partners.

- Bring in people from companies in other segments of your industry that have been affected more quickly by e-business changes to warn employees about what is coming.

Actions that signal crisis and danger will help shake people out of their complacency. A sense of urgency must replace their comfort with the status quo.

One type of bad news that may cause the organization to retrench rather than change is a mistake or failure in some part of the business operation. The mistake itself is not the problem, but if the leaders are quick to fix blame and punish, they will create a culture of fear and cynicism. A business unit president of a large service industry company was famous for fixing blame. According to the senior managers reporting to him, "He's never made a mistake in his entire career. Just ask him." He always blames them. Their favorite stories are the numerous times he has taken one of them to task in front of the entire management team for a failure. And everyone in the room, except the president, remembers the last meeting when the guilty party argued against the plan and was ordered to do it anyway. Needless to say, this reaction to bad news does not inspire an open-communication, risk-taking culture. This culture will have a very hard time moving at Internet speed.

ALLOCATING RESOURCES

Where leaders allocate resources such as time, money, employee talents, and equipment speaks volumes about the leader's true beliefs. The allocation of resources should be based on the business strategy, but it may not always be the case. Some organizations may allocate resources based on the previous year's expenditures without regard to changing conditions or new opportunities. If companies talk about moving to the Internet world but allocate few resources to the initiative, no one believes in the effort. A consulting company that claims people is its most valuable resource had gone years without even a mid-level executive responsible for human resources. The company's turnover rate was very high, and leadership had a reputation among employees for caring more about protecting their stock option wealth than about ensuring that employees were treated well. When this same company hired an executive for the human resources position and called the department "human capital," it was met with skepticism.

On the other hand, when traditional companies pour vast amounts of resources into R&D efforts geared toward entering the e-business arena, employees get the message that this is a serious issue. This book contains numerous stories of companies making massive resource commitments to their e-business efforts. These examples include P&G starting a .com subsidiary called Reflect.com, Charles Schwab transforming its entire operation to incorporate on-line trading, GE launching its "destroyyourownbusiness.com" initiative, and Whirlpool entering the e-commerce arena with its new subsidiary, brandwise.com. There are dozens of examples of companies using resource allocation as a leadership tool to send the message that e-business is important and "the way we do things around here."

BEING A ROLE MODEL

Leaders are visible symbols of the organization's culture, which is most obvious in start-up organizations or with a charismatic leader. Charismatic leaders gain followers by inspiring them with a vision or personal magnetism. By Hollywood or Washington standards they might not be viewed as charismatic leaders, but Bill Gates at Microsoft, Steve Jobs at Apple, Andrew Grove at Intel, and Jack Welch at General Electric are certainly role models and symbols for their organizations. Their styles are consistent with the culture of its organizations, and when they live the stated values of the organization, it creates a momentum and a pressure for everyone else to follow their lead.

REWARDING THE RIGHT PEOPLE

Another way leaders define the corporate culture is by who they reward and for what behaviors. It is critical that these people and their behaviors are consistent with the culture the leaders want to develop. The .com world requires high-speed operations, risk taking, and teamwork. People who produce these actions in ways that are consistent with the values of the culture are the ones that must be rewarded.

If a core value for a company is extraordinary customer service then the employee that goes out of the way to assist a customer should be recognized and rewarded. American Airlines provides their frequent fliers with small cards to give to employees that they feel provide exceptional service, and the airline employees can then turn the cards in for free flights. The right people are recognized and rewarded for acting in a way that provides good customer service. In the transition to a .com culture, if a project team time boxes a project and accomplishes the goal in half the usual time, then that team should be recognized and rewarded for their success at the new, faster way of operating in the company.

The types of people recruited or promoted into leadership roles go to the core of the culture. Selection for a senior management position is one of the highest rewards a company can bestow on an individual, and this selection has a significant impact on the organization's culture. It sends a powerful symbolic message about what is really important to the CEO or board of directors. This new leader also has a direct practical effect on shaping the future culture, and hiring a new leader can signal that a change in the culture is taking place. For example, when the board or CEO hires a new leader with a very different background or personality than in the past, the message is clear: things are going to change. If you use a promotion as a catalyst for change, tell people that you purposely selected a "different" kind of leader and you support this leader as a catalyst for change. Otherwise, employees may wonder if you simply made a hiring mistake or they may think they can resist the new leader efforts with no adverse consequences.

Jim Hammock, CEO of Hire.com, told a story about an experience with a company he led earlier in his career.

"Another company acquired our company. The chairman of the purchasing company told me that the number one thing he wanted was our corporate culture. 'You're nimble, customer-oriented, and so forth. We're becoming bureaucratic. I want you to come in and change our culture.' Now that was what the chairman said to me. If it was communicated to the rest of the chairman's staff, it did not get through. The message was never converted to actions. So from day one, we came in working for the chairman, thinking we were going to change things. And the rest of his organization was trying to get control of us. It was a less than rewarding experience for all concerned."

If leaders are brought in to change the culture, that has to be stated explicitly so that it is clear to everyone involved. If the CEO brings in a staff of Generation Xers to create a .com culture, she better make sure everyone understands why they are there. The sponsorship must be very visible and high enough in the organization to legitimize the change. In a bricks-and-mortar company, people brought in to speed up the culture face resistance at every turn unless the sponsoring leader reminds the organization of the reason for the change and holds people accountable for cooperating. If this new group of employees is brought into the existing organization and the sponsor does not stay involved then everyone that is threatened by the new group or wants to maintain the status quo will block the efforts to bring about change. During the transition from bricks-and-mortar to an e-business enterprise, this type of resistance is likely to be much more intense than in the past because the change is so dramatic and threatening to employees with traditional skills and work habits. If a group of stereotypical techies with nose rings and ponytails is brought into the marketing department of a Fortune 500 company to create their Web presence, these people with their strange work habits and new age skills will seem like alien beings to the veteran corporate employees. Without active sponsorship they might even have difficulty getting access to office space or other resources then need to do their jobs.

USING INFLUENCE MORE AND POWER LESS

Power, influence, and authority are closely related concepts. Formal authority legitimizes the use of power, while informal authority must rely on influence. In a .com culture, relying on formal authority and power as a primary tool to lead an organization or a team seldom works. Formal authority, of course, still exists, but the role it plays in the culture is not as central as it was in the old command and control world. The .com culture is informal in structure and style, and teams self-manage most aspects of their projects. The demand for speed makes it logistically impossible for formal leaders to monitor enough details of employees' work to exert formal authority and power on a constant basis.

The contrast of these two types of leadership styles was very apparent between two leaders in a large, very traditional corporation. In this case, they were both formal leaders, but one relied on a command and control approach, and the other relied heavily on leading through influence and encouraged everyone in his organization to do the same. The president, who had worked for the company most of his career, was nearing retirement. The senior vice president of one of the divisions who reported to the president had worked for a number of companies during his career, including start-ups. Drawing on the power of his position, the president insisted on approving nearly all decisions and frequently gave specific orders to the vice president and other leaders on exact actions to take to address specific business problems. He even went so far as to script what his direct reports were allowed to say when then went to quarterly briefings with the entire senior management staff of the corporation.

The younger division vice president's leadership approach was dramatically different. His philosophy was to hire the right people, keep everyone well informed about key issues in all areas of the company, and trust them to do their jobs well. The leadership meetings in his company were primarily discussions of issues. The vice president was adamant in these meetings about issues that were important to him and problems that had to be solved. He would often have ideas for how to go about solving those problems but did not give orders. His opinions carried a great deal of weight with every member of the leadership team, but it was clear from the behavior at meetings that they did not hesitate to speak up and disagree with him when they believed it was necessary. The president and the vice president clashed frequently about these different leadership approaches causing a great deal of stress for both of them. Clearly, the vice president was much more suited to lead in a .com environment that requires speed, risk taking, and independent decision-making down through the ranks. It is no accident that he was one of the leaders in the corporation that was extremely frustrated at the slowness with which the company was embracing e-business technologies, but made no progress in convincing the president of the urgency of the company's outdated technology strategy. This kind of tug-of-war between contrasting leadership styles is taking place in many organizations as the transition to e-business unfolds. The old guard and new guard almost always differ on the priority they place on the use of power versus influence in how they lead.

The Difference Between Power and Influence

The exercise of *power* changes the individual's situation or concept of the situation but not the individual's preferences.

The exercise of *influence* entails an authentic change in the individual's preference.[9]

---

[9] Marvin E. Olsen and Martin N. Marger, eds., *Power in Modern Societies* (Boulder, CO: Westview Press, 1993), 27.

It is particularly difficult to rely on formal authority and power in a booming economy when most knowledge workers can easily move on to work for another company. This is especially true of your most talented employees, who stay with your company only as long as they choose to. They might hang around long enough to exercise the next round of stock options, but then they leave, unless the company is a good place to work.

> **TIP** THINK of e-business employees as volunteers, because to a great extent they behave like participants in a volunteer organization.

In this work environment people can be influenced, but cannot easily be ordered to comply. Leaders, managers, and others in positions of formal authority still have the short-term capacity to use power to change people's behavior. But if you are trying to build a .com culture, power is best used in small doses because the long-term effects will be the loss of your most valuable employees.

The Nine Types of Influence[10]

Rational Persuasion—based on facts, logic, and rational arguments.

Exchange—do something for the person or group so they will reciprocate at a later date.

Coalition Building—seek the help of others to persuade them to do the desired act.

Inspiration—use appeals to the organization's values or the aspirations of the person you are trying to influence.

Empowerment—ask the person or group being influenced to assist in planning or helping with the project.

Admiration—use praise to encourage the person or group to be receptive to the new idea.

---

[10] Gary Yukl, *Leadership in Organizations*, 3rd ed. (Englewood Cliffs, NJ: Prentice Hall, 1994), 225.

Moral—seek the person or group's commitment based on ethics or values. It is the right thing to do.

Coaching—offer to provide opportunities or teach the person or group something new.

Persistence—refuse to give up and try repeatedly to convince the person or group to commit to the project.

Because individuals and groups respond to different influence tactics, it is best to develop skills for using a variety of tactics to influence behavior. People who are highly analytical such as engineers and accountants usually respond better to rational persuasion based on facts and figures rather than inspiration. People that are more expressive and like the big picture are usually bored by a purely rational presentation. They would be more likely to respond to an inspirational appeal. Exchange is one of the most effective tactics because when you do something for someone they usually are willing to do something for you in return.

DEVELOP your skills in using the nine types of influence described above. In a .com culture you will likely need skills in all nine areas.

- Use the list of nine types of influence as a checklist to assess your current influence skills.

- Pick out the three that you think are your strongest skills and three that are your weakest or least used skills.

- Ask two or three trusted colleagues to tell you what they think are your strong and weak suits.

- Use your strongest skills whenever you can—you are likely to have the best outcomes with them.

- Train yourself on your weak suits through seminars, books, or coaching. There is no reason you cannot become proficient at all types of influence.

Many times leaders overlook the influence or persuasion step when trying to bring about change. Because leaders have worked with the new ideas for some time before they are announced to employees, they are familiar with these ideas and convinced of their merits, and they may forget that the employees have not been exposed as much to the new information. Announcing the new approach and stating that it is a good plan is not likely to trigger enthusiastic buy-in for the new idea. Leading employees through the transition from a traditional company to an e-business company requires highly developed skills in the art of influence.

E-BUSINESS REQUIRES MORE LEADERSHIP AND LESS MANAGEMENT

A woman in the audience of a Warren Bennis lecture for AT&T said, "I have a deaf daughter, so I've learned American Sign Language. In ASL, this is the sign for manage." She held out her hands as if she were holding onto the reins of a horse or restraining something. She then said, "This is the ASL sign for lead. She cradled her arms and rocked them back and forth the way a parent would nurture a child."[11]

The root of the word *manage* means to control, while the root of *lead* means to take on a journey. Managers control people or projects, while leaders motivate and inspire people. The manager tries to produce predictability, order, and control, while the leader strives to produce flexibility, commitment, and organizational identity. All organizations require both management and leadership to stay on course, but the move into e-business demands more leadership and less management than most traditional organizations because of the uncertainty, complexity, and fluid nature of the e-business environment. If the opposite happens and a company uses more management

---

[11] Warren Bennis and Joan Goldsmith, *Learning to Lead: A Workbook on Becoming a Leader* (Reading, MA: Addison-Wesley, 1994), 5.

than leadership, the organization lacks the agility to respond at the necessary speed. In times of uncertainty, leadership is more effective than management. All the recommended activities described in the previous section of this chapter focus on leadership not management.

Differences Between Management and Leadership[12]

Management	Leadership
Planning and budgeting	Establishing direction
Organizing and staffing	Aligning people
Controlling and problem solving	Motivating and inspiring

PEACETIME MANAGEMENT AND WARTIME LEADERSHIP

Many books compare the business environment to war and apply the principles of war to the business world. There are no conditions in the business world as extreme as the conditions experienced in war, but the metaphor is helpful when considering the move from traditional to e-business conditions. Both circumstances have high levels of uncertainty. And some of the same leadership skills are required in both settings.

> At Southwest Airlines many of the cultural aspects of the .com world like speed, creative thinking, communicating in a dynamic environment, and being customer-focused have been part of our culture for decades. Because of the competitive nature of the airlines industry we feel we are always at battle. We talk about the warrior spirit a lot. [CEO] Herb Kelleher stresses that the competitive nature of the business is with other companies not inside with each other.
> —*Ross Holman, CIO, Southwest Airlines*

---

[12] John P. Kotter, *Leading Change* (Boston: Harvard Business School Press, 1996), 26.

Many accounts of combat refer to the "fog of war." This means that you are focused on a very small area and concerned with accomplishing your mission and staying alive, which gives you little time to pay attention to the bigger picture. The speed and uncertainty of the Internet environment can cause this "fog." In peacetime, the changes usually come in small measured doses, but in wartime the degree of uncertainty is at the highest level people may ever experience. Someone must keep track of the big picture, and this calls for leadership.

The US Army uses the following model of leadership for training all levels of leaders from the newest junior noncommissioned officer to the four-star general who is the Chief of Staff of the Army. It has developed this training based on a framework of be, know, and do.[13]

US Army Model for Leadership in Action

BE
Be a person of strong and honorable character.
Be committed to the professional Army ethic.
Be an example of individual values.
Be able to resolve complex ethical dilemmas.

KNOW
Know the four factors of leadership—the leader, the led, the situation, the communications.
Know standards.
Know yourself.
Know human nature.
Know your job.
Know your unit.

DO
Do provide purpose.
Do provide direction.
Do provide motivation.

---

[13] Field Manual 22-100 *Leadership* (Headquarters, Department of the Army, 1990), 53.

It always has been a challenge for the armed forces to train for war in a peacetime world. In peacetime, the management aspect of the job takes priority over the leadership aspect. In peacetime, many officers that rise to the top are exceptionally good at administrative management. The individuals classified as warriors (i.e., people with the skill to lead in combat) are less likely to receive promotions during peacetime. This works during the times of stability, but the downside occurs during the transition from peace to war. The officers with good management skills who excell during peace time are the first to lead the troops into combat during the time when the military is transitioning to the warrior officers. At the start of every war, unnecessary causalities occur because people are managed in combat rather than led. This has resulted in a universal adage in the military that captures the difference in priorities for peacetime and wartime officers: no combat-ready unit ever passed inspection and no inspection-ready unit ever passed combat.

The parallels to wartime conditions in the business world today are based on the complexity, volume, and velocity of change caused by the Internet. Organizations trying to adjust to Internet speed are faced with a similar problem when they have too many administrators and not enough leaders. Companies trying to move to warp speed in the complex and chaotic world of the Internet must have leaders who can think fast, take risks, and function well under extreme pressure. Whether you recruit new leaders or discover ones already in your organization, you must find them somewhere.

INFORMAL LEADERS AND EMPOWERMENT IN A .COM CULTURE

In a .com culture, leaders are everywhere in the organization. Informal leadership on teams and in work units provides the direction that keeps the company moving at top speed on a daily basis. The recommendations in this chapter apply to informal as well as formal leaders. Informal leaders can use the eight key activities of leaders described earlier in this chapter. In fact, the activities may be more effective when practiced by informal leaders close to the action of teams or work units. Because they are on-site where the action is taking place, their reactions are more timely. The informal leaders are also well-known to the employees and have earned their respect. This is why they are informal leaders in the first place. When informal leaders take a stance on an issue, the group is likely to follow their lead.

Informal leaders have always performed an invaluable role in all organizations. But as company's transition from traditional to e-business operations, the need for them is even greater. Companies need more informal leaders working throughout the organization, and these people must be empowered to take action without getting bogged down in bureaucratic red tape. Empowerment is a word that has been used in business for years, but the promise of the concept rarely has been translated into action with great success. This is not surprising. It is a difficult concept to implement skillfully. Empowerment initiatives often have been introduced with great fanfare but little training or follow-up. Often these initiatives were little more than announcements of a new program with a round or two of seminars to introduce the topic. This is not enough to have any effect on the cultural habits of the organization. You must find ways to empower informal leaders, or you will not be able to build a culture that moves at Internet speed.

Empowerment is the concept of sharing the power, authority, and responsibilities with employees.

There are four components that you must address to effectively implement the concept of empowerment:

1. trust
2. training
3. setting limits
4. time

The first underlying concept is *trust*. The managers and the leaders in the organization must trust the employees to do the correct thing. The employees must in turn, trust their leadership and the organization to provide the resources necessary to be successful.

Major General Michael Kostelnik, Commander of the USAF Air Armament Center at Eglin AFB in Florida, gave an example of the important role trust and empowerment plays in his operation.

"We use a computer based Executive Management Information System (EMIS) to communicate 'virtually' within our organization at all levels. This system facilitates both top-down and bottom-up information flow, and makes our operation very 'efficient.' It does not, however, handle some management situations, which are still more 'effectively' handled in the 'physical' world. We have developed a corollary rule set. This management rule set states that routine organizational communications will flow 'virtually' through EMIS, but if one of five 'filtering' criteria is met, a phone call, meeting, or personal video teleconference must take place. The five criteria, which require a 'physical' forum: political, high risk, high value, in trouble, or those that an employee wants his supervisor's involvement or help for his own reasons. Since the employees are the only ones who will decide what real world events fall into any of the above criteria, this approach is obviously built heavily on trust and empowerment. You would be amazed at how well our workforce has responded to this approach. Managers are empowered to establish their own levels of managerial risk, and our leadership team is seldom surprised by real world events. Once empowered, our employees tend to be more forthcoming with real problems, which should be brought to management's attention. Our organization is a strong performer on par with top peer competitors, and I credit our success to the trust and empowerment cornerstones of our management philosophy!"

The second component of empowerment is *training*. Since empowerment requires the sharing of power and responsibility, this may be new behavior to most organizations. Training on how to share is critical. There are training program and books available that can be used to teach cooperation and sharing. For example, in the book *Thinkertoys*[14] Michael Michalko describes a Japanese method called *Rice Storm* that can be used to open communications, break down isolation, create alliances, and a spirit of collaboration. This training must include decision making, project planning, and resource allocation. There are excellent training programs available from many sources on the development of collaborative negotiation skills, which is the most complex version of this cooperative strategy development and communication.

The third component is *setting limits* of empowerment. If leadership does not establish limits at the beginning of a project, it must accept the results or risk destroying trust. In an academic setting one organization eliminated formal management positions and created self-directed teams empowered to develop the curriculum and deliver the courses. No limits were established beforehand. The results were a perfect distribution along a bell-shaped curve. One third of the group made a mad dash to discover the outer limits to the point of creating an entirely new mission that did not require students. The center third tried to move forward to create new courses and expand the number offered but within the existing mission of the organization. The third group found the whole exercise so unsettling that it insisted on continuing to do business as it had always been done. The leadership could have eased this transition from the start by setting limits and giving direction.

Empowerment is not an abdication by the formal leaders. When you fail to set clear goals for a team and to set limits within which they are to function, you are abdicating your leadership responsibility. This usually results in one of two undesirable outcomes. Either the team takes off in some misguided direction that is not useful to the company or it flounders and accomplishes nothing at all. Another example of this problem took place in a large federal government department in Washington, DC. It created a self-directed work team and empowered

---

[14] Michael Michalko, *Thinkertoys: A Handbook of Business Creativity for the 90's* (Berkeley, CA: Ten Speed Press, 1991), 294.

the members, but limits were not set ahead of time. The team's charter was so vague that when management tried to provide direction the team did not believe it had to listen because it was a self-directed work team and was doing its thing.

The fourth component of empowerment is *time*. It is important to remember that empowerment is a relatively new concept in many organizations, running counter to the historical culture of these companies. If you are sharing power and responsibility for the first time, it is not likely that everyone will have it right in, say, 90 days. If this is a significant cultural change, it will take time for people to learn the leadership skills required and trust that the formal leaders of the organization are serious about this culture change.

COMPLEXITY OF THE E-BUSINESS WORLD: LEADING AT THE EDGE OF CHAOS

Throughout this book we have described the cataclysmic changes shaping the new world of business and professional life. The environment we live in today, in both our personal and work lives, is vastly different from the one we experienced in the early 1990s. Five key trends have changed the workplace in the past decade. And the coming decade promises to bring many more changes.

Figure 10.1: Leadership

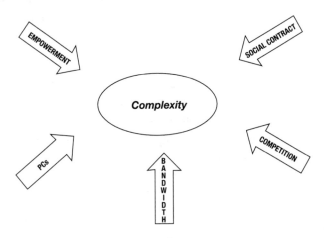

1. The vastly expanded bandwidth capacity of the Internet is changing the nature of business.

2. Web-based start-up companies are posing a competitive challenge to bricks-and-mortar companies.

3. The arrival of the personal computer moved computing power from the hands of the information technology professionals to the masses.

4. The democratization of the workforce resulted in the empowerment of employees.

5. The massive layoffs of employees in the 1980s and 1990s broke the social contract between organizations and employees.

These five dynamics occurred during a very short time period and have created high levels of uncertainty and ambiguity. In the 1970s and 1980s scientists from around the world and from many professions began to study patterns of order in irregular events and unpredictability just below the surface of order. This scientific effort became known as chaos theory and was translated into layman terminology for an audience outside the scientific community by James Gleick in his book, *Chaos: Making a New Science*.[15] Additional work took place at the Santa Fe Institute, a New Mexico think tank that developed complexity theory. These two theories have been applied to the study of organizations as well as to science.

According to this theory, the Internet is a development that has created a pull between traditional models (rigidity) and newly morphing models (chaos) of the .com world. The balance point is called the edge of chaos.

Complexity is a class of behaviors in which the components of the system never quite lock in place, yet never dissolve into turbulence either. These are the system that are both stable enough to store information, and yet evanescent enough to transmit it.[16]

---

[15] James Gleick, *Chaos: Making a New Science* (New York: Penguin Books, 1987).

[16] M. Mitchell Waldrop, *Complexity: The Emerging Science at the Edge of Order and Chaos* (New York: Simon & Schuster, 1992), 12.

Faced with leading the transition to the Internet era, many traditional leaders feel overwhelmed. They often express their frustration by wondering why all of this had to happen when they were at the helm. There is, however, some good new in the chaos. The edge of chaos or complexity is the point in systems or organizations where creativity takes place. The ambiguity and uncertainty provide the catalyst for new ideas and challenges to the status quo. If there is ever a time when a leader can take a traditional company and transform it into a leading edge innovator, it is now. All the rigid systems and cultures are coming unglued, which provides the opportunity to reconfigure the pieces into a new enterprise. The key is to resist the temptation to hang on to the old ways and look for a safe place to hide.

In his book on leadership, Ronald A. Heifetz wrote "In times of distress we turn to authority... We look for direction, protection, and order."[17] There is no safe shelter in the transition to the .com world. The business world is one grand experiment, and there is no going back. It is the chance of the epoch for companies to participate in changing the way the world does business. To participate in the journey, companies need skilled and committed leaders with the courage to lead the way.

APPLYING THIS INFORMATION IN YOUR ORGANIZATION

Below are questions to help you diagnose the current patterns of leadership in your company. The old world emphasizes formal leaders who rely on command and control while the .com world that needs both formal and informal leaders who rely more on influence and less on formal power.

1. Can the employees of the organization state the guiding principles? When is the last time you heard the guiding principles and vision of the organization discussed? By whom?

---

[17] Ronald A. Heifetz, *Leadership Without Easy Answers* (Cambridge, MA: Belknap Press, 1994), 69.

2. Are the formal leaders of your organization symbols of your corporate culture? What are their personal traits that match the cultural characteristics?

3. What do the leaders in your company pay attention to? How do the leaders react to bad news? Who has been rewarded or promoted recently? What do these leadership actions tell you about the culture of your organization?

4. Does your organization make a distinction between leadership and management?

5. What do you do to encourage informal leadership?

6. What kinds of power or influence do formal and informal leaders use in your organization?

7. Is there a sense of urgency in your company about making the transition to e-business?

Ten Final Tips on Building a Corporate Culture for the Connected Workplace

At the beginning of this book, we promised to give you practical advice on building a high-speed corporate culture that can survive in the .com world. Each chapter ends with questions to diagnose your company's current situation and key tips for using the ideas in that chapter. We end the book with one last round of practical advice. The three of us sat down and asked ourselves, "What would we say if a reader asked for a few quick pieces of advice that capture what we learned from researching and writing this book?" So here is our parting advice as we finish *Culture.com*.

> Success depends, in a very nonhierarchical way, upon information flowing through the organization and coalescing in the right place. This doesn't happen by fiat. It's a function of culture. Culture is the software that drives an organization.[1]
> —*Richard Friedman, Managing Director of Goldman Sachs and Co.*

---

[1] Sunny Balker, "Global E-Commerce, Local Problems," *Journal of Business Strategy* (July 7, 1999), 37.

1. RECRUITING FOR CULTURAL FIT

Building and sustaining a corporate culture that fits your needs requires a critical mass of employees who are committed to the culture's core beliefs and values and have work habits matching the culture you are trying to create and maintain. It is much easier to hire people with those traits than to change their personalities, beliefs, and behaviors once they are hired. Ask questions in the interviews and listen carefully to their stories about previous work experiences. Listen for cultural fit. If you do not hear it, beware: you may be hiring the technical or professional skills you need but damaging your chances of building a strong culture.

2. SPEED UP YOUR CULTURE

Time-box your next project. Pick a high-priority project and decide to set a firm deadline for completion that is shorter than normal. Do your own version of the 100-Days Project described in Chapter 2. This will require you to change your thinking about time. You no longer will be able to ask, "How much time will it take to complete this project?" Instead, you now will be asking, "What is our completion deadline? How do we manage this project so we can meet the deadline with a high-quality outcome?"

3. WHEN CHANGING YOUR CULTURE, YOU GET ONE POINT FOR EACH ACTION

Changing a culture does not happen as a result of a one big corporate meeting to announce the new direction and inspire the troops. A culture changes because of hundreds of small actions taken throughout the organization. People hear the announcement about the new culture, but they wait to see if the actions match the announcement before they believe in the new culture. Think of it this way: you get one point for each new behavior that represents the new culture. It takes many detailed actions throughout the company to accumulate enough points to trigger a real change in the culture.

4. LEAD MORE, MANAGE LESS IN A .COM CULTURE

Lead your organization or team like it is a workforce made up entirely of volunteers. This requires you to use more leadership skills and fewer management skills. A .com culture has informal leaders throughout the organization at all levels. The formal leaders must set the direction, inspire, and empower those informal leaders to create a fast, innovative e-business culture.

5. PICK CREDIBLE ROLE MODELS

One of the best tools for building a corporate culture is to identify role models. These employees are stellar examples of the cultural traits you want to encourage (e.g., speed, risk taking, customer service, team skills). Be sure you pick people that employees respect. There must be general agreement among managers and employees that this person deserves to be honored. Mistakes in picking role models lead to cynicism about the culture.

6. PROTECT THE .COM TEAMS
FROM THE CORPORATE IMMUNE SYSTEM

When teams are working on e-business projects or other innovative efforts, the traditional groups within the organization tend to be hostile toward those groups and their ideas. An organization has an immune system just like the human body. If it senses a new idea in its midst, it surrounds that idea like white blood cells and kills it. Teams working on these projects need strong sponsor support to protect them in the early stages. They also must keep a low profile. Too much publicity about new ideas will set the immune system in motion. Keep the team out of the limelight until it has enough momentum to withstand controversy and resistance.

7. INCREASE THE COLLECTIVE IQ OF YOUR COMPANY

Start holding your own version of After Action Reviews used by the US Army. Bring people together to discuss events when they are finished and to learn collectively from your mistakes as well as your successes. Many traditional companies have a culture that encourages employees to hide mistakes for fear of retribution, so you have to create rituals like After Action Reviews to change that message. A company will have a difficult time increasing its collective IQ if it cannot discuss and learn from its mistakes. The next time a team tries something new and it turns out to be a mistake, reward the people on that team. Have them tell their story and what they learned from the experience that others can benefit from. Create a few heroes out of high-profile mistake-makers, to demonstrate the kind of corporate IQ you want in your company.

8. ENHANCE YOUR COMPANY'S KNOWLEDGE MANAGEMENT SYSTEM

Do a knowledge management assessment. If you want to improve your organization's methods for managing knowledge, start by determining your current state. Use the 18-question assessment at the end of Chapter 7 on knowledge management to find out what is working well. That way you can spotlight the successes and clone them and identify the gaps so you can start developing strategies to address them.

9. PLAN THE INTEGRATION OF YOUR PARALLEL CULTURES

Temporary groups can form such strong cultures that it is difficult to disband them later. If you are setting up an Internet division or another type of separate group to do the early development work on your Internet business, plan for the group's integration into the larger company from the project's beginning. Make sure everyone knows this is a temporary structure for the early phase and make plans early about how and when this group will merge with the larger organization.

10. CLARIFY EACH PARTY'S COMMITMENT LEVEL IN ALLIANCES

When you set up an alliance with another company, be sure you both have the same understanding of the commitment level. You may think you are entering into a full-blown partnership with flexible give and take in the way you will work together, but if the other company sees the alliance as simply a contractual relationship in which it is not obligated to do anything not spelled out in the contract, you may be headed for trouble. As the relationship progresses, make sure you stay at the same commitment level.

WE WILL KEEP YOU POSTED AS THE STORY UNFOLDS

As we said in Chapter 1, the story is just beginning for most companies. We will continue to research the topic and interview the people who are living through the transition to e-business. Our Web site, www.culturedotcom.com, will update you on our latest findings and ask you questions about what is happening in your world. We are all living through a grand experiment that is changing the way the world does business.

> To turn the hype of e-commerce into reality involves placing a higher priority on dealing with corporate culture, which is vitally important but often pushed aside in favor of speeds and feeds. "I don't think people are going to be successful on whether or not they nail the technology. They are going to be successful if they nail the sociology."[2]
> —*Lee Dingel, Vice President of Interactive Solutions of Cambridge Technology Partners*

Corporate cultures will continue to change as companies race to implement their e-business strategies. We remind you once more that the two must work in sync. If your business strategy and your corporate culture are pulling in two different directions, the culture will win no matter how brilliant your strategy is.

---

[2] Teri Robinson, "Reinventing the Business Wheel—Ready or Not, Companies Must Be Prepared for a Major Overhaul," *Information Week* (June 21, 1999), 6.

Index

TO CONTACT THE AUTHORS

Peg C. Neuhauser
PMB 504
3267 Bee Caves Road, Suite 107
Austin, TX 78746
512-328-8896
pegneu@earthlink.net

Ray Bender
PMB 504
3267 Bee Caves Road, Suite 107
Austin, TX 78746
512-347-0660
raybender@earthlink.net

Kirk L. Stromberg
StarCompass Group
PO Box 404
Glen Echo, MD 20812-0404
301-229-0287
Kirk-L-Stromber@usa.net

For further information on *Culture.com* and the authors
visit their Web site at **www.culturedotcom.com**.

Under**DATE DUE**

The Library Store   #47-0107